I0796723

U.S. Special Forces Commando

Other Titles Available by the Author

An O.S.S. Secret Agent Behind Enemy Lines,
Frontline Books/Pen & Sword Books Limited, Barnsley, 2024

U.S. Special Forces Commando

From OSS Agent in the Eastern Bloc to Airborne Soldier in Korea and Green Beret – The Cold War Service of Leif Bangsbøll

Brook G. Bangsbøll

Frontline Books

First published in Great Britain in 2025 by
Frontline Books
An imprint of Pen & Sword Books Limited
Yorkshire – Philadelphia

ISBN 978 1 03611 947 8

A CIP catalogue record for this book is available from the British Library.

Typeset by Mac Style
Printed in the UK by CPI Group (UK) Ltd, Croydon, CR0 4YY.

The Publisher's authorised representative in the EU for product safety is Authorised Rep Compliance Ltd., Ground Floor, 71 Lower Baggot Street, Dublin D02 P593, Ireland.
www.arccompliance.com

For a complete list of Pen & Sword titles please contact

PEN & SWORD BOOKS LIMITED
47 Church Street, Barnsley, South Yorkshire, S70 2AS, England
E-mail: enquiries@pen-and-sword.co.uk
Website: www.pen-and-sword.co.uk
or
PEN AND SWORD BOOKS
1950 Lawrence Road, Havertown, PA 19083, USA
E-mail: uspen-and-sword@casematepublishers.com
Website: www.penandswordbooks.com

U.S. Special Forces Commando *is dedicated to four of my ancestors that I never met: Grandmother Rigmor and Grandfather Frederik, and their two daughters, Inga and Jytte Bangsbøll – my father's family…he loved them dearly.*

This book is also dedicated to my father, the remarkable character – Leif Bangsbøll.

He was a sailor, aviator, soldier and secret agent.
But he also was a son, brother, husband, father and grandfather.

Testimonial

"When our nation must turn to war, we turn to warriors like Leif Bangsbøll to carry the fight to our enemy. Consistent with his Viking ancestry, in this detailed recounting we see the warrior's journey through the adventures and tragedies that war throws at those in the brawl. Read *An OSS Secret Agent Behind Enemy Lines* and its sequel: *U.S. Special Forces Commando* and remember those we have a duty to never forget."

General Jim Mattis, U.S. Marines (ret.)
and 26th Secretary of Defense

Contents

Captain Leif Bangsbøll, United States Army Special Forces, 1955.
(*Courtesy of the United States Army*)

Acknowledgements

Like most major literary endeavors, the creation of *A US Special Forces Commando*, the sequel to *An OSS Secret Agent Behind Enemy Lines* took the dedicated efforts of many people – family members, friends and professional colleagues, all contributed to bring this story to life. To my two big brothers, Chris and Mark, your knowledge of our family history, and in particular Dad's extensive military career was invaluable and aided me to focus on the key elements of each story within each chapter – adding details, such as dates and locations to many of the stories Dad recounted. Our Danish cousin Jeanette Dunn has been instrumental in providing not only the record of the Bangsbøll family lineage, but access to the Danish archives and the Danish Resistance Museum along with many old family photos which were crucial to telling the full story. Creative advice and encouragement from my sister-in-law Nancy and my nephew Bradley Bangsbøll were inspiring and kept me slogging through the tough times and focused during the successes. Likewise, I cannot understate the value of those who I call my *beta readers* – Brian Wrong, Neil Bolt, and my nephew Bryce Morawiec, who read the rough drafts and first cuts of each chapter and provided insightful feedback on what worked and what didn't.

To the wonderfully talented Jennifer Yates, my first editor, whose passion for the literary word was inspiring. Jennifer's editing skills and enthusiasm for the original work, entitled *Onward to Valhalla*, was crucial to our success – keeping track of our edits during the COVID-19 pandemic was a herculean task! Likewise, my dear friend and colleague, Cathy Priestman, and her technical guru Daniel whose limitless energy and creative ideas brought the story on-line through our webpage, and managed the inventory of photographs which are now in *An OSS Secret Agent Behind Enemy Lines* and *U.S. Special Forces Commando.*

Finally, to the three most important people in my life – my wife Jan, son Garrett and daughter Emily – thank you from the bottom of my heart for your continuous support over the 15 years it took me to research, write and complete this important family record. Without your love, support and encouragement, I could not have reached the finish line.

Foreword

Many sons have written books about their fathers, but few have had such a richness of substance or strength of impact to convey as Brook Bangsbøll.

Brook's father, Army Lieutenant Colonel Leif Bangsbøll, himself the son of a Danish Navy Admiral, was an accomplished man who lived a fascinating life. Leif Bangsbøll was born in Denmark, served in the Danish Navy, the Norwegian Air Force, the Office of Strategic Services and the United States Army. His story is one of heroic actions in two wars and important service as an original member of the Army's Green Berets.

Brook was too young to understand his father's impact until after all of this had occurred. But as he got older, he realized that Leif's life as a sailor, soldier and spy was worthy of his fullest admiration and respect. He learned that at one point, Leif had started to write his autobiography but didn't get very far. By writing these books, Brook is telling the full story that he wished his father had written.

Leif Bangsbøll's story gets better with each chapter, and Brook has done a masterful job in creating this narrative. Written more than 20 years after his father's death in 2001, Brook has crafted two books in which the main story lines and all major events are true and verified, but many of the details are constructed from the recollections of himself and others, augmented by written accounts in various forms. The result is two historical works: *An OSS Secret Agent Behind Enemy Lines* and its sequel: *U.S. Special Forces Commando* – both factual and inspired by grand memories. Both books are well-researched, informative and entertaining.

I never knew Leif Bangsbøll but as a former Navy SEAL officer and descendant of Norsemen, I felt a special link to him. I dove into this book and read it with ever-growing awe. It is, simply, a son's wonderful account of his legendary father, told with both loving care and attention to its historical significance. Brook also connects the reader to his father's Viking ancestry, sure that retired Lieutenant Colonel Leif Bangsbøll resides in the Halls of Valhalla, where the most courageous of Vikings live forever as celebrated heroes.

In life, Leif Bangsbøll was awarded the Army's Distinguished Service Cross and Silver Star Medal, his adopted nation's second and third highest awards for valor against the enemy. In death, he has been acclaimed with awards and distinctions by both the Army's Special Forces and the United States Special Operations Command – two organizations that trace their roots directly back to the secretive Office of Strategic Services in which Leif Bangsbøll served so heroically.

And now he is honored by his son, Brook Bangsbøll, in a two-volume opus that merits all of our careful attention. I salute both the father and the son.

Admiral Eric Thor Olson,
United States Navy (Retired) -
Former Commander of the United States
Special Operations Command (USSOCOM)

If

If you can keep your head when all about you
Are losing theirs and blaming it on you,
If you can trust yourself when all men doubt you,
But make allowance for their doubting too;
If you can wait and not be tired by waiting,
Or being lied about, don't deal in lies,
Or being hated, don't give way to hating,
And yet don't look too good, nor talk too wise:

If you can dream – and not make dreams your master;
If you can think – and not make thoughts your aim;
If you can meet with Triumph and Disaster
And treat those two impostors just the same;
If you can bear to hear the truth you've spoken
Twisted by knaves to make a trap for fools,
Or watch the things you gave your life to, broken,
And stoop and build 'em up with worn-out tools:

If you can make one heap of all your winnings
And risk it on one turn of pitch-and-toss,
And lose, and start again at your beginnings
And never breathe a word about your loss;
If you can force your heart and nerve and sinew
To serve your turn long after they are gone,
And so hold on when there is nothing in you
Except the Will which says to them: 'Hold on!'

If you can talk with crowds and keep your virtue,
Or walk with Kings – nor lose the common touch,
If neither foes nor loving friends can hurt you,
If all men count with you, but none too much;

If you can fill the unforgiving minute
With sixty seconds' worth of distance run,
Yours is the Earth and everything that's in it,
And – which is more – you'll be a Man, my son!

Rudyard Kipling, 1943

Abbreviations

AKA	Also Known As
ALO	Army Liaison Officer
APC	Armored Personnel Carriers
ARCT	Airborne Regimental Combat Team
ATAF	Allied Tactical Air Force
BOQ	Base Officers' Quarters
CIA	Central Intelligence Agency
CO	Commanding Officer
COS	Chief of Staff
DC	District of Columbia
DNA	A Person's Genetic Code
DPR	Democratic People's Republic
DSC	Distinguished Service Cross
Ex-O	Executive Officer
FBI	Federal Bureau of Investigation
FDR	President Franklin D. Roosevelt
GDP	General Defense Plan
HALO	High Altitude Low Opening
ID	Identification
Int & Recon	Intelligence and Reconnaissance
JCOS	Joint Chiefs of Staff
KGB	Committee for State Security – Soviet Union's Security Service
KIA	Killed in Action
MIA	Missing in Action
MP	Military Police
MS	Motor Ship
NATO	North Atlantic Treaty Organization
NCO	Non-Commissioned Officer
NKVD	Soviet Secret Police
OSS	Office of Strategic Services
PIR	Parachute Infantry Regiment
PoW	Prisoner of War

RCAF	Royal Canadian Air Force
ROK	Republic of Korea
S-3 Officer	Principal Staff Officer – Operations
SCUBA	Self Contained Underwater Breathing Apparatus
SF	Special Forces
SFG	Special Forces Group
SI	Secret Intelligence
SOE	Strategic Office Executive
SSU	Strategic Service Unit
TRS	Tactical Reconnaissance Squadron
UN	United Nations
US	United States
USA	United States of America
USAAC	United States Army Air Corps
USAF	United States Air Force
USAAF	United States Army Air Force
USMC	United States Marine Corps
VE Day	Victory in Europe Day

Introduction

U.S. *Special Forces Commando* continues the story from where *An O.S.S. Secret Agent Behind Enemy Lines* left off – in May 1945, as First Lieutenant Leif Bangsbøll, codenamed Alexander Hudson and alias Jorgen Bech, OSS field agent, has just successfully led the attack to capture the German garrison at Ryvangen, Denmark.

Then, with the war in Europe over, Leif faces the reality that he will be sent to the Pacific theater of war to face the Japanese. But to his shock and amazement of the entire world, American President Harry S. Truman orders the use of a new most-powerful weapon: the atomic bomb. Shattered by the immense destructive power of the splitting-atom, Japan surrenders unconditionally. Believing the Second World War is finally over, Leif looks to Dorothy-Jean Henry to start a new life together.

However, the United States Department of War and the OSS have a critical assignment in Soviet-occupied Germany to which they believe Lieutenant Leif Bangsbøll is ideally suited. In December 1945, after three months of clandestine operations within the Soviet Sector of occupied Germany, a deadly encounter with the KGB changes everything.

This is the true account of my father's incredible life and military career. Each story in every chapter of this book is based on oral recollections conveyed by my father to me, my siblings and family friends, many times over – recollections that were at times very emotionally difficult to articulate, despite the long passage of time. All the central events described in the book have been corroborated by extracts from military records or other documented media or reference materials, including medal citations, letters and photographs with handwritten notes on the back.

Throughout the book I have taken literary license to generate the dialogue between characters. All characters are real. However, some names have been created as their true names were unknown to the author. The entire storyline of events within *US Special Forces Commando* is based on historical facts and colorfully augmented by the detailed description of events recounted by my father and his friends and military colleagues during his lifetime.

Chapter 1

The End and the Beginning

'We know what we are, but not what we may be.'
William Shakespeare, *Hamlet*

On 7 May 1945, after five years of Nazi occupation, Denmark was liberated by British and Canadian troops under the command of Field Marshal Bernard 'Monty' Montgomery. Two days earlier, First Lieutenant Leif Bangsbøll, of the United States Army, operating under the direction of the OSS, had successfully planned and lead a heroic attack, capturing the main German encampment at the Ryvangen garrison in Copenhagen. With the capture of the Ryvangen garrison, organized German resistance within the capital crumbled. The war and Denmark's painful and humiliating occupation were over.

Having successfully carried out his eight-month OSS mission behind enemy lines in occupied Denmark, and with his homeland liberated, Leif's first and foremost objective was to locate and be reunited with his father, Commodore Frederik Bangsbøll. It had been over five arduous years since he had laid eyes on his father, the most important person in his life. On 10 May 1945, at the Danish Admiralty building at the Holmen Naval Base in Copenhagen, Leif felt the warmth and strength of his father's embrace once more.

Five years of Nazi occupation had taken its toll. Leif thought his father had aged twenty years since he last saw him. His hair grayer, his face still tanned with a well-worn, leather-like quality, but with many more, deeper wrinkles around his eyes. But Frederik was alive and well; his steel-gray eyes still with the sparkle of his youth, as if he were still a young Naval ensign. But now, those eyes glistened with tears of joy at the sight of his son – alive, home, and a war hero. Frederik beamed with pride at the sight of his son and thought he looked fit and strappingly fine in his United States Army uniform, adorned with the blue and red arm band, denoting his affiliation with the Danish Resistance.

Father and son spent the afternoon reminiscing and from time to time, filling in each other with some of their respective wartime activities over the past five years. 'Where do I start?' said Leif and slowly pieced together the various trials and tribulations and course corrections of his life and military career. Frederik did the same and at one point they both came to the realization that over the past year, they had both, unbeknown to each other, been working with the same resistance leader: codenamed Gold. Clearly, their clandestine cover stories had held up, as it was only now that their codenames were unveiled to expose their true identities: Leif Bangsbøll was Agent Alexander Hudson, alias Jorgen Bech, and Frederik Bangsbøll was The Shepherd. 'Look at us Jocom – secret agents!' They laughed, long and hard, wiping away tears of joy.

At the end the day, Leif and Frederik were driven home to Nærum by Frederik's driver, passing through the Øterbro district of Copenhagen, driving near to Ryvangen garrison, which was once more manned by Danish soldiers, where less than a week earlier, Leif had successfully led the resistance force in a life and death struggle with its German occupiers. Now Denmark was liberated, and Leif and his father were once again free to move about their beloved Copenhagen as they wished.

Later that day, back in the comfort of their home, Leif and Frederik continued to fill in their separate experiences of the last five years, recounting the challenges of the war and some of the remarkable feats achieved. Frederik was so proud to hear of his son's leadership role in the capture of the Ryvangen garrison from the Germans. In turn, Leif was elated to hear his father recount his performance at the Copenhagen railway yard, when he retrieved the OSS weapons that Leif had sent on the German supply train. Then, after a lull in their conversation, Frederik commenced a more serious topic, indicating that he had heard that an American OSS agent had been responsible for the recent capture and elimination of a traitor, aiding the Nazis from within the Danish Ministry of Foreign Affairs. Leif's demeanor changed noticeably; he had not spoken of this event since he debriefed his partner, Agent Bjorn Toller the day after the mission – that was eight weeks ago.

> "Yes, that was my dirty work father. Not very pleasant business." Leif chose not to mention that the traitor he had been ordered to eliminate had been a former school mate. Leif felt that some of this war's details should be left behind, buried and forgotten. "However," Leif continued, "I must admit that as I interrogated Victor Larsen, it became apparent that he had pointed the Gestapo in your direction, Father; in the direction of the Royal Danish Naval Reserve Fleet, as being the lead in the secret transportation system of Danish Jews to the safety of Sweden. Knowing Larsen's culpability made the task much easier, but knowing he had led the Gestapo towards you, made it my revenge."

Leif said no more on the subject. He did not want to share the details that he had previously known and befriended Larsen, during his school days at Sølvgades School. His father did not need to be burdened with these facts.

Looking to lighten the mood, Frederik searched for a safer topic. 'Leif', he asked, 'what of your old girlfriend, Sophie? Have you seen her?' Leif could not hold back the grin stretching across his own face, and his father noted his son's eyes roll in mock exacerbation as Leif went on to explain the circumstances of Sophie's sudden incarceration in the sanitorium in Jutland. When Leif had finished explaining how it was a choice between either killing Sophie as a collaborator or secret her away for the remainder of the war, the room was silent, and the two men stared at each other for a long moment. Leif looked for an acknowledgement from his father that surely it was the only rational choice that could have been made. Frederik remained pensive for a moment, stroking his white beard as he processed the circumstances of the situation described. Suddenly, Frederik's large, callused hand rose and came down flat on the table with a crash, rattling the table settings and with a wink of his eye he bellowed, 'BY GOD, THAT'S A HELL OF A TALE SON! I don't suppose you two will be dating any time soon.' Frederick added, 'That story calls for a drink!' Frederik got up from the kitchen table and pulled the half full bottle of Akvavit from the ice chest.

After the schnapps and a few beers were consumed, along with half a dozen cigarettes, father and son leisurely prepared a simple supper together. It was a beautiful, warm evening, so they sat in the back yard, watching the sunset, overlooking the Kattegat Strait – the entrance to Copenhagen harbor. There, father and son enjoyed the simple pleasure of each other's company. After dinner, just as the Scandinavian sky's violet horizon began to reveal a universe of stars, Frederik brought out two fresh glasses and the bottle of Akvavit, its sides frosted and damp. They toasted the end of the war and the coming of peace. They toasted their fallen comrades. They toasted family and friends. Then Frederik made a final toast of the evening: 'Jocom, a toast to our parents' children.'

This was a toast his father had taught Leif as a child, which he said was created especially for Leif and his two sisters. Secretly it was Leif's favorite toast. Following a long, reflective silence, Leif said, 'Father, I plan to take the ferry tomorrow and spend the weekend on Bornholm – to pay my respects to Mother and the girls. Would you come with me?' Frederik's demeanor suddenly changed.

> Leif, you have obviously not heard the latest intelligence reports – you cannot go to Bornholm. Yesterday, Russian forces landed on Bornholm. They've rounded up the German garrison of 400 soldiers who had been occupying the island during the war. The Russians are staking a claim to our island.

This disturbing news brought an otherwise wonderful evening to an abrupt and unsavory end.

Later that night, laying in his bedroom, Leif could not fall asleep. He was relieved that the war was won and over and seeing his father alive and well was of great importance to him. But the thought that their little island in the Baltic – the final resting place of his mother and sisters and countless other Sørensen-Bangsbøll ancestors was now occupied by another foreign invader ate at his soul. Leif had planned to travel out to Bornholm, hopefully with his father, to stay at their family's summer home in Sveneke and to pay his respects at the gravesite of his mother and two sisters. It had been fifteen years since he last stood over the family plot hand in hand with his father. So much had happened since then and so much had changed. Leif needed to return to Bornholm, but it was clear that such a visit would have to wait.

As a result of the news of the Russian occupation of the Bornholm, Leif chose to remain with his father for a few more days. The next morning, Frederik went back to the Admiralty to make arrangements to bring back the many Danish naval ships that had been dispersed to the safety of neutral Sweden at the beginning of the war. His son continued with his interrogation of German prisoners and commenced the search for known Danish collaborators and traitors. Justice must be served.

Leif's plan to stay a few days with his father stretched into two weeks. Father and son reveled in this new, calm atmosphere within Denmark. During the last week of May 1945, after spending a rejuvenating stay at his boyhood home with his father, Leif, knowing he would soon receive new orders from the OSS, took the opportunity to travel back to Jutland and the towns of Aarhus and Horsens to visit and bid farewell to Hans Fletcher and the rest of his former resistance team members. While in Jutland, Leif also made a special detour to visit the village of Skive, to pay a visit to Olaf and Ragla Gustavsson, the farmer and resistance member whose farm Leif had landed on during his initial insertion mission in the early morning of 6 October 1944. Olaf and his wife – who had also assisted Leif with the Sophie Halverson situation – were immensely glad to see Leif again and spent an evening getting news of how Copenhagen had been liberated and together recalling the adventures of the past few years.

By early June 1945, Leif and the OSS and their SOE colleagues were wrapping up their investigations and post-war reports in Copenhagen. On 17 June 1945, OSS and SOE agents and staff in Denmark held a victory dinner to celebrate the Danish Resistance, and the accomplishments of the OSS and SOE in defeating the Nazi occupiers. Approximately 100 fellow agents and support staff assembled in the grand ballroom of the Wivex Hotel in Copenhagen. The Danish hosts put on a spectacular meal – a true Danish smorgasbord. The beer and Akvavit flowed freely and the victorious comrades in arms celebrated late into the night.

A week after the victory dinner, Leif received orders from the OSS headquarters in London, calling him back there. There, his assignment was to complete detailed reports on his activities as an OSS/SOE agent while in occupied Denmark, and to contribute to the collection of lessons learned from other OSS and SOE agents. Those documented lessons would later be used to educate and train new agents.

London, despite the obvious scars of war, was remarkable, observed Leif. The collective pride at enduring five years of German onslaught and the elation that Britain had been victorious were palpable on every street corner and in every setting. Leif enjoyed reuniting with his fellow OSS and SOE colleagues and made an effort to frequent many of the sites of London, including his favorite clubs and pubs. One evening he stopped by the Café de Paris, which was owned by Martin Poulsen, a fellow Dane. Upon arrival at the café, Leif was disappointed to find that the building was boarded up. Apparently, the damage done during the blitz had weakened the building's foundation and major repairs, or possibly even demolition, were in its future.

Then, in mid-July, Leif received new orders, directing him to return to OSS headquarters in Washington DC, where he was to prepare for a deployment into the Pacific theater of war against the Japanese. Once back in Washington, knowing he would be shipped out again in the near future, Leif felt that he needed to take some leave and visit some special war-time friends. On 1 August 1945, Leif was granted six weeks leave by his supervisor at OSS headquarters.

* * *

The first thing Leif did with the large bundle of cash – backpay that he had earned for his time in Denmark the previous year – was to buy a car. He chose a Ford Super Deluxe Coupe, two door, canary yellow convertible. With a brand-new car at his disposal and money still to spare in his pocket, Leif drove north up Interstate Highway 95 towards Canada. His destination was 231 King Street East, Oshawa, Ontario. True to his promise when he had bid farewell to Margaret and Clifford Henry in November 1942, Leif returned for a long-awaited visit. There, Leif reacquainted himself with the Henry family and particularly with Dorothy-Jean Henry, now 18 years old. The sweet young girl he had met three years earlier was now a beautiful young woman. Dorothy had enrolled at Branksome Hall College, an all-girls school in Toronto, and was spending the summer with her family in Oshawa when her secret love returned from the war – just as he had promised.

On 15 August 1945, while still on leave in Canada, to the great fortune of Leif and so many other Allied soldiers, news of an atomic bomb and the unconditional surrender of Japan was announced. The Second World War was over. Now, with the prospect of being assigned to fight the Japanese lifted from his thoughts, Leif was able to truly relax for the remainder of his leave with the Henry family. Or so he thought.

Less than a week later, on 20 August 1945, a cablegram addressed to Lieutenant Leif Bangsbøll was delivered to the Henry residence on King Street. Leif was ordered to report for duty to OSS headquarters in Washington DC immediately. A situation in the Soviet Zone of occupied Germany was developing for which the United States Department of War and Colonel "Wild Bill" Donovan, the Director of the OSS, believed Leif was ideally suited.

* * *

The seeds of this new mission had been planted five months earlier, in March 1945, during a meeting at the White House, when Colonel Donovan had addressed President Franklin D. Roosevelt.

> Mr. President, we must not allow the Soviets free reign in Europe or anywhere else. When this war is over and won, Stalin's paranoia over a resurgent Germany and the prospect of the emergence of freely elected governments in Eastern Europe, coupled with his visceral suspicion of American motives, make any possibility of working cooperatively with us or our Western Allies extremely remote.

FDR replied,

> You may be correct, colonel, you usually are about such matters. However, until this war is concluded, both in Europe and in the Pacific, the Russians are our allies.

Donovan knew the meeting was over as the president concluded, 'Thank you for coming in to see me this morning, Bill.' Donovan stood up and came to attention, as is standard military protocol. However, breaking with protocol, he did not immediately take his leave but spoke again. 'I understand, sir', he said, then insisted,

> Mr. President, after what our nations have just been through, I don't believe that the Soviets will want or risk open warfare with the West. At least not for a while. For those reasons, we need to have our agents inside the Soviet zone. These agents will be the first to 'fight' in this new conflict. It will be

> a cold war, because it will not be about direct conflict of hot metal being struck into our enemy, but much more a game of wits and brinkmanship. It will be a war of secrets and of spies, of threats and provocation, of calculated, clandestine missions within and amongst the enemy to glean vital intelligence as to what our adversary is doing, and just as important, what they are planning on doing. For the safety of our nation, we need to have our people inside the Soviet Zone so we can learn what they are really thinking and what they are truly intending to do.

FDR thanked Donovon and said, 'I will consider your recommendations'. Now the meeting was over.

So it was, on 8 May 1945, two months after Donovan's last meeting with FDR and just a month after the president's death, that war in Europe was over. The six years of bloody conflict was an extremely heavy burden to many nations, in terms of not only lives lost but also the physical destruction of national resources and the weakening of their economies. Almost 7.5 million Germans had died during the war. Most German cities were in ruins and the country's transportation network was virtually non-existent, having been pounded to rubble by the Allies' relentless aerial bombardment campaign. People who had lived in cities or any of the larger towns had either died in bombing raids or been displaced and were either refugees or living in squalor within the bombed-out remnants of their homes. Germany's capital, Berlin, was mostly an enormous pile of rubble and burnt-out buildings. Eight hundred thousand homes and apartments had been destroyed, and only 2.1 million of the city's original population of 4.3 million still lived within the city's perimeter by August 1945. Despite the ravages of war, the victorious major Allied powers – Britain, the United States, Canada, France and the Soviet Union – all knew that the centrally located Germany needed to be rebuilt and was still of vital importance to the future of Europe. But few, if any, realized that it would be the epicenter of the impending Cold War, a conflict that would last for the next forty-five years.

In accordance with the Potsdam Conference, the victorious Western Allies ceded roughly 25 percent of Germany's pre-war territory to Poland and the Soviet Union. As well, the agreement signed by the Allies divided the city of Berlin, which was located deep in the middle of the Soviet controlled sector of Germany, into four sub-sectors administered jointly by the occupying powers of Britain, the United States, France and the Soviet Union. As Donovan had expected, in an effort to assert its dominance, the Soviet Union quickly restricted movement across the intra-German borders and security zones. Soon after Berlin was subdivided, conflicts of interest emerged between the victorious Allied powers with regard to the post-war order in Europe in general and concerning the management of Germany in particular. Little did these world powers realize that this was the initial phase of a new type of geo-political war. Germany was poised to become the lightning rod of intense competition between East and West ideologies. The transition from declared war with a known enemy to the murkiness of the shadow war between East and West, communism and capitalism, rapidly took shape as this 'cold war' emerged and enveloped Europe and other parts of the world.

As early as June 1945, it became evident to American military leadership in the American Zone of Germany that the capabilities of the OSS in Germany would be best put to use in keeping the American commanders abreast of what developments were going on in the adjoining zones and, in particular, in the Soviet Zone. As such, at the end of the Second World War, the OSS had shifted to a new mission in Germany, with a strong emphasis on counterintelligence: the gathering of evidence for war crimes trials of Nazi officials, the rounding up of members of the Nazi underground movements and the recovery of lost and stolen art that had been looted by the Germans throughout Europe. All these efforts required OSS personnel and resources. With orders from the president, Donovan, the OSS director, ordered that all OSS assets be refocused on implementing a penetration agent program with a balanced network of counterintelligence and counterespionage agents operating in and near the Soviet Zone. It was becoming apparent that this war was going to be fought with spies, not soldiers, at least in the immediate future.

The growing concerns over Soviet intentions in central and eastern Europe meant that the OSS needed to revise its *raison d'être* and initiate new agent assignments. It was amidst these concerns and a direct result of this refocusing of effort that Leif was recalled from his leave in Canada on 20 August 1945 and ordered to return to Washington DC as soon as possible. Upon reporting to OSS headquarters, Lieutenant Bangsbøll was given intelligence briefings on the military and political situation in Europe and orders to report to the new OSS station chief, Mr. Allen Dulles, in Bierbrich, Germany, by 1 September 1945. Dulles was under top secret orders to use his OSS agents to infiltrate and spy on the Soviets now occupying regions of Germany. Leif would be working directly for United States Navy Commander Frank Wisner, department head of the SI Section, who was tasked to develop a new network of OSS infiltrators within the Soviet Zone. Leif was immediately put to work developing an insertion plan to enable him and his OSS colleagues to establish and operate a small intelligence gathering cell within the Soviet Zone of Berlin and adjoining Soviet controlled Germany. Under Operation Cambridge and known as a 'P' unit (P for intelligence production), the insertion teams were tasked with collecting information on Soviet forces' orders of battle (troop composition, organizational structure and locations) and assess all new military installations under construction in and around east Berlin. Relying on captured, former German intelligence agents for advice and critical contact information, Leif developed a plan and cover story that would support his infiltration of the Soviet Zone of East Berlin, within East Germany. He would transform into Agent Jorgen Bech once more. Leif would have the support of two other OSS agents who were already secretly operating within the Soviet Zone of Berlin. This three-man OSS team was designated as the Hudson cell.

Back in late July 1945, when Dulles had arrived in Berlin, the new OSS station chief for Germany – soon to be director of the relabeled SSU – had found that Soviet intelligence operations were far more advanced than he had anticipated and well ahead of the United States and its Western Allies' current capabilities. His counterpart within the KGB (the Soviet equivalent to the American OSS), Colonel General Ivan Alexandrovich Serov, was known to run a ruthless and efficient operation in occupied Germany, using terror and intimidation tactics to coerce former German officers and security police to aid the Russian efforts against the West. In a briefing to his OSS agents, Dulles made it clear that the Russians were playing hardball, and although the war was over, America was not at peace – a new era of dangerous, secret warfare was at hand, and his agents needed to always keep that at the forefront of their objectives. Familiar with counterinsurgency tactics, the message was clear – Leif did not have to be told this twice.

The necessary accoutrements for spying on the Soviets had to be put in place to allow American agents to operate in Soviet held territory. Fortunately, during the final stages of the Second World War, some of Dulles's OSS agents in charge of counterespionage had discovered, amongst captured German stores near Berlin, two truckloads of printing equipment, fake Soviet identity documents, official stamps for producing the forged signatures of senior Red Army officers, and an inventory of telephone books for Russian towns, all of which they put to good use in creating covers for OSS agents.

In early September 1945, far from the cold face of the tactical realities of counterinsurgency operations in Europe, and with the former vice president, Harry S. Truman, now occupying the Oval Office in the White House, uncertainty in Washington coincided with a re-examination of American intelligence policies, targets and operations not only within Europe but for all parts of the globe. President Truman was gravely worried about the spread of communism. In early September 1945, OSS field stations received the following directive:

> The conversion of this agency from a wartime to a peacetime basis brings with it a shift in emphasis in counterespionage targets. No longer are the German and Japanese Intelligence Services the focal point of our attention. Instead, all, repeat – all, foreign intelligence services, and personnel connected thereto, now become the legitimate objective observation and study for this Branch.

* * *

After completing his preparations with Dulles and his team of intelligence officers, Lieutenant Bangsbøll, travelling as Mr. Jorgen Bech, took one of the few scheduled trains still operating within Germany, from Frankfurt, Germany to Copenhagen, Denmark, where he would join a team of Danish Red Cross workers preparing to travel to Berlin to assist with the International Red Cross' efforts in the war-torn country. Though it would be a great deal of traveling for Leif just to end up right back in Germany, he knew it was important that he arrive in Berlin with the incoming Danish Red Cross team from Denmark to minimize questions from the already suspicious Soviet security and their customs authorities.

On the morning of 8 September 1945, upon his arrival in Copenhagen, Lieutenant Leif Bangsboll, in civilian clothing presented himself as Jorgen Bech, and was met at the central train station by his former boss within the Danish Resistance. Director Gold, who had received the request from Dulles, on behalf of the OSS, had facilitated the approval and creation of Leif's credentials as an accredited Danish Red Cross engineer and his assignment on the up-coming Red Cross team's deployment to Berlin. Bech's first order of business in Copenhagen was to meet briefly with his fellow Red Cross workers as they prepared to travel to Berlin. But before he could truly focus on his upcoming entry into Soviet-held Germany, he knew that he needed to take the opportunity while he was in Copenhagen to see his father. After his meeting with Dr Petre Magnusson, the Danish director of the Red Cross, and the rest of the Red Cross deployment team, Leif took a taxi to the Holmen Naval Base to locate his father.

Upon arrival at the main gate of Holmen Naval Base, Leif was met and escorted by a young junior Danish naval officer to the Royal Danish Naval Reserve Fleet headquarters building where his father, Commodore Frederik Bangsbøll, commanded all Royal Danish Naval Reserve activities. Leif walked the familiar cobblestone roads and passageways and was comforted by the calm atmosphere of freedom and peace that prevailed amongst the busy, goings on of this large naval base – a dramatic contrast to the draconian conditions that existed during the previous five years of occupation under the Nazis.

Upon entering his father's office, Leif, despite being in civilian clothing came to attention at the doorway. Frederik looked up from his massive oak desk, and with a broad smile that made his gray beard stretch, and exclaimed, 'Jocom! Come in, son! Come in!' As father and son embraced, the young ensign pulled the door to the office closed so as not to disturb his commander's reunion with his son. Though not exactly famous, details of Leif's war-time exploits had begun to spread, and with the recent awarding of the United States Army's Distinguished Service Cross (DSC) medal, honouring his combat actions against the Germans in Denmark, had gained some notoriety and certainly had impressed the young Naval Ensign who had been assigned to escort Lt Bangsbøll during his brief visit to Holmen Naval Yard. The ensign had heard rumours that the Danish-American soldier was even being considered for several Danish and Norwegian medals in recognition for his wartime accomplishments.

After a hearty embrace, father and son – commodore and first lieutenant – moved to the comfortable sitting area of Frederik's spacious office. Seated adjacent to the window which ran the length of the office, providing a spectacular view of the Holmen Naval Yard and the bustling activities of the Copenhagen harbor. They sat in the high-back leather chairs around a beautiful oak coffee table, which was prepared with coffee in Royal Danish Navy china and brightly polished silver cutlery – clearly Frederik wished to make his son welcome and comfortable. The two exchanged pleasantries and filled each other in on their activities over the past few months since they had last seen each other at the war's end. Leif conveyed that after departing Copenhagen in June 1944, he had spent time in London and Washington DC. Leif's eyes lit up as he explained that he had spent most of his post-war leave in Canada with the Henry family, who had befriended him during his time as a trainee and then instructor at Camp X. Frederik, who, despite his stoic nature, could tell that there was more to the story, pressed Leif for further details of his personal life. Eventually Leif succumbed to his father's inquiries and admitted that he had, in fact, fallen in love with a young Canadian girl named Dorothy-Jean Henry.

As Frederik stood up and set his gaze over the bustling naval yard, under a bright-blue, cloudless sky, he said:

> Your mother would be so pleased, Leif. You know, I can still see her standing right down there on pier No.1, waving to me each time my ship left, and again when we returned to port. She was a wonderful woman, and I can scarcely believe that it has been fifteen years since she passed. Much has happened since, and so much has changed.

Frederik turned to his son and asked, 'So, to what do I owe the pleasure of this visit? Will the Americans assign you back here now that the war in the Pacific is over?' Leif stood up and moved beside his father, who continued to survey the activities of the base and seaport below. It was now late afternoon, the sun was low on the horizon and the water in the harbor was a shimmering, golden orange. Leif paused and took in the simple beauty of the scene, then replied without emotion, 'Father, I'm being sent into Germany tomorrow. Into the Soviet Zone of Berlin to be precise.'

Unable to provide details or explain the circumstances of his assignment, Leif divulged only that their mutal wartime Resistance colleague Gold had facilitated support from the Danish government and that Dr Magnusson, a well known and respected sociology professor from the University of Copenhagen, was his sponsor/director with the Danish Red Cross. Magnusson, also a wartime member of the Danish Resistance, was known by Leif's father and was obviously trusted to provide cover support to this developing OSS mission. Frederik could fill in the gaps of the information that Leif could not share with him. The Soviets had been allies of necessity, united in cause against the Nazis, only to protect the Motherland until the defeat of Hitler. The Soviets had no intention of remaining aligned with Western objectives. As a result, the rift between the Soviet Bloc and the Western alliance would descend through central Europe like a mighty axe splitting a kiln-dried piece of wood. Frederik's heart sank as he realized this was another dangerous and secret OSS-related mission that must involve the Soviets.

'Dear God, has my son not given enough already?' lamented Frederik to himself. Then, feigning enthusiastic support of his son's new assignment, Frederik smiled and nodded his head and then called to his assistant to bring in the food – a good distraction to this ominous news. After a wonderful meal of traditional open-faced Danish sandwiches, including Leif's favorites of steak tartare and pickled herring, assorted cheeses, all accompanied by Danish beer and a shot of premium Aalborg Akvavit, father and son spoke of the trials and tribulations that had befallen Denmark during the Nazi occupation and the optimistic hope that better things were to come now that the Germans and the Japanese had been defeated. They finished their meal with strong black coffee. After a few minutes of an awkwardly growing silence, Leif indicated to his father that he would have to leave soon, as he needed to order a taxi to the airport to catch his flight to Berlin.

'Stay a few minutes longer, son. I will have my driver and staff car take you directly to the airport.' Frederik called for his assistant, who immediately appeared at his office doorway. 'We'll need the staff car in fifteen minutes to take Lieutenant Bangsbøll to the airport.' His assistant nodded and disappeared back into her office, shutting the office door behind her. After a few minutes of small talk, which avoided the obvious, Frederik rose to walk his son to the door. Then he stopped. With both arms outstretched, Frederik grasped his son by his broad shoulders and looked longingly at his face. With eyes glistening, Frederik could not find the words to speak. Frederik stoically smiled, nodded his fatherly approval and gave a final grip and release of his son's shoulders. The sentiment was clear – no words needed to be spoken. Slowly and reluctantly Frederik dropped his hands from his son's shoulders, releasing him to his fate. But as Leif turned towards the door, his father quietly and unexpectantly announced, 'Leif, son, I've met someone – a woman.'

Leif looked back at his father, allowing a small crack of a smile to appear and just nodded his head ever so slightly – no words could be spoken. A soft knock at the door broke the moment between father and son. The young naval ensign appeared at the doorway to the office to say that the staff car was ready and waiting. Leif continued to look at his father with love and understanding, suppressing all the childish urges to revolt against his father's announcement of a new women in his life. 'I'm happy for you, Father', he allowed, with a forced smile, 'I hope I will have the chance to meet her soon.' It was all he could muster. They shook hands, more formally this time, and Leif turned to follow the young and eager ensign to the waiting car.

As the ensign escorted Leif to his waiting transport, he could not help but think to himself how exciting his guest's wartime experiences must have been and how lucky he was to be going back to America – as a hero. Little did the ensign know that this Danish-American hero was not destined for the safety of his new home in America. Quite the contrary, Lieutenant Bangsbøll was heading east, back into harm's way.

Chapter 2

The Tiergarten Incident

'The life of a spy is to know, not to be known.'
George Herbert, 1640

Later that night, at 2300 hours, on 8 September 1945, Leif, using his well-established, yet fictitious persona, along with ample supporting false documentation regarding Jorgen Bech, Danish engineer and now an International Red Cross representative, stepped off a United States military C-47 Dakota transport aircraft at Berlin's Tempelhof Airport. Tempelhof Airport was situated within the United States sector of Berlin, deep inside the Soviet Zone of what would later be called East Berlin. There was no doubt that Soviet agents were monitoring the flow of Western 'Allied' passengers arriving and departing from within the Soviet-controlled area. Though most of the airport's buildings and hangars were nothing but burned-out shells, the airfield's runways had been repaired by the United State Army Corps of Engineers and had reopened a few weeks earlier, allowing desperately needed resupply flights to land. The aircraft that delivered agent Bech and the five, real Danish Red Cross workers was flown by United States Army Air Force (USAAF) pilots, was part of the International Red Cross effort to relieve the suffering of the destitute and dislodged civilians and refugees across Europe who needed food, water, medical attention, shelter and clothing – the essentials of life. Several weeks earlier, the Soviet Union had reluctantly approved the West's offer to send the International Red Cross supplies and aid workers to help relieve the growing famine and refugee crisis in central Europe, and particularly within the Soviet-controlled area of Germany. Leif and the five other Danish Red Cross workers on the flight from Denmark were still stiff and tired from their two-and-a-half-hour flight to Berlin. They each had had to find suitable seating amongst the several tons of cargo that filled the compartment. Pallets of food, medical supplies, blankets as well as engineering and surveying equipment filled almost every space in the aircraft's cargo compartment. The six Danish Red Cross workers were designated to join the other 200 International Red Cross workers already in Berlin, and assist with the distribution of both the Red Cross and Western Allies supplies as well as the set-up of a Red Cross office and a warehouse and distribution center somewhere in the shattered confines of the city of Berlin.

Leif was assigned to the latter, to assist Dr Magnusson, the assistant director of the Danish Red Cross and former member of the Danish Resistance himself, with the set up of the Red Cross relief distribution and engineering office. Leif's cover story was that he was part of Magnusson's engineering and administrative team assigned to assist him with locating and setting up a proper Red Cross office from which distribution of supplies could be organized and controlled, as well as conducting engineering assessments on critical infrastructure repair projects. Also joining the Red Cross headquarters set up team were two other real Red Cross workers. Two other OSS agents, who would assist Leif and who, together, made up the Hudson cell, had already been in Berlin for several weeks, also under the guise of Danish Red Cross workers.

During his first week in Berlin, Leif and his two OSS colleagues – support agents, William Jacobsen and Carl Vestegaard – focused exclusively on solidifying their cover stories. To accomplish this, they worked long hours as Red Cross workers, assessing the best location to set up the Red Cross office and improving the temporary Red Cross warehouse and distribution center at Berlin's Tempelhof international airport. If they were being watched by the KGB, which they had to assume they were, they had to appear to be hard-working Red Cross employees. However, during their daily travel through the city between their humble accommodations, the airport warehouse and the new Red Cross office, the three OSS agents gathered as much intelligence as they could – observing and reporting upon many on-going Soviet military activities. Some of the Soviet work efforts were clearly basic recovery efforts, such as clearing streets of rubble left from the Allied bombings. But oftentimes the 'when and where' the Soviets were working provided valuable intelligence as to which areas of the city and surrounding areas were their priority, and that priority could provide clues as to the Soviets' strategic objectives.

* * *

During the past five years, Leif had learned to expect the unexpected and to adapt well to the changing circumstances that his wartime / military affiliation threw at him. In September of 1945 another major change was looming for him and his fellow OSS agents. On 20 September 1945, a Presidential decision was made over 4,000 miles away, across the Atlantic Ocean, that would change the US intelligence program forever. It was a decision that came without warning and would have a profound impact on Leif and all his fellow OSS colleagues. On that day, President Truman disbanded the OSS. With the stroke of a pen, the OSS ceased to exist, only to be quickly reborn as the new Strategic Services Unit (SSU), which fell under the Department of War. A new era of American intelligence activities had commenced. The SSU – which would soon be renamed the Central Intelligence Agency (CIA) – shifted its efforts to collect information on personnel, activities and goals of all foreign intelligence services, with particular emphasis on the Soviet Union.

For Lieutenant Bangsbøll and his Hudson cell colleagues, operating behind enemy lines once again, this time in Soviet-occupied Germany, the disbandment of the OSS and its resurrection as the SSU had no direct impact on their current mission. In fact, the Hudson cell would not learn of the organizational change until nearly a week after the fact – during its weekly encrypted report submitted by shortwave radio. What they were called and who they reported to did not matter, the important fact was that Lieutenant Bangsbøll, and the Hudson cell, had slipped through the Soviet security net as ordered and were operating within the Soviet Zone in relative obscurity as members of the Danish Red Cross assigned to help the German population rebuild their country. Lieutenant Bangsbøll's orders were to observe, assess and report as much as he could about Soviet military units and their intentions within Germany, at all levels – strategic, operational and tactical – and identify, if possible, any Soviet intelligence probes – agents or initiatives – operating within Western Allies' zones of Germany. Though his initial infiltration into Soviet-occupied Germany went smoothly, Leif's cloak of anonymity would not last for long.

In the autumn of 1945, Soviet security officials expected that the Western Allies would attempt to infiltrate the Soviet Zone with their agents in order to obtain military and political intelligence on the Soviet Union and Soviet-occupied regions of Germany, just as their Soviet counterparts were attempting to do with the Western Allies. To counter this Western infiltration, the Soviets' secret police – the Soviet's Commissariat for Internal Affairs (NKVD) and the Committee for State Security (KGB) relied on a broad network of surveillance methods and multiple protocols of identity verification and identity pass renewal processes – and, of course, frequent, no-notice demands for personal documentation (not unlike the German Gestapo methods) to verify the identity of all personnel inhabiting the Soviet sector of East Germany. Though Lieutenant Bangsbøll's cover story as a Danish Red Cross member was effective to get him into the Soviet Zone and for the first few weeks of his assignment there, the vigilance of the KGB would eventually put Leif and his two fellow OSS/SSU team members on the Soviet security network's sphere of interest. By mid-November 1945, approximately ten weeks after entering Berlin's Soviet Zone, Leif's antennae were up – he knew someone was watching them with more than a casual interest.

Lieutenant Bangsbøll, now operating as Agent Bech, along with Agents Jacobsen and Vestegaard, had already established a detailed protocol of verbal and non-verbal code phrases and visual signals that would subtly convey warnings or all clear messages to each other. As well, they had established several safe house locations throughout the city and the surrounding area of Berlin where they could find shelter and relative safety in an emergency and exchange clandestine communication. Granted, with so much of the city in ruins, some of the safe houses were just vacant cellars of bombed homes or office buildings, but they served their purpose. Regardless, the agents routinely reviewed and practiced their clandestine communication system to ensure that when the time came, they would be able to warn each other of impending danger and have a sequence of procedures and rendezvous locations to meet or leave messages to give themselves time to assess their circumstances in relative safety and without compromising the rest of the OSS/SSU network of agents.

Most vehicles moving about Berlin were military ones, some of which had been German citizen-owned vehicles, confiscated by the Allies and given to aid agencies such as the International Red Cross. Most of the Red Cross's vehicles were former German Army vehicles – trucks and staff cars, with the German swastika painted over with a red cross on a white background. When Bech, Jacobsen and Vestegaard traveled about the city conducting engineering assessments, they did so with caution, alert to any signs of being followed by the NKVD or KGB, and routinely changing their routes and doubling back to shake off anyone who might be following them. The Berliners they encountered during their daily work, who had survived the Allies' onslaught, usually looked weak and cowed. Many Berliners who remained within the city were war weary. Most of the citizens on the street looked emaciated, frightened and had a dazed appearance. Many had still not yet recovered from the shock of the battle for their capital and the years of war related hardship, death and destruction. Thankful to have survived and adapting to this new world order of Soviet occupation was a new but similarly stressful nightmare for Berliners and German citizens in many other German cities and towns.

The months of September and October 1945 had been legitimately focused on getting the new Red Cross headquarters set up and improving the distribution system, though some valuable OSS-related intelligence gathering was gleaned as a result. It was essential that the OSS agents appeared to be dedicated relief workers before they began initiating any substantial, clandestine intelligence-gathering operations. Towards the end of November 1945, Agent Bech had received some unsubstantiated intelligence reports indicating that the Soviets were constructing several large military airstrips east of Berlin. As a result, Leif tasked Jacobsen and Vestegaard to investigate, using the cover story that they were seeking supply routes to transport desperately needed Red Cross supplies further into the Soviet Zone of eastern Germany.

It was expected that the reconnaissance mission would take two days. During their absence, Agent Bech focused on a major engineering project to repair the Leipziger Straße bridge over the Spreek Canal, in the center of Berlin. Leipziger Bridge was located in the Soviet Zone of Berlin, close to the Soviet-American crossing point, known as 'Checkpoint Charlie'. While conducting the engineering assessments of the bridge repairs, Bech was able to secretly pass an encrypted written report to American contacts within the American Zone. The report detailed the intelligence he and his team had gathered in the previous weeks within the Soviet Zone and included the ongoing investigation into the possible large Soviet air bases being constructed to the east of Berlin.

Two days passed since Bech's two colleagues had departed on their mission without word from them. Understanding that in autumn 1945, the German telephone system was still being rebuilt and as such was unreliable, Leif went to each of the agents' apartments, located in the famous Tiergarten district of Berlin, to see if his colleagues had returned unannounced. They had not. Concerned at their overdue status, Leif then drove by the primary and secondary safe houses, but the associated message drops were empty, and the pre-agreed signal was not evident that the safe houses had been or were active.

At the end of the third day, without any contact from either Jacobsen or Vestegaard, Leif, facing the possibility that his cell might have been compromised by the KGB, began preparations for possible close down of his cell and the potential of an emergency repatriation to the American Zone. By the book, Leif's response was the appropriate and logical course of action. However, Agent Bech could not accept the possibility that he might have to abandon two of his colleagues, who he feared might now be in Soviet custody. That night, Bech transmitted a brief, encrypted message to the SSU operations center in the American Zone indicating the basic situation:

> Two agents on reconnaissance mission north-east of Berlin are twenty-four hours overdue. Consider possibility that agents have been captured. Consider cell closure protocols and evacuation of remainder of the team to be imminent.

The next morning, 28 November 1945, the office of the International Red Cross received a telephone call from Vestegaard. Fortunately, Bech was in the office and was able to speak directly with him and learned that the reconnaissance mission had been successful but had taken longer than expected. Furthermore, while on route back to Berlin the two agents had run into some trouble with the KGB.

They were now safe, having just cleared the Soviet security checkpoint at the Friedrichstaße bridge over the Falkenseebach river in the southeastern quarter of Berlin. 'Some trouble with the KGB?' wondered Bech. He knew that any contact with the Soviet KGB or NKVD was to be taken seriously, but 'some trouble' could mean a broad spectrum of disasters for the SSU mission or for his cell. Immediately concerned, but unable to speak openly over the possibly compromised telephone line, Bech took a moment to pause and think through the options he had been considering as he waited to hear from his agents. Bech wrote down the following coded message: 'MPC, SH, RP-1, TL5'. Then in a calm, clear voice, he ordered the two returning agents to initiate their return protocol in accordance with the phonetically coded instructions: 'MPC, SH, RP-1, TL5.'

The coded message translated to:

> **M**ission **P**robable **C**ompromise (MPC) – return via **S**afe **H**ouse (SH) – use **R**everse **P**riority **-1** (return to the safe house, one location up from the bottom of the memorized list of safe houses) (RP-1) – the **T**hreat **L**evel (TL) is considered high: Level **5** (5).

Speaking slowly and deliberately, Bech stated, once more, using military phonetics,

> I say again, initiate your return protocol in accordance with plan: **Mike, Papa, Charlie,** [pause] **Sierra, Hotel** [pause], **Romeo, Papa, minus one** (pause) **Tango, Lima, five.** I'll meet you there tonight at 1800 hours sharp. Don't be late.

The added timing instruction was also part of the code. By adding the word 'sharp' Bech was telling the agents to add four hours to the prescribed time stated. If anyone was listening in on the telephone call, the information would be challenging to decipher, at least in the short time before their planned rendezvous.

'Do you understand those instructions?' asked Bech. After a moment's delay, Vestegaard said, 'Affirmative.' Then the telephone line went dead. Vestegaard slowly released his hand from the telephone handle and looked at his partner, Jacobsen. He smiled awkwardly.

> Bech thinks we have been compromised and are probably being followed by the KGB. He has ordered us to return to one of our safe houses – with extreme caution.

Both Vestegaard and Jacobsen mentally went through the encrypted instructions that Bech had given them. They both realized that the code order MPC5

(Mission Possible Compromised Level 5) that they had received was serious and was only one degree lower than 'MC6', which meant that:

> The mission has been compromised, disperse immediately and make your way out of Soviet Zone to any friendly (Allied) area as soon as possible, using any means at your disposal.

Jacobsen, the eternal optimist, shrugged his shoulders and said,

> He's just being cautious, Carl. I'm sure we lost our tail – those KGB agents who were following us back near that village when they had pulled the U-turn off the autobahn are nowhere to be seen.

Earlier that day, Vestegaard and Jacobsen had completed their reconnaissance of two suspected Soviet airfields being constructed near the German towns of Neuhardenberg and Müncheberg, east of Berlin. Having taken a series of clandestine photographs of the ongoing construction and recording map coordinates of the two sites, the agents were returning to Berlin via Autobaun Number 1 as planned. They had initially planned to cross back into the city limits via the bridge in the Hoppegarten district, however, two hours earlier, just prior to arriving at the security checkpoint, Jacobsen confirmed that they were being tailed. If they continued to the security checkpoint, they knew they would be caught for certain. The KGB agents following them would take advantage of the security stop to close in on the suspected foreign agents. Vestegaard recalled the sequence of events. They spotted a car following them as they departed Neuhardenberg. Thirty minutes later, as they approached the outskirts of Berlin, at the Hoppegarten Bridge, over the Strausberger-Muhlenflies River near the entrance to Autobahn 10, they had executed a drastic, high-speed U-turn to escape the Soviet secret police. The evasive manoeuvre caught the KGB agents off guard and Vestegaard and Jacobsen quickly put distance between themselves and their pursuers as they sped southbound on the autobahn. Vestegaard and Jacobsen drove south-west towards their planned, alternative city entry point via the Friedrichstaße bridge in the southern district of Berlin. Though there was another security checkpoint at the Friedrichstaße bridge to cross, the two agents' false documentation as Red Cross workers proved effective as they passed through after a cursory review of their identity papers by the Soviet Army guards.

Once back within the Berlin city limits, in the perceived relative safety of the busy streets, Jacobsen pulled their car over near the central train station to allow Vestegaard to make his telephone call from one of the few reliably functional public telephone banks in that part of the city. His telephone call was to the Red Cross headquarters, at which time they received their caution and reintegration orders from Bech: 'MPC, SH, RP-1, TL5.' Vestegaard repeated the coded instructions to himself once again.

'Are we still being followed?' wondered Vestegaard, as he casually scanned the surrounding streets. Aside from the many hungry and exhausted looking people walking down the middle of the road (since most of the street remained impassable) hauling their carts full of meager, personal belongings, there were few vehicles on the streets of Berlin. 'Surely, we would be able to notice if we were being followed?' he thought. Vestegaard and Jacobsen sat in their car and reviewed the instructions that Bech had just given – they needed to mentally review the list of safe houses (in their proper order) to determine the location where they were to meet up with Leif that evening at '2200 hours: 1800 hours plus four hours equals 2200 hours.' Both agents went through the list of safe houses in their minds, and both agreed that the second to last safe house on their list (**S**afe **H**ouse, **R**everse **P**riority **-1**) was the second-floor apartment, Apartment D, located at 121 Schelling Straße in the Potsdamer Platz complex. This safe house was situated across the street from the Bluemax Theater. The theater had been a popular venue before the Second World War, and despite having been mostly destroyed, was still a distinctive, recognizable landmark. Though they had only visited and inspected this safe house once several weeks earlier, they were familiar with its location as it was not far from the Hotel Maratim on Hitzgalle Straße where their assigned apartments were located.

Vestegaard and Jacobsen had several hours to pass before their rendezvous with Bech, so they found a small *Gasthaus* (guest house and restaurant) within walking distance of the safe house that served a basic but well-presented meal, given the limited food supplies available. Both agents discussed various possible scenarios that might confront them in the hours to come – likely confrontation with the police or KGB on route to, at or after entering the safe house. Jacobsen said, 'We should expect that Bech will have cased out the safe house to ensure it is in fact safe, but we need to be prepared if things go wrong.' Both agents had their service revolvers with them and would not hesitate to use them if necessary. They recalled Allen Dulles's warning: 'The Soviets play hardball. If you are in a fight, they will not offer you quarter.'

Vestegaard and Jacobsen agreed that if they became separated, they would forego going to their apartments – that would be too easy a place to trap them. They agreed to meet at midnight back at the car they had already parked in a nearby, darkened alley. While Vestegaard and Jacobsen were eating their simple meal of boiled potatoes and beets and the questionable piece of meat that was advertised to be pork chops, they discussed their rendezvous plan. At that same time, Bech was only a few blocks away, cautiously approaching the designated safe house on Schelling Straße. Once he was certain he had not been followed or was not being observed, he entered Apartment D. When he entered the safe house, he determined that the apartment was secure and as far as he could tell, it had not been compromised. Bech left a handwritten note detailing his instructions in the drop box – an empty kettle on the stove in accordance with their pre-agreed communications plan, and then departed. He had not spent more than two minutes in the apartment. Once again, he assumed that he was being watched by the Soviets, so he cautiously departed the apartment building via the basement, where he crawled out of the coal shoot into the debris-filled alley behind the apartment. When he was sure he had not been observed and was not being followed, he proceeded towards the actual rendezvous point on Tiergarten Straße and the expanses of Tiergarten Park, a massive park located in the heart of downtown Berlin. Tiergarten Park, Berlin's oldest and largest, consisted of 200 hectares of wide expanses of tree covered parkland and was surrounded by such notable landmarks as the Reichstag (the German parliament buildings), the Berlin polytechnic university, the Kaiser Wilhelm Memorial Church and the famous Brandenburg Gate.

Bech considered the safe house at Apartment D on Schelling Straße to be too confined a space, with restrictive access and exit points for a safe rendezvous location for a possibly compromised team of agents returning from a sensitive mission. As such, Bech had decided that the nearby Tiergarten Park would be the actual rendezvous location. Bech walked the grounds of the south-east corner of Tiergarten Park to refamiliarize himself with the terrain. Despite the massive destruction inflicted upon the city of Berlin, Tiergarten Park had remained relatively unscathed. As there were only a few, small pavilion buildings within the confines of the park with no strategic value, the park itself had been spared any intentional targeted attacks by Allied bombers. Bech walked by several large bomb craters and toppled trees that had been damaged during the later stages of the Allied bombing campaign. This damage seemed to be confined to the edges of the park, adjacent to the city's buildings and boulevards.

The instructions Bech had left for Vestegaard and Jacobsen in the safe house drop box would direct the agents to this dark and secluded rendezvous point from which Bech could observe their arrival from a distance and, more importantly, observe anyone that might be following them. Leif recalled 'Dangerous Dan' Fairburn's words of warning from his Camp X training days: 'Trust no one, kill or be killed.' They were cautionary words of macabre wisdom. Leif's memory neurons were firing up like a Christmas tree and this would be his mantra until this situation was resolved.

As Bech waited for his fellow SSU agents to arrive, he had time to contemplate his surroundings.

> It was less than nine years earlier, that my father and I walked through this beautiful park together. We had taken the walk following the spectacular military parade we had witnessed, honoring the Führer's fiftieth birthday. How young and naïve I was back then… and how correct Father had been to be so concerned at the meteoric rise to power of Hitler and his maniacal and seemingly unlimited ambitions for world domination.

Leif recalled, with a degree of embarrassment, how exhilarating it had felt to see and hear the thousands of goose-stepping troops of the Third Reich's military forces marching up Tiergarten Straße in 1936. Now, here he was again, in 1945, back in the heart of Hitler's Third Reich – well, what was left of it. And now he was playing a real-life, dangerous game of cat and mouse with the Soviet NKVD and KGB. 'Will this madness ever end?' thought Leif. 'When will I get my life back?'

Bech froze – he thought he heard something, and his mind and instincts snapped back to his current situation. The darkness that fell over Berlin at night was unnerving in its eerie profoundness. With the extensive damages to its electrical grid and gas lines, less than 10 per cent of the city had any semblance of functional lighting. The darkness that enveloped the city, and Tiergarten Park, which was only sparsely lit prior to the war, was a virtual black cloak of concealment. Ideal if you wished to hide in the shadow but challenging to conduct any anonymous movement or activity. Bech had chosen this rendezvous location well. As he stood under the canopy created by a large stand of mature oak trees whose leaves now blanketed the ground around him, he scanned the various approach routes. Always vigilant to the slightest security vulnerability, he realized that the temperature had dropped several degrees since he had arrived, and he could now see his breath. This realization made him instinctively lean back into the shadow to ensure his condensing breath would not give away his location – it was those little details that could mean the difference between success and failure, life and death. Agent Bech identified the source of the noise he had heard – it was just a mangy, half-starved dog moving through the night in its endless seach for sustenance. The dog seemed to sense Bech's precence in the shadows and immediately altered its course of travel to give the unknown human a wide birth.

Bech pulled up the collar of his coat and was grateful that he had put on his long overcoat. The warmth of the coat was comforting, but more importantly, its loose-fitting style allowed him to easily conceal both the pistols he carried on his person; his ever-reliable OSS-issued Walther PPK and a newly acquired 9-millimeter Husqvarna pistol. He had just recently obtained the 9 millimeter by trading it for a carton of American cigarettes with a former Wehrmacht army sergeant he had met. Leif had encountered this entrepreneurial German soldier soon after arriving in Berlin, and immediately liked his honest, forthright and professional manner. It was clear that he had been a reluctant combatant of the Third Reich but had all the requisite skills and was a natural soldier and survivor. The former Wehrmacht sergeant turned out to be resourceful in various and nefarious endeavors during Bech's tenure in Berlin as an International Red Cross worker. He was in his late fifties and had been pressed into service with the German army in 1943 and was lucky and talented enough to survive the Allied onslaught until Germany's capitulation in May 1945. The former German soldier had quickly realized that upon the collapse of the Third Reich the Western Allies would be far more civilised than their Soviet counterparts. As such, he had been keen to assist the young Danish Red Cross worker who was looking for advice on various aspects of Berlin, including usable office space, apartments for rent and ultimately the acquisition of a personal firearm – the 9-millimeter Husqvarna. According to the German sergeant, he had 'liberated' the pistol in the final days of the war from a Russian soldier who no longer had the capacity to use the weapon. Both Leif and his alter-ego Jorgen knew what that meant: 'War is hell, kill or be killed.'

Bech, still standing in the shadows at Tiergarten Park, figured that he had about twenty minutes to wait until Vestegaard and Jacobsen arrived. During that time, he reviewed their activities over the past few weeks to see if he could discern how and when his SSU team might have been compromised. He thought back to the many routine encounters with the Soviet security forces during his time in the Soviet Zone, when they had been ordered to present their identity papers daily, at checkpoints or just randomly as they navigated the cluttered streets or even while sitting in a café or restaurant. Then he recalled an event in early October, when he had had his first serious encounter with the NKVD and KGB. On that day, Bech had just completed an inspection of a large warehouse that had sustained bomb damage during the Second World War and had undergone structural repairs to its roof and floor by his engineers. The warehouse, located only a few miles from the Tempelhof airport, had miraculously sustained relatively minor damage compared to some of the surrounding, industrial structures. This warehouse was chosen by the International Red Cross leadership because it was ideally located near to the airport and a major autobahn route, which would facilitate and improve Red Cross storage and aid distribution capabilities. On that day, just as Bech was exiting the newly repaired Red Cross warehouse, he was confronted by two Soviet officials, one army major in uniform and one 'inspector' dressed in civilian clothes, who was undoubtedly with the KGB. They intercepted Bech and demanded to see his identity papers. Though they attempted to convey that their sole concern was for the structural integrity of the warehouse and the safety of future Red Cross staff occupants, Agent Bech immediately knew otherwise, but he played along with their amateurish ruse. Bech answered all their personal and technical questions without hesitation. Initially, the conversation was conducted in broken Russian and broken Danish, but they quickly determined that German seemed to be the best common language for the three 'allies' to converse.

As the civilian-dressed Soviet official reviewed Bechs papers, the Soviet Army major peppered Bech with questions regarding his activities in the Soviet Zone since his arrival from Copenhagen on 8 September 1945. After twenty minutes of questions regarding dates and places around Berlin that they had observed Bech working, the Soviet officials seemed to be satisfied with his answers and the interview appeared to be coming to a successful conclusion. The Russian major handed back Bech's papers. They shook hands, and the KGB agent turned and began to walk away. The Russian inspector/KGB agent suddenly stopped, looked back at Bech, and in perfect English attempted to test Jorgen Bech's identity with a sly, yet simple trick.

'Mr Bech', the KGB agent asked in perfect English, 'do all American agents speak German as well as you?' Without a moment's hesitation and basing his following response on the theory that the best defense is a good offense, Bech replied with great assertion, at first in Danish and then switching to German.

> Who is American here, sir? I am a Dane, and you are a Russian. You are a member of a barbarous nation, who claim to be an ally, but have invaded my Danish homeland island of Bornholm without provocation and which is an affront to international law!

As Bech stepped forward towards the KGB agent in a menacing manner, he pointed at the Russian official's chest and using their common language of German, said emphatically, 'Listen here, comrade, if you are looking for Americans, I'm sure that there are several hundred thousand of them just a few miles over in that direction.' He gestured over his shoulder towards the American Zone. 'I am a Dane, and damn proud of it. Don't you forget it!' Jorgen Bech continued his diatribe in German for his final and closing rebuke towards the two Soviet officials:

> I'm a Danish engineer, here with the International Red Cross and I'm going to certify that this warehouse is ready for use and recommend that we start occupying it tomorrow. Do you have a problem with that, comrades?

The intensity of Bech's response was so spontaneous and vehement that, although neither of the Soviet officials fully comprehended the Danish portion of the tirade that had been unleashed upon them, its passion was clearly from the heart of a Dane, and both Soviet agents recoiled from the verbal assault. The Russian major immediately attempted to reassure the over-zealous, yet patriotic Dane that they meant no offense and that they were just ensuring his identity and that his engineering report on the hangar was thorough and accurate. 'The Red Cross operations at this location can commence as soon as you are ready.'

Relieved, Bech nodded and turn and went back into the warehouse, thinking to himself that being confident in the face of these aggressive Russians could be respected, though he may have overplayed his cards with too much zeal. A fundamental rule taught to OSS and SOE agents specifically and to military personnel in general who might become PoWs is to be the 'gray man' to improve your odds of survival. The 'gray man' is the quintessential, non-descript, non-interesting, blend in with the crowd nobody. To avoid attention of your captors – the prison guards, the police, border guards or, in the worst case during the Second World War, the Gestapo – the best technique was to be relatively invisible or totally forgettable in your appearance, mannerisms and conduct. In Leif's situation, during the identity check, the two Soviet officers had asked some general, personal questions of Jorgen Bech, to which he provided the necessary information, including his nationality, his date and place of birth, the names of his parents and their current address in Denmark – all true information concerning the real Jorgen Bech. They also asked for the name of his employer, to which he replied: the Danish Red Cross, and his superior, Dr Petre Magnusson. All of which was also true – to a degree. Though Leif's performance for the two Soviet officials at the new Red Cross warehouse was extremely effective – it convinced both the Soviet Army intelligence officer and the KGB agent that Jorgen Bech was a legitimate Danish engineer working with the International Red Cross – his aggressive diatribe concerning the Soviet occupation of Bornholm convinced the Russians that he was clearly a patriotic Dane, though it had breached a fundamental rule normally followed by an agent and all those others who wish to remain undetected by the authorities: do not bring attention to yourself. Normally, providing this type of information to security officials would not be of concern to Leif because of the thoroughness of their OSS-fabricated cover story and associated files. However, given that the Soviet Union currently occupied the island of Bornholm where the actual parents of his dead friend Jorgen Bech, now resided, this was enough open-source information available to the Soviets, which could and would eventually cross reference to Jorgen Bech's active, Soviet-issued, International Red Cross worker permit for working within the Soviet Zone of Germany. A cross reference that would expose the OSS/OSU subterfuge.

* * *

The Soviet's cross-referencing of intelligence would result in a red flag being attached to Jorgen Vejlby Bech's identity file. This unfortunate mishap occurred as a result of the Soviet Army's thorough application of their mandatory registration of all residents and visitors to the now occupied Danish Island of Bornholm. This mandatory registration had been implemented by the Soviet Army during the first month of the twelve months occupation of the island. All residents of the Bornholm, including Mr. and Mrs. Nicolaus Bech, the parents of the real and deceased Jorgen Bech, were required to provide family background details. When it came to their dearly departed son, Mr. and Mrs. Bech said that their son Jorgen had died on 7 December 1941, at Pearl Harbor as a member of the United States Navy. The reminder of this fact made both Mr. and Mrs. Bech simultaneously proud and sad. The information was annotated on their file for follow-up research by the KGB. This would be Leif's undoing as an OSS/SSU agent and placed Leif and the Hudson cell in grave danger.

Leif surmised that the Soviet security analyst who would eventually review and process the report might make the connection between Mr. and Mrs. Bech of Bornholm, Denmark, formerly of Copenhagen, who reported their son Jorgen V. Bech deceased, with another file from the Soviet Zone of Berlin Germany listed a Jorgen V. Bech with the same parents as a current, living member of the Danish office of the International Red Cross who had been issued a valid and active Soviet Zone permit. However, the information that initially caught the attention of the Soviet security personnel who read the file was the mention by his parents of Jorgen Bech as a member of the United States Navy. It was inevitable that once the Soviets had interviewed the Bechs, red flags would be raised on the Bech file.

While Soviet security processes were thorough, fortunately for Bech and his SSU team they were also incredibly bureaucratic, cumbersome and slow, so the manual cross referencing of the Soviet registration of Bornholm residents with Red Cross permit holders in the Soviet Zone in Berin did not occur quickly.

* * *

As of mid-November 1945, Leif (Agent Jorgen Bech) continued to operate under the Soviet-approved work permit with relative anonymity. However, in late November, just two days prior to Bech assigning Vestegaard and Jacobsen with the mission to investigate the possible Soviet Air Force installation east of Berlin, Vestegaard had innocently triggered a separate Soviet security investigation when his landlord had reported, during another routine Soviet security probe, that although Vestegaard was a polite and quiet tenant, he frequently left his apartment at night, along with another tenant and Danish Red Cross worker, Mr Jacobsen. Although this information was not remarkable in itself, given the decimated condition of the city and the fact that there were limited things to do at night in post-war Berlin that a normal, law-abiding citizen could do, it raised the question: 'Where did Vestegaard and Jacobsen go at night and what were they doing?' These unanswered questions prompted the KGB to follow Vestegaard and Jacobsen during their reconnaissance mission of the Soviet airfields under construction. The Soviets were now actively tightening the noose around two of the three Hudson cell team members.

At precisely 2200 hours, as per their coded, verbal instructions from Bech, Vestegaard and Jacobsen entered the safe house at 121 Schelling Straße. After reading Bech's instructions, which he had left in the empty kettle (their message drop-box) on the stove in Apartment D, Jacobsen walked over to the apartment's fireplace and there in the cold, gray ashes was the object, wrapped in burlap cloth as Bech had indicated in his note: a camera with a flash attachment retrieved from Leif's engineering equipment. Bech knew that Vestegaard and Jacobsen had started their mission with a camera, but he couldn't be sure that they would still have it with them and the flash component was going to be essential for this evening's purposes.

Exactly as Bech had instructed, the two agents exited the apartment building the way they had entered, by way of the main entrance. Bech's rational was, if his agents were being followed – which he was certain they would be – he did not want the KGB to know that the SSU agents knew that they were being followed.

Bech's final instructions read,

> Exit casually but cautiously. And if you spot a tail, continue to our rendezvous point, and I will be there to intercept and eliminate any opposition. Don't forget the camera with the flash.

Vestegaard lit a match and burned Bech's note and threw it in the fireplace and said, 'Let's go to Tiergarten.'

If his plan was going to work, Bech knew they would have to catch the Russians by surprise and take advantage of a precious few moments of sudden chaos in order to maximise the likelihood of success and their safe escape. At 2230 hours, from his concealed location in the Tiergarten Park, Bech, whose night vision had completely adapted to the darkness, observed two men crossing the Tiergarten Straße, one holding a small burlap parcel in his left hand, the signal that the two of them believed that they were being followed. As per Bech's instructions, the two SSU agents entered the park at the south-east entrance and proceeded just far enough to be in the deep shadows of the trees within the park. They were now unobservable from the built-up area across the street from which they had just come and from the KGB agents who had followed them.

Without giving up his place of concealment, Bech gave his two agents a quick, step by step outline of his plan to intercept the Russian agents, who were expected to show up at any moment. Vestegaard and Jacobsen acknowledged their assignments and moved another ten paces into the park where they were completely concealed by darkness, as perscribed in Bech's instructions. There, they stood, lit and began to smoke cigarettes as instructed. Within a minute, after observing the two cigarettes being lit by the Red Cross members, one of the two KGB agents who had been following Vestegaard and Jacobsen since they had crossed back into Berlin earlier in the day moved forward from the shadows across the Tiergarten Straße. Seeing the two cigarettes being lit and remaining stationary, the Soviet agent assumed the two foreign agents were in place for their rendezvous with their handler. The KGB agent surmised that it was time for him to move in and confront these amateur foreigners. Following the same, yet slightly parallel route that Vestegaard and Jacobsen had used, the first Soviet agent walked towards the Tiergarten Park entrance with his Russian-made pistol in his right hand and clearly visible to the three American agents. The second KGB agent remained concealed in the shadows of the doorway of the building directly across from the park entrance observing the scene. The second Soviet agent also held his pistol in hand, ready to respond if his partner gave him the signal or if any unusual or suspicious activity were to occur.

Bech watched the Soviet agent approach. The Russian was 100 yards away and closing. Leif's thoughts went back to one of the distract and deter lessons at Camp X.

* * *

During that nighttime outdoor class, in an inky field surrounded by heavy trees and bushes, their instructor had casually pulled out a cigarette, closed his eyes tightly and lit a match. Unbeknownst to the trainees, the match had been produced with three times the usual ignition chemicals and included bits of magnesium to further amplify the chemical reaction. Once lit, the super match ignited the entire box of matches and produced such a sudden, explosion of bright light that it startled the entire class, all of whom had jumped to their feet, their night vision compromised. By the time the students had recovered their senses, their instructor was nowhere to be seen. The students were astonished by the dramatic disappearance of their instructor before their very eyes, and again, several minutes later when the instructor sauntered back into their field of view with a cigarette in his hand. 'What seems to be the bloody problem here?' he asked innocently. The explosion of unexpected light had been so remarkable that it virtually blinded all twenty of the students to the point that they had not noticed their instructor walk straight out of view between them and then suddenly reappear amongst them in the darkness of the outdoor classroom.

* * *

Leif was counting on the pitch black of the park in which they stood to provide an even more dramatic effect, if his two colleagues could pull off their assignment in a timely, effective manner.

The approaching KGB agent was now only 50 yards away. Vestegaard stood silently smoking his cigarette, facing Jacobsen, with his back to both Bech, who was 10 yards behind him and to his right, and to the approaching KGB agent. The seconds passed and the Soviet agent was now only 25 yards away and closing. Jacobsen was facing Vestegaard and knew that Bech was somewhere to his front, between him and the approaching Russian, standing beside one of the large oak trees whose silhouettes were just barely visible in the darkness of the park. Vestegaard and Jacobsen's eyes had adjusted somewhat to the darkness, but the glow of their cigarettes managed to slow their visual adaptation to limit their night vision. Jacobsen could just make out the figure walking towards them from across the Tiergarten Straße – he knew who it must be. 'That must be our Soviet tail.'

Determining that he had to prepare for his next move, Jacobsen tossed his cigarette to the ground and watched the orange-red sparks of the cigarette bounce on the cobblestone walkway as he grasped the camera hanging from his neck with both hands, gently moving his fingers on the edge of the camera to feel, but not press the activator button. Jacobsen recalled Bech's last instructions:

> Let the Russians approach to the point that you believe that they are adjacent to or just past my location and activate the flash. Both of you must keep your eyes closed until after the flash. I will do the rest but come and assist me if there is a struggle beyond a few seconds. But one of you should keep your eyes trained on the far side of Tiergarten Straße, as the next danger may come from there soon enough.

The SSU interception of the KGB agent was as shocking as it was brief. As expected, the KGB agent had cautiously entered the park with his pistol drawn. With heavily accented English, the KGB agent, unaware of Bech's presence, called out to Jacobsen and Vestegaard directly in front of him – telling them to remain where they were and raise their hands. The darkness being almost complete, the two SSU agents appeared to the Russian agent as mere smudges against a larger murky expanse. As ordered, Vestegaard slowly raised his hands, one of which still held his lit cigarette, to the Soviet agent, the upward movement of the glowing cigarette was the only true indicator that he had complied with his order. Simultaneously, Jacobsen stepped slightly to his left and, with the camera pointed directly at the KGB agent, Jacobsen, Vestegaard and Bech closed their eyes and Jacobsen pressed the shutter button, which activated the flash mechanism of the camera. The sudden 'pop' sound of the bulb igniting and the explosion of intense, bright white light – 100,000 lumens – caught the Russian agent totally unprepared. Reacting instinctively, the KGB agent began to raise his empty left hand to protect his assaulted eyes and brought up his right hand, with his Russian-made Korovin service pistol in it, up and forward while bending his knees to crouch into a proper firing position. At that same instant, a figure moved with lightning speed from the Russian's right. The Russian agent had only a fraction of a second to register that the threat was not from the light source – several yards in front of him, but incoming from his immediate right – only 2 feet away.

The Russian's response was fast, but not fast enough. As the KGB agent's weapon came up to an almost horizontal firing position, pointing towards the initial threat and source of the bright white light, Bech's left hand came down hard and he grabbed the Soviet agent's right wrist with vice-like effectiveness. Bech, whose eyes had completely adapted to the darkness over the past thirty minutes and had been tightly closed at the moment of the camera flash, could clearly make out his unsuspecting Russian adversary's face, which was contorted with a mix of surprise and fear. Grasping the Russian agent's right wrist, thereby immobilizing the immediate danger of the weapon, Bech wrenched, with brutal force, the Soviet agent's right hand upward and twisted the wrist and elbow far beyond their natural, physical range. With sudden and intense pain shooting through his arm, from fingertips to shoulder, the Russian agent managed to squeeze the trigger enough to discharge its 6.35-millimeter round. The bullet struck the cobblestone walkway 2 yards forward of his position – ricocheting into the dark void.

The pistol's discharge did not distract Bech from completing his interception and immobilization of the threat. In fact, it only added to Bech's already heightened adrenaline rush, as his grip on the Soviet agent's wrist tightened even further. Using all his strength, Bech now raised his left arm as high and as violently as he could, pulling and twisting his opponent's arm up and away. The natural reaction of the human body in such circumstances is to take the path of least resistance and so the Russian agent raised up onto the balls of his feet in a futile attempt to relieve the searing pain and pressure on his wrist, elbow and shoulder that this unseen menace had suddenly inflicted. This self preservation reaction, however, exposed his upper torso and throat. With lightning speed and a force that he himself was surprised by, Bech brought his right hand – open palm and fingers straight and taut – crashing down on the exposed throat of the Soviet agent. The force of the blow cut short the Russian's brief cry of pain, while the impact of the strike crushed his larynx, driving broken cartilage through the trachea and esophagus, rupturing blood vessels and putting his neck muscles into spastic shock. The KGB agent's body immediately went limp and collapsed to the ground. His hand involuntarily released the pistol, which clattered on the cobblestones. The Russian agent was unconscious and out of the fight. Bech did not realize in that moment, that the force of the blow he had just delivered had actually ruptured the Russian agent's carotid artery. The Soviet agent was bleeding internally and, with the interruption of oxygenated blood to the brain, would be dead within three minutes.

Standing over his now immobile adversary, assessing if, in fact, he was truly out of the fight, Bech heard sounds of distress coming from his two SSU colleagues behind him. Bech picked up the Russian agent's pistol and took a moment to carefully scan across the Tiergarten Straße but saw no movement or imminent threat. He then turned towards his two colleagues. The ricochet of the 6.35-millimeter round from Russian service pistol had grazed Vestegaard's calf muscle, tearing a 6-inch gash in his leg – non-life threatening, but a wound that needed to be dressed to quell the bleeding and which would limit his mobility. As Jacobsen tied his handkerchief around his colleague's wound, Bech scanned the approaches, in particular the Tiergarten Straße intersection that the Soviet agent had approached from. Bech knew that the Soviet agent would not have come alone.

About a minute after the interception event, Bech and Jacobsen observed three brief flickers of a flashlight from across Tiergarten Straße. At the sight, Jacobsen tensed up in anticipation of another adversary approaching. Surprisingly, Bech calmly said, 'Good, we're safe, let's move out.' Somewhat dazed himself and unsure of their current circumstances, Jacobsen followed Bech's directions. Relying on Bech's calm, confident manner, Jacobsen helped lift his wounded colleague to his feet and assisted Vestegaard across the Tiergarten Straße towards the shadowy building where they had seen the flashlight signal a few moments earlier.

The three SSU agents lumbered across the broad expanse of the Tiergarten Boulevard, Vestegaard limping and supported by Bech and Jacobsen. They approached the darkened buildings on the far side of the boulevard, where a lone figure stepped out of the shadows to confront them. The initial reaction of both Jacobsen and Vestegaard was to stop and prepare to defend themselves, but Bech continued to move forward without hesitation as a calm, friendly and familiar voice emanated from the shadowy figure.

'Follow me, gentlemen', they heard, 'I have a car nearby and will get you to safety.' To Vestegaard and Jacobsen, the sudden appearance of Dr Magnusson from the shadows of Tiergarten Straße as their rescuer was quite unexpected but much appreciated. Neither of these agents knew of Magnusson's previous association with the Danish Resistance during the Second World War. In those days it was a need to know basis only and the less you knew, the better for all concerned. It was only after the four of them piled into the doctor's Red Cross-issued Sedan, a well used Volkswagen, and were almost back to the new, designated safe house that the recent events began to fall into place for them. Leif had known and worked with Dr Magnusson in Denmark during the last year of the war. Given the dire situation that Leif found himself facing with his two SSU colleagues returning under duress and being followed by the KGB, Leif knew he needed the assistance of a tested resistance operative who could handle himself in stressful situation. Magnusson was that man. Though Magnusson was more accustomed to intelligence gathering work, mission planning and coordinating the efforts of other 'real' agents, his calm and professional demeanor had always impressed Leif, who was confident that the doctor could handle a high stress operational situation if called upon and this night he was doing just that. The previous day, when Leif had outlined his concerns about his two returning agents, Magnusson had volunteered his services and was clearly willing and able to assist in any way he could.

Earlier that evening, as the two Soviet KGB agents observed and followed Vestegaard and Jacobsen from the safe house at 121 Schelling Straße towards the Tiergarten Park, Magnusson had, in turn, followed the two Russian agents. Though Bech's plan counted on the two Russian agents separating for mutual support prior to engaging his SSU agents, he was not absolutely sure that they would do what he expected. Fortunately, when one of the KGB agents went forward into Tiergarten Park to confront Vestegaard and Jacobsen, Magnusson was in position to intercept the second Russian agent before he could come to the aid of his partner. Anticipating the flash from the camera as the initiating event in the interception of the Russian agent who had followed Vestegaard and Jacobsen allowed Magnusson to be one step ahead of the second Soviet agent who was waiting in reserve. Fortunately for Magnusson, the unsuspecting second Russian agent was so surprised at the sudden flash of light from the park and the appearance of Magnusson, armed with a pistol at the ready, that when the Russian agent stepped from the shadows of the Tiergarten Straße building, his capitulation was all but complete before he knew what had happened. Both Russian agents had underestimated their prey.

Leif knew, as did Magnusson, that the doctor was a man who had spent his live saving lives and was not accustomed to handling weapons. Confronting the Russian agent with a loaded weapon was nothing more than a calculated bluff. Had the Russian KGB agent reacted differently and made a defiant move against Magnusson, the situation could have had a much different outcome. However, the good doctor was convincing in his role and got the drop on the Soviet agent and had him disarmed and locked in the trunk of the agent's own car in short order.

Leif had not expected, nor did he want the outcome of this encounter between KGB and SSU agents to result in the death of anyone; a dead Russian agent was regrettable and would be problematic for the SSU and the United States. However, it was far better than three captured or dead American agents. Leif knew that this was now a matter of getting out of this situation before all hell broke loose. They estimated that they would have between two and three hours before the Tiergarten Park scene was discovered or the Soviet agent freed himself from the trunk of his car. Either way, the three SSU agents knew they had to move quickly if they were to cross back into the American Zone before the Russian security forces increased their vigilance at all the checkpoints. Looking for foreign agents who might be spying on Russian activity in the Soviet Zone was one thing; looking for foreign agents who had just killed a Russian KGB agent was quite another situation.

Recalling their field director's previous warning, 'The Russians play hardball…' they understood that the Russians would direct all of their local assets to close off all of Berlin's checkpoints and tighten their security network until they found the culprits. The KGB agents had already been on the trail of Vestegaard and Jacobsen and the anomalies in Jorgen Bech's file had not yet been discovered. However, as all three men worked together, there would be no doubt that the KGB and the Russian's security forces would know exactly who they were hunting for, soon enough.

After arriving at a nearby safe house – a separate one that only Leif was privy to, Magnusson used a first aid kit that Leif had handed to him to bandage Vestegaard's wound. Leif had pre-positioned emergency supplies at each safe house. In this case, he had hidden them under the floorboards in the kitchen. As Jacobsen stood watch at the window facing the street, Leif went through the inventory of supplies… two canteens of water, a few chocolate bars and a modest cache of money – about $2,000 in both American and Russian currency. Also stowed away, wrapped in brown paper, was a spare set of clean clothes – shoes, slacks, button shirt and jacket, all in Leif's size. Once his wound was bandaged, Vestegaard put on the new pair of trousers that were slightly too large but helped conceal his injury. Magnusson took over sentry duty and stood near the narrow window adjacent to the front door of the apartment that led directly onto the street while the three agents made their final preparations.

The safe house was six blocks away, about midway between the incident site at Tiergarten Park and Checkpoint Charlie. Bech's objective to gain access back over to the American Zone was to reach Checkpoint Charlie. It was one of only two checkpoints between the Soviet Zone and the Western Allies' zones that was open 24/7 and the only Soviet-American checkpoint that was always open. As well, it was only a short distance away. It was easy walking distance for the uninjured... but possibly a problem for Vestegaard. Bech attempted to use the safe house telephone to contact the SSU operations center but the telephone circuit was dead – a common situation in Berlin. Setting up the wireless radio – also pre-positioned and hidden under the kitchen floor – took a couple of minutes, but soon enough, Bech had transmitted an urgent, coded message that outlined the situation. The Hudson cell had been compromised; one times KGB, status black (meaning dead); two times OSS agents, status green, and one yellow (meaning two uninjured and one injured agent) requiring immediate repatriation to American Zone through Checkpoint Charlie in two hours.

It was 0030 hours, so there would be less cross-border traffic at this time of night and the checkpoint sentries would be tired and less alert. Leif aimed to make the crossing attempt in one hour, at 0130 hours. As Dr Magnusson was the only legitimate Red Cross worker of the four men and there was no evidence to believe that he was suspected by the KGB, he planned to remain in the Soviet Zone and would feign surprise to the authorities at the sudden disappearance of his three Red Cross colleagues. In fact, the next day, Magnusson, in his capacity as the Danish Red Cross director, would report the three men missing to his Soviet counterpart, conveying grave concern for their safety and whereabouts.

At 0100 hours they were ready to go. Magnusson shook each man's hand and wished them well. He paused with Leif and squeezed his old resistance colleague's hand just a little bit tighter and a little bit longer. Their eyes met and a message of mutual respect passed between them. A moment later, the doctor stepped into the darkness of the street and was gone. Before departing the safe house, Leif collected all their weapons and went one last time back to his hidden storage space in the kitchen. After removing an item from a burlap bag, Leif placed all their weapons into the sack and tucked it back into the hole. After securing the floorboards back into place, Leif returned with the item. It was a bottle of Danish Akvavit – his last bottle. Once again, Leif would rely upon his old, reliable tool – alcohol – to facilitate his next act. 'Drink up, gentlemen,' said Bech, 'we need to look and smell like three drunken Danish Red Cross workers when we get to the Soviet checkpoint.'

Vestegaard's leg injury was painful, swollen, stiff and difficult to walk on. The Akvavit helped numb the pain, but his injured leg slowed their pace of travel for the short distance from the safe house to the security checkpoint. Fortunately, at that time of night, the streets were dark and void of other pedestrians or vehicle traffic. The three American agents made their way along Leipziger Straße and then crossed over to Mauer Straße, which merged onto Friedrich Straße and positioned them just 100 yards from their intended crossing point between the Soviet Zone and the American Zone. After twenty minutes they neared their destination. By then, half of the bottle of schnapps had been consumed. As they stood in the shadows observing the access point to the Soviet security checkpoint, Bech took the bottle from Jacobsen and splashed a few ounces of the clear fluid onto the front of Vestegaard's coat. 'Act drunk', he instructed, 'really drunk, and we'll help you across the street to the checkpoint. Maybe they won't notice your limp.' At that, they each took one last swig of the Akvavit. Bech looked at both Vestegaard and Jacobsen and said, 'It's been an honor to serve with you gentlemen.' He then grabbed Vestegaard's right arm, pulled it over his shoulder and stepped out into the open street. The deserted street leading to the checkpoint was lit by several portable light stands hooked up to a diesel generator.

About halfway across the intersection, Vestegaard began to sing, quietly at first but soon he was loudly slurring the words of a traditional Danish folk song, one that both Bech and Jacobsen knew and began to sing along. As they approached the checkpoint, two Russian army guards stepped forward towards the three oncoming men. With their rifles raised to waist height, the guards gave the trio of late-night drunkards an order to halt. After a few additional and unsteady steps, the three drunken companions complied. Bech and Jacobsen stopped singing, but Vestegaard, whose head was facing the ground and wobbling loosely from side to side, continued to belt out the chorus as a solo.

When the Russian guard asked for their papers, Bech, who had one hand holding Vestegaard's arm over his neck and the other holding the bottle of Akvavit, casually handed the bottle to the Russian sentry, who was caught off guard by the action, and fumbled with his weapon in order to grab the bottle. Bech reached into his jacket pocket for his identity papers and then did the same for Vestegaard who continued to serenade the gathering with a garbled rendition of another Danish song. As Jacobsen passed his papers to the guard, he unapologetically urged his fellow Dane to shut up. At which time, the drunken singer momentarily stopped singing, looked up at the Russian guard, smiled and said enthusiastically, 'Good evening, comrade! What are you doing in Denmark?'

The Russian guard ignored the drunken Dane as he passed the identity papers to his second sentry to review. Vestegaard then spoke again, exclaiming, 'Oh look, our Russian friend has a bottle of Akvavit too! Let's drink!' Vestegaard attempted to grab the bottle from the Russian, but both Bech and Jacobsen pulled their drunken colleague back out of reach while at the same time, the Russian guard took a step back from the trio of drunken Danes.

'Vestegaard is putting on quite a performance!' Leif thought appreciatively. Then, speaking in German, Bech suggested that the Russian guard should keep the bottle, as they had drunk far too much already. The Russian did not react. Bech then used the few words he knew in Russian and pointed at the bottle and then to the Russian sentry and then to his partner and said in stilted Russian: 'Sorry – you please – drink – night cold – good Danish schnapps – like vodka.' Looking around at the night sky, Bech added, 'Cold, cold like Russia – yes?' and mimicked a shiver. The Russian guard looked at Leif and replied, 'Da. Yes, cold, but not like Russia cold.' Then he smiled at the friendly, drunken Dane. The second Russian guard who was reviewing the three Danes' identity papers asked why they were wanted to cross at such a late hour, to which Bech replied that they had been celebrating their drunken friend's departure – that he was due to fly back to Copenhagen early the next day, and needed to collect his belongings from the Red Cross Office in the American Zone before going to Tempelhof Airport. As they waited for the second Russian guard to consider this story and to complete his review of their papers, the phone rang in the Russian guard house. Bech's body immediately tensed up as he prepared himself for a potentially serious confrontation. He suspected that that telephone call was the KGB reporting the incident in Tiergarten Park and to warn the guard post of a possible escape attempt by three agents posing as Danish Red Cross workers who had killed one of their comrades. As the Russian army officer stepped out of the guardhouse and walked towards them, Bech tried to read the Russian officer's demeanor – nothing.

Bech thought, 'Russians always look serious and angry.' He also began to question his logic of concealing his Husqvarna pistol in the waistband of his trousers at the small of his back. Killing a KGB agent in the heat of a confrontation is one thing, but having a shoot out with battle-hardened Russian soldiers at an international checkpoint is an entirely more serious matter. The Russian officer in charge of the night shift at Checkpoint Charlie moved with purpose but did not appear to be overly concerned with these three drunken Danes. He quickly conferred with the guard holding the Red Cross workers' identity papers, grabbed the documents abruptly from the Russian guard, approached the three men and compared their faces to those on the identity papers. After a moment of prolonged silence that seemed like hours, the Russian Guard Officer handed all three sets of documents back to Bech and as he turned, grabbed the bottle of Akvavit from his Russian comrade. 'Let these fool's pass. There is a convoy of Red Cross packages and supplies from the American side that is on it's way over.'

As the three SSU agents stepped over into the safety of the American Zone, United States Navy Commander Wisner, the region's senior SSU operations officer, stepped out of the American guardhouse. 'Welcome home, gentlemen.' Watching the three cargo trucks approach from a nearby warehouse, he continued,

> We thought the timely arrival of Western supplies for the Russkies to pilfer before being distributed to the needy Germans would make those guards drop any interest in three Danish Red Cross workers. Clearly, I was correct.

While at the United States Army field hospital waiting for Vestegaard to be stitched up, Leif and Jacobsen were interviewed separately by a panel of SSU and army intelligence officers led by Captain William Colby. Captain Colby, who would go on to become the Director of the CIA in the mid-1970s was there to determine what had transpired in the Soviet Zone that night, and during the preceding seventy-two hours. His findings would initiate the imediate repatriation of the Hudson cell to the United States for a more thorough de-briefing and the cell's eventual dissolution. With their preliminary interviews concluded and after Vestegaard had been stitched up by a qualified United States Army medic, all three SSU agents were handed food ration packs and fresh canteens of water, transfer into the back of an olive-drab, canvas-covered United States Army transport truck and driven to Tempelhof Airport to catch the next flight to the American air base at Frankfurt. There, the three fugitive SSU agents were immediately escorted to a waiting C-47 Dakota aircraft destined for Washington DC. Aside from the aircrew, they were the only persons authorised on the flight. The SSU senior leadership and the United States Department of Defense did not want this potentially destabilizing political incident to be discussed with anyone until the director of the SSU could hear the report for himself. After which he would brief the JCOS – Joint Chief of Staff – before the story became public knowledge. Which, thankfully, it never did.

The newly constructed Soviet airfield near Neuhardenberg, east of Berlin, that Vestegaard and Jacobsen reported on would later be called Maxwalde Airfield. It would play an important role in Soviet and East German military operation facing the Western Allies during the entire Cold War era. The photographs of the installation and details of its design and construction provided the Allies with vital operational and strategic intelligence about how the Soviets intended to defend their territory and, equally as important, how and where they would forward deploy many of their offensive military assets to confront the Western Allies over the next four decades.

In late December 1945, with the Tiergarten incident now only a painful memory, Leif was assigned temporarily to the SSU headquarters in Washington DC, which inhabited the former OSS headquarters building on E Street, overlooking the Potomac River and Arlington Virginia. Regrettably, the fatal incident in Berlin would have a major impact on Leif's career path. It was determined that his cover as a SSU agent was irrevocably damaged, as the Russian KGB would inevitably piece together the various cover stories and false history of Jorgen Bech, and would eventually determine his true identity: First Lieutenant Leif Bangsbøll, Danish-born, now United States Army officer, had killed a KGB agent on Soviet-controlled territory.

* * *

Remarkably, the Bangsbøll family's involvement with the KGB did not end on that December night in 1945. Over thirty-five years after Leif's deadly encounter with the KGB in the Soviet sector of Berlin, an incident would occur involving Leif's son, First Lieutenant Mark Bangsbøll that would rekindle Leif's Cold War concerns and shed new light on his son's understanding of his father's past. The incident would also prove beyond a doubt that the Russian KGB had a long corporate memory.

It was early summer of 1981, First Lieutenant Mark Bangsbøll, an infantry officer in the United States Army and a recent graduate of the United States Military Academy – West Point, class of 1978, was on leave from his NATO assignment with the United States Army in West Germany. Mark, accompanied by his new bride, Veronica, a Canadian-born woman from Toronto, of Hungarian descent and with the permission of his CO, visited Hungary, an Eastern-bloc/Warsaw Pact nation to visit his wife's relatives. Immediately upon their arrival in Hungary, Mark had the uncomfortable feeling that they were being watched. After several days of touring the country and visiting his wife's extended family, Mark was sure of his suspicions – they were being followed, every day and everywhere. But knowing that he was just a junior infantry lieutenant, Mark could not understand the efforts and resources being employed to follow and watch him while on a family holiday.

On the eve before their departure from Hungary, following a wonderful meal at a restaurant in downtown Budapest, Mark, channeling the well-documented and well-known boldness of his father, decided to confront his Soviet shadows.

As they were exiting the restaurant, Mark stopped beside the suspected secret police agent sitting alone at a table close to the exit and asked if he and his comrades had enjoyed their time following him and his wife around Hungary. The KGB agent grinned through his tobacco-stained teeth but did not reply. A few seconds later, as Mark and his wife walked down the street, the Russian agent stepped out of the restaurant and called out,

> Lieutenant Bangsbøll! Send the KGB's regards to your father! I trust he is enjoying his retirement in Toronto. I hope his damaged knees aren't bothering him too much.

Mark stopped in his tracks and turned to look back. The Soviet agent stood in the doorway of the restaurant and smiled as he lit another foul-smelling Russian cigarette and added, 'It's so sad to see a once strong and bold warrior reduced to walking with the aid of a cane. Maybe someday he will come to visit us, we would very much like to speak to him.'

In accordance with proper United States military protocol, on his return to his military unit, Mark reported to his CO that during his leave he believed that he had been in contact with members of a foreign secret service agency – likely the KGB. After explaining the details of the encounters during his leave in Hungary, a subsequent report from the United States Defense Intelligence Agency confirmed that Lieutenant Colonel (Retired) Leif Bangsbøll was still believed to be on the KGB's hit list for an incident in East Berlin back in December 1945.

* * *

It may have been because it was that incident that ended his career as a special agent, or it may have been for more personal reasons; for the fact remained that it resulted in the unintentional taking of a life – even though the KGB agent posed a direct threat to himself and his two SSU colleagues and he had intended to only disarm and temporarily incapacitate the threat, not eliminate it.

In his heart, Leif knew that he had done the right thing and took solace in the fact that 'Dangerous Dan' Fairbairn would probably say that he executed his duty flawlessly. Regardless, Leif bore the burden of what he perceived as the unnecessary death of an enemy agent on his conscious for the rest of his life.

In June, 1981, upon returning to their home in Mainz, Germany, from their eye-opening trip to Hungary, Mark, a person who was known to never overreact or act impulsively, was eager to speak to his father. Mark placed his and wife Veronica's luggage in the hallway of their apartment and walked immediately into their kitchen and picked up the phone and made a long-distance call to his father, in Toronto Canada. After a few minutes of pleasantries and sharing a few tourist highlights of his trip to Soviet controlled Hungary, Mark's tone became serious. "Dad, I have to talk to you about something that happened during the trip. We were followed – followed every day – everywhere. We were followed by the KGB Dad!" "Well son, its not everyday an American Army officer gets permission to visit a Soviet Bloc country – I'm sure they just wanted to keep an eye on you" said Leif in an intentionally light, dismissive tone.

"No Dad, they were following us because of you!"

Both father and son remained silent for a long moment as the long distance line crackled with static during their pause in conversation. "Are you still there Mark?" ask his father. "Dad, they knew where you lived, they knew your rank, that you had retired and lived in Toronto and that you use canes to walk because of your damaged knees. They..." Leif interrupted Mark and said: "I have to tell you about something I did a long time ago, something I have never spoken about to anyone another than my OSS leadership back in 1945. Something I am not very proud of..."

When his father had finished outlining the events of his heroic encounter with the KGB, Leif concluded their conversation with his usual fateful resolve: "For the first few years following that incident, I'll admit, I did watch over my shoulder, expecting to see some Russian thugs approaching me with clubs, and revenge on their faces, but it never happened, they never came.

As the years went by, the events of that night all faded into the background of life's routine for which I am grateful. I'm old now son, the Russkies had their chance, but didn't take it – they won't bother this old man now."

Of all the stories about his life's adventures, Leif rarely spoke of the fatal incident in East Berlin. In fact, the author, probably because he was the youngest of Leif's children, was never told of this event, and only learned of it during the writing of this book when the author's brother Mark, having just read an early draft of the book, said to him: "Brook, your book is missing an important story about Dad...something happened in Berlin in the Fall of 1945 that you need to know...

Chapter 3

Yokohama and Che Je Do

> 'Men who are familiarized to danger, meet it without shrinking, whereas those who have never seen military service often apprehend danger where no danger is.'
>
> General George Washington, 1776

Following the dramatic incident with the KGB in Berlin in December 1945, and his subsequent daring escape from East Germany, Leif would have to undergo another career transformation. The SSU, formerly the OSS, as well as the Department of War and the United States government were unsure of what facts the Soviets knew of the fatal incident in Tiergarten Park and of those involved. What the Department of War did know is that they wanted to get Lieutenant Leif Bangsbøll and his two SSU team members as far away from Berlin and the Soviets as possible. The Soviet security forces were notorious for being relentless and unremorseful in their efforts to inflict retaliatory measures or revenge killings. And while they did not publicly admit that they had lost an agent, the elimination of a KGB agent on their own territory would undoubtedly create a myriad of potential retaliatory responses against the United States.

What became of agents William Jacobsen and Carl Vestegaard and where the US Army sent them is unknown. Leif expected that they too were being secreted away into the massive conglomeration of the United States Army for their own safety. As for Leif, he was immediately reassigned to one of the safest locations in the United States. He was ordered to the 504th Parachute Infantry Regiment (PIR), as part of 18th Airborne Corps and the United States Army's 82nd Airborne Division, known as the 'All Americans', based at Fort Bragg, North Carolina. There, the former agent, now on the KGB's most wanted list, would disappear amongst the sprawling 160,000-acre military installation and integrate himself amongst the 45,000 other United States Army uniformed service personnel. Leif would be anonymous to the outside world and a tough target for the KGB to locate, let along reach.

The United States Department of War understood that Lieutenant Bangsbøll had specialised training with the OSS, along with his wartime experience and proven combat capabilities, which were valuable assets that needed to be preserved – and exploited. His assignment with 82nd Airborne Division would offer him a chance to continue to serve and put his knowledge and skills to good use, while allowing him to remain hidden from Soviets whom the American government presumed were searching for him and his two SSU team members. The Soviet government does not accept failure well and its KGB were undoubtedly seeking to reap some revenge for the loss of one of its agents. When, where and how were the questions.

Far from Berlin and the Eastern Bloc nations that were soon to be referred to as the 'Warsaw Pact' countries, Leif would go on to have a productive and excitingly challenging tour of duty as a member of 82nd Airborne Division during the period of January 1946 to November 1947. With his All American brothers, he honed his skills as a paratrooper and refined and shared his unique combat skills and clandestine methods of confronting and frustrating the enemy. Working for the brigade commander, Colonel William Westmoreland, Leif learned to be a strong, well-organized staff officer, while becoming one of the most proficient parachutists in the battalion. His love of parachuting was insatiable, often performing two or three training jumps in a day. Eventually he earned and was most proud of the coveted 'Master Parachutist' badge, which would adorn his uniform.

* * *

During this period, Leif was able to visit the Henry family, as he had promised, mostly to foster his relationship with Dorothy-Jean, the love of his life. Over the next two years, while assigned to 82nd Airborne Division at Fort Bragg, Leif left his clandestine life as a secret agent behind in the the shadows of the past and enjoyed his new career path as an airborne soldier – in the light of day, for all to see. During that time, he consumed all his available leave visiting Dorothy at her parents' home in Oshawa or visiting her in Toronto as she completed her education at Branksome Hall College. By autumn 1947, Dorothy, who was now 19 years old, and Leif, 28, were contemplating their future together. However, Leif believed that he had at least one more year at Fort Bragg before another assignment, and although he was deeply in love with his Canadian sweetheart, he was in no rush to press for marriage. That perspective would soon change.

* * *

In November 1947, Leif received orders transferring him from his assignment with 82nd Airborne Division at Fort Bragg, to 1st Cavalry Division, Eighth

United States Army in Japan as part of the post-war United States occupation force. Along with his new military orders also came a letter from the United States Bureau of Immigration and Naturalization…Leif's service in the United States Army during the war had earned his U.S. citizenshp – Leif Bangsbøll was now, officially an American. Prior to reporting for duty to his new assignment, Leif decided to take a few weeks of leave, with the plan of going to visit his girlfriend and unofficial fiancée who was in her graduating year at Branksome Hall College in Toronto. However, during a long-distance telephone call to Dorothy to make his travel plans to Canada, the plan changed. Instead of going to Canada, Leif and Dorothy decided to meet in San Francisco where they would get married. Was it impetuous? Yes, but they were young, and with the blessing of her parents, Clifford and Margaret Henry, Dorothy flew to San Francisco to meet and marry Leif. Dorothy's mother, Margaret, traveled with her and would be her daughter's matron of honor at a small wedding ceremony. Dorothy's father, Clifford, gave his blessings to the union but was too frail to travel that far and remained in Oshawa.

Leif, Dorothy and Margaret spent a week prior to the wedding as tourists in San Francisco and the surrounding area, taking day trips up the coast and into the hills of northern California. It was a wonderful time that they would recall fondly for years to come. Leif, having lost his mother early in life, embraced Margaret as a welcome surrogate mother. 'Margaret Henry was so very kind to me and so fun and full of adventure. I was so lucky to have met her and the Henry family.' Time and time again, through word and deed, Leif would convey how fortunate he was to have such wonderful in-laws.

On 10 December 1947, at a simple ceremony at the army chapel on Camp Stoneman, located just outside of San Francisco, Dorothy-Jean Henry of Oshawa, Ontario, Canada, with her mother at her side, married First Lieutenant Leif Bangsbøll of Copenhagen, Denmark. Standing beside Leif was his best man, Second Lieutenant John McGuire, a fellow member of the 504th PIR who was also on route to his assignment with the 1st Calvalry Division in Japan. Following the ceremony, a small but elegant wedding celebration dinner was hosted at the St Francis Hotel in San Francisco. Life was good and the world was at peace.

The newlyweds spent their honeymoon in Santa Barbara and Los Angeles. A week later, Leif and John McGuire flew from San Francisco to the Far East to their new assignment in Japan. Dorothy-Jean flew home to Canada to complete her final semester at Branksome Hall College. Four months later, once Leif was settled into his new assignment with 5th Cavalry Regiment in Yokohama Japan, and after Dorothy had graduated, she traveled to Japan to be reunited with her husband. There, the newlyweds commenced a wonderfully exciting life together.

Leif and Dorothy were extremely fortunate, the United States Army assigned them to a palatial home in the town of Hayama, located on the outskirts of the port city of Yokohama. Though only a first lieutenant, as part of the United States Army's Occupation Force and responsible for security coordination and reconciliation with the Japanese in the Yokohama region, Lieutenant Bangsbøll wielded a great deal of influence and power among the local community administrators and population. As such, he was assigned a traditional Japanese home – an impressive mansion – which had previously been the provincial governor's official residence. It was one of the most welcome dividends of the assignment.

As well as this wonderful home, with spacious gardens and treed property, Leif and Dorothy were assigned four local servants: two women – who dressed in traditional Japanese embroidered silk kimonos – who looked after the cooking and cleaning, one man, the gardener/handyman, who tended to the maintenance of the house and grounds, and lastly there was Hiroshi, the houseboy, self-proclaimed 'boss servant' and interpreter. Hiroshi also appointed himself as Dorothy's personal bodyguard. Despite Hiroshi's later claim, a small detachment of local Japanese police constables were assigned to guard the house. A Japanese guard was always present at the residence day and night. Just a few weeks into this assignment, however, Leif realized that there was no tangible threat and asked his superiors to discontinue the Japanese police presence at his home, but to no avail. The commander insisted that all American married officers living outside of Camp McGill would have Japanese police assigned to provide security, no matter how low the threat level was.

Despite their defeat by the Allies, the Japanese remained proud and fiercely loyal people. Japan's failed ambitions to dominate and subjugate the whole of Asia and Indonesia, led to a humiliating state of armed occupation by foreign military troops. The Japanese people could have easily shown defiance at the foreign occupation. Upon Leif's arrival in January 1948, Japan was still very much a conquered nation. Despite its once zealous and ferocious military aims and, at times, inhumane conduct during the Second World War, Japan and its people were now a docile, subservient nation and the United States and its soldiers were the absolute and unquestionable authority. Once the Japanese emperor ordered the nation's surrender, the capitulation was virtually absolute and unquestionable. Hiroshi was one of the vast majorities who accepted their fate as a conquered people and as such, he and the rest of the house staff honored the victors with enthusiastic energy and dedicated loyalty. Hiroshi would care for Dorothy, whom he affectionately referred to as 'Young Missy-San', as if she were his own mother, even though he was ten years older than Dorothy.

Dorothy, just 20 years old and for the first time in her life living outside of Canada, found herself transported into the life of a princess. She was a privileged young woman living in an exotic foreign land, far away from home and in a place so different from anything she could have imagined. She loved it and embraced the opportunity given her. Dorothy quickly blossomed into the role of quintessential hostess and consummate army officer's wife. She was witty, beautiful, engaging, glamorous and always willing to host formal or casual social functions in support of her husband's military career and his current duties for security coordination and reconciliation with the Japanese.

Dorothy admitted that hosting a dinner party for a dozen army officers and local officials was easy. 'For goodness' sake, I had four full-time staff who would do everything for me.' With Dorothy's simple upbringing, she referred to her helpers as 'household staff', as she did not like the commonly used title of servants, frequently used by the Americans.

'The household staff became like family to me and would not let me do any manual work. And later, when it became known that I was pregnant with little Leslie, oh my, did the staff go overboard for me. The staff would not let me lift a finger. I think that when I was pregnant with my first born and I went into labor – dear Hiroshi got more worked up than Leif! As a young girl, far from home, I was so fortunate. Hiroshi and the rest of the household staff were wonderful to me. Japan was a very special time in our lives.'

Leif's assignment was with 1st Cavalry Division, Eighth United States Army as part of 2nd Battalion, 5th Cavalry Regiment (infantry), stationed at Camp McGill, 20 miles from Yokohama. This was the first military assignment that had been given in the past ten years that did not involve risking his life in high-stress, combat situations or clandestine duties that put his life in danger as a matter of routine. The 5th Cavalry Regiment (infantry) was assigned guard duties and security missions in and around Tokyo and Yokohama as part of the reconstruction plan for Japan.

Despite the generally amicable relations between the Japanese population and the American occupational force, there were occasions when unrest did manifest itself in noticeable and potential conflict. In May 1948, Japanese trade workers in Tokyo began protesting certain work restrictions applied on the population by the Americans. On one occasion, a protest rally was organized by Japanese laborers and the assembly point for the protesters was a modest-sized sports stadium on the outskirts of Tokyo. As Leif prepared his plan to address and possibly confront the assembly of several hundred angry Japanese workers, he surprisingly asked his wife Dorothy and their houseboy, Hiroshi, to accompany him to the protest site. The idea of bringing a young, blonde Caucasian women to such an event baffled many of the other American officers and soldiers. However, Leif understood that the Japanese, despite being a defeated nation, were proud and tremendously polite people and saving face was important in the Japanese culture. Knowing that the authority and military might of the United States Army of occupation would rule the day regardless of what the Japanese protesters said or did, Leif surmised that the unexpected presence of a foreign woman and wife of an American officer at the frontline of the stadium protest assembly point might catch the protesters off guard and just might help defuse the situation.

With Hiroshi's assistance as guide and interpreter, the head of the Japanese union of workers was located within the stadium and invited to meet Lieutenant Bangsbøll to discuss the Japanese workers' concerns and grievances. It was clear that the workers' leader was immediately disarmed by the presence of a young, foreign woman at the meeting. Evidently, he thought that if the American officer considered it safe enough to bring his young wife to such an event, then the American intended to negotiate in good faith, so the least the Japanese workers could do was to respect her presence and avoid any uncivilised conduct or agitation between the workers and the American troops. With Hiroshi's interpretation skills, each side's point of view was conveyed to the other; and with Dorothy's nearby presence, the Japanese workers' leadership accepted the American employment rules with no further complaints. In return, Leif was able to lift a few of the work and travel restrictions, which allowed for an acceptable, mutually face-saving compromise to the situation. Whether the situation would have unfolded differently in the absence of Dorothy and Hiroshi we will never know, but Leif was sure that their presence made the difference between reasonable compromise and a heated – possibly violent – confrontation.

* * *

In July 1948, Lieutenant Bangsbøll, along with a small cadre of other officers of 1st Cavalry Division, were temporarily assigned duties in South Korea with 24th Infantry Division under Major General William Dean. Their mission was in support of the United States government's efforts to stem the growing communist insurgency of South Korea. The reason the United States government was so interested in Korea and had stationed some of its forces in South Korea is relatively straightforward: the long political and military history of Korea was one of being caught between neighboring influences and rife with conflicts involving Japan, China and Russia. Now, the United States intended to have political influence in the region. It began by providing massive aid to the South

Korean people, sending in military advisors. In so doing, the United States would gain a strategic foothold in the region and influence the small, yet strategically important nation.

China has had a long history of influence over Korea. However, the First Sino-Japanese War (1894–1895) saw the Japanese military forces crush the Chinese military, who were occupying Korea. Ten years later, after similarly defeating Imperial Russia in the Russo-Japanese War (1904–1905), Japan made Korea its protectorate and completed its annexation in 1910. Three decades later, Japan considered Korea to be an integral part of the Japanese Empire, as an industrial colony along with Taiwan. The Japanese Asia-Pacific Empire was expanding and would ultimately lead to Second World War conflict in the Pacific.

Throughout the Second World War, Japanese troops occupied Korea and enslaved its people, while exploiting many of its natural resources to keep its war machine running. As the Second World War approached its final phase, the Japanese government had withdrawn most of its military forces from Korea in order to protect the home island of Japan. During the Yalta Conference in February 1945, as the Second World War was approaching its end, the Soviet Union promised to join the Western Allies in the Pacific theater of war within three months of the victory in Europe. Germany surrendered on 8 May 1945, VE Day. Subsequently, and as promised, the Soviet Union declared war on Japan on 9 August 1945 and immediately began occupying the northern region of the Korean peninsula with Soviet troops. On 8 September 1945, Korea was divided at the 38th parallel, forming two distinct nations, North Korea (DPR) and South Korea (ROK), aligned with the Soviet Union and the United States of America, respectively.

With the end of the Second World War, the Chinese Civil War resumed between the Chinese communists, led by Mao Zedong, and the Chinese nationalists, which resulted in the victory of Mao's communists and the formation of the People's Republic of China in 1949. The Soviet Union continued to retain influence over North Korea and now with communist China, a juggernaut of expansionist power on North Korea's border, the region was a powder keg of potential conflict. It was during this time of Cold War posturing between the United States, the Soviet Union and the newly formed People's Republic of China that Leif found himself in South Korea, along with a few hundred other United States Army troops who were assisting the South Korean government by bolstering their defenses and conducting anti-communist insurgency missions.

* * *

After working for three weeks at the United States Army's 24th Infantry Division headquarters in Seoul, acclimatising himself to the strategic and tactical situations, Lieutenant Bangsbøll was transferred to 59th Military Government Headquarters Company as the public safety officer and was assigned a mission that involved traveling on his own to the southern island of Che Je Do to assess the level of communist insurgency in that island province. While in Che Je Do province, Leif would report his findings to Major General Dean directly.

The island province of Che Je Do is located 80 miles offshore of the southernmost tip of the South Korean peninsula. On this assignment, Leif was accompanied by special police investigator Inspector Han Joon Dak from Seoul, a police officer who had worked closely with the United States Army over the past three years and spoke impeccable English. Inspector Han had studied at the University of Southern California from 1935 to 1939 and subsequently worked as an investigator for a law firm in San Francisco during the Second World War, while Korea was under Japanese occupation. Inspector Han accompanied Leif to the island of Che Je Do to act as his translator, to ensure full cooperation of the local authorities and to report their findings back to the South Korean police and military commands in Seoul. Inspector Han would become an indispensable colleague, friend and ally to Leif over their five-month mission on the island. Their official host while in Che Je Do was Chief of Police Superintendent Kim Bong Ho, who would prove to be a man of swift action with deep anti-communist views. Superintendent Kim had a ferocious manner when it came to matters of defending his homeland from external or internal threats. Both Lieutenant Bangsbøll and Investigator Han realized that they would have to tread carefully around Superintendent Kim.

Leif, dressed in his US Army Class A uniform, along with Investigator Han were met upon arrival at Che Je Do's Jeju airport by Superintendent Kim on 7 June 1948, who would work closely with Leif and Inspector Han over the next five months. He proved to be a valuable and powerful ally during their investigations and threat assessments of possible communist infiltration of the Che Je Do province. He was also a key proponent and coordinator of the infamous, government-led, anti-rebellion massacre in Che Je Do, which had occurred just a few months earlier, in April 1948, during which the South Korean army and police forces killed over 15,000 Che Je Do residents, including women and children.

After a brief indoctrination by the South Korean police superintendent, Lieutenant Bangsbøll and Inspector Han were escorted to meet Captain James Leach, a United States Army MP officer, and the senior ranking United States officer on the island. Captain Leach was responsible for American-Korean security cooperation on the island of Che Je Do and was glad to have the additional support, as he was woefully understaffed, especially given the provinces recent uprisings. Lieutenant Bangsbøll and Inspector Han were advised that it was believed that the vast majority of suspected North Korean insurgence were infiltrating Che Je Do from the south-west region of the island and that Leif and Inspector Han should concentrate their threat assessment in that region. At their initial meeting, Superintendent Kim also pledged to provide the two official visitors with police resources to protect them and assist them in their duties. Initially, they were assigned five South Korean constables, all of whom were natives of Che Je Do.

Counterinsurgency operations are incredibly challenging missions. Discerning friend from foe from within a homogeneous population was difficult and both Lieutenant Bangsbøll and Inspector Han recognized that being assigned a team of native police constables would make it difficult to bring in new ideas from the mainland and a challenge to detect those constables who might have underlying sympathies with the growing communist insurgents' influence on the island. Leif realized that the South Korean government had recently killed 10 per cent of the population of the island of Che Je Do based purely on a perceived internal counter-insurgency threat. Though Inspector Han would earn Leif's respect and unreserved trust through various acts and deeds over the next five months, Leif remained ever cautious of the true allegiance of the South Korean police force on the island. An old OSS saying was once again his guiding principle: 'Trust no one.'

Being one of only a dozen Caucasians on the island made Leif's presence standout, so he made no attempt to disguise himself or underplay his presence – he wanted everyone to know who he was and why he was there. In addition to the squad of Che Je Do police constables given to Lieutenant Bangsbøll and Inspector Han, Superintendent Kim also arranged for their use of a modest three-room house, on the outskirts of the town of Moseulpo to use during their assignment. The traditional, thatched roofed dwelling, located in the foothills of the southwestern mountain range of the island, was an ideal location to establish a base camp from which to mount coastal surveillance operations and inland foot patrols into the hills where the insurgents were believed to be operating from.

During the first month of operations, Leif set up several observation posts along the western coastline, adjacent to the most sea-accessible beaches and the most probable North Korean insurgent entry points. Within two weeks, his constables had observed two separate incidents where a North Korean fishing trawler came in at night close to shore with the vessel's navigation lights turned off and dropped off between eight and a dozen personnel. In early September 1948, one of their observation posts photographed what appeared to be a submarine that had surfaced 1 mile offshore and dropped off three individuals who rowed ashore in a rubber raft. The photographs were sent to Seoul for analysis at the South Korean army headquarters and United States Army liaison and intelligence office, which quickly confirmed that it had been a Soviet submarine.

With this new intelligence evidence, Leif's mission took on new and greater importance in the defense of South Korea and the United States' sphere of Cold War posturing. The following week, in response to the effectiveness of Leif and Inspector Han's work, Superintendent Kim assigned an additional twenty constables to Leif's team and gave him the authority to intercept and engage in force, any illegal activities, including North Korean pirates landing on Che Je Do shores. Furthermore, he authorised them to mount patrols into the region's mountain villages where they believed many of the North Korean insurgents were now hiding and secretly developing their insurgent network.

During the last week of August 1948, one of their coastal surveillance posts identified a fishing trawler that approached close to shore and discharged eight armed North Koreans. Ready for this encounter, and supervised by Inspector Han, ten South Korean constables surprised the insurgents by immediately engaging them as they set foot on the South Korean beach. Five of the North Koreans were killed and three were arrested and taken prisoner. That same week, after prolonged surveillance of suspected insurgent cells working in the mountains, Lieutenant Bangsbøll and Inspector Han led a twelve-man team into the mountains and arrested a number of suspected North Korean communist ring leaders, confiscating a large cache of Soviet and Chinese weapons and reams of incriminating documents, including pro-communist pamphlets.

Two nights after their successful patrol into the mountains and late in the evening, Lieutenant Bangsbøll and Inspector Han's home came under brief but heavy direct small arms fire. The enfilade of bullets caused a cacophony of sudden noise, penetrating the thin plaster walls of the house and impacting the interior walls, sending clouds of plaster and wood splinters into the air. When the attack started, Leif immediately and instinctively rolled out of his bed onto the floor and found himself scrambling to locate his United States Army issued Colt 45 gun to return fire. But by the time he had gathered his wits and armed himself, the attack was over. Rattled, neither Leif nor Inspector Han, nor their police constable guarding the house, were injured, however the barrage of projectiles destroyed the few pieces of furniture that came with the safe house. The North Korean insurgents had fired 80 to 100 rounds into the house and in so doing, had sent an unmistakable message. As Leif saw it, they had just upped the ante to his mission.

Following the late-night attack on their modest, now bullet ridden quarters, Inspector Han arranged for several local and trustworthy laborers to come to the house to repair the damage. At Lieutenant Bangsbøll's insistence, the workers were also ordered to dig slit trenches in each of the house's three main rooms. As the floors consisted of only mat-covered earth, the workers were able to quickly dig three, 3-foot-deep trenches in which the safe house occupants could take cover in the event of another attack. Always the cautious one, Leif would sleep in his fox hole during the remainder of his stay on Che Je Do. He also arranged to have additional defensive measures put in place, such as layers of barbed wire strung out behind the house where the most likely attack route would be launched from. In addition, and with the approval of Captain Leach, the United States Army Military Police (MP) officer and senior American on the island, Leif drew several carbine rifles, a medium machine gun and plenty of ammunition along with a case of hand grenades from the island's United States Army supply depot. If there was another attack, Leif would be ready to respond with lethal force.

To demonstrate their commitment and resolve to their mission, the following night, Lieutenant Bangsbøll and Inspector Han led a police force of thirty constables up into the mountains to confront the insurgents. Using stealth and the element of surprise, they inflicted heavy casualties on the North Korean insurgents' suspected headquarters, killing half a dozen, wounding several more and making a number of arrests. Two nights later, the North Koreans, in a show of their resolve, reattacked Leif's and Inspector Han's quarters. This time they were ready to defend themselves. After a few sporadic shots into the house by the insurgents from the hillside behind their house, Leif returned fire with his newly acquired 30 caliber machine guns. With a sustained burst raking across the scrub brush-covered slope behind the house, he effectively suppressed the insurgents' ability to accurately fire upon the safe house. While Leif was keeping the surprised North Koreans' heads down with an enfilade of machine gun fire, Inspector Han made his way out the side door of the house and along the stone garden wall towards the insurgents. With a hail of bullets emanating from the safe house behind him providing cover, Inspector Han launched half a dozen hand grenades into the insurgents' suspected positions. Within five minutes the insurgents' attack had been thwarted. For safety reasons, Leif and Inspector Han chose to wait until daylight to inspect the battlefield. The next morning, they found four dead North Koreans along with blood trails of at least another three wounded insurgents. If Leif had any doubts about Inspector Han's loyalty, trustworthiness or capabilities under fire, his brave actions that night against the North Korean insurgents put them all to rest.

As a result of the unexpected and overwhelming defensive firepower from the safe house, the North Koreans never attempted another ambush of that magnitude again. However, every week or so, some brave North Korean insurgent would be sent down from the hills to fire a pot shot or two into the house. Those nocturnal raids, though ineffective, kept both Leif and Inspector Han on their guard, and both became quite accustomed to the routine of sleeping in a trench, inside the house and being harassed from time to time by their unwelcome and now cautious communist neighbours.

During the period from June to October1948, the intelligence they gathered of the North Korean communist insurgents' activities through passive observation, direct engagement during raids on the insurgents' headquarters, and the interrogation of the many prisoners they captured, enabled Lieutenant Bangsbøll and Inspector Han to produce a detailed and enlightening report that outlined the depth of the North Korean infiltration of the western half of the island of Che Je Do. The verification that the Soviet Union was supplying intelligence, weapons and logistical support to the North Korean insurgents who were actively infiltrating South Korea was critically important intelligence. The report predicted that if unabated, the insurgents would be sufficiently well organized, equipped and manned to initiate significant offensive action within twelve to eighteen months. Given the animosity between the island's population and the South Korean government owing to the government's previous actions and the brutal way it had quelled the political protests less than a year earlier, it was believed that a strong communist movement could lead to widespread rebellion and the loss of Che Je Do as a South Korean province. Such a turn of events could be strategically perilous to South Korea and its military, as it would place communist enemy forces on two sides of the South Korean peninsula.

Leif believed that his intelligence report would be useful to the South Korean government and the United States Army intelligence headquarters in Seoul, and that appropriate steps would be taken to address the growing threat. As such, Leif and Inspector Han returned to Seoul with expectations that sufficient warning had been provided and their work in that regard was complete. With his assignment completed, Leif was sent back to Japan to rejoin his unit, 2nd Battalion, 5th Cavalry Regiment (infantry), in Yokohama. Waiting patiently for him was his wife, Dorothy.

* * *

At about the same time, and as agreed to by an accord between Russia and the United States, the Soviet Union began to withdraw its troops from North Korea while the majority of United States troops would withdraw from South Korea the following year, leaving only a relatively small deterrent force, headquarters personnel and liaison staff in and around the cities of Seoul and Busan, totaling 10,000 American troops.

Following his assignment with the South Korean police, and a few weeks after returning to Japan, Leif's CO at headquarters, 2nd Battalion, 5th Cavalry Regiment (infantry), received a letter from Chief Superintendent Kim, Che Je Do Police Department:

To American 5 Cavalry Commanding Officer,
I would like to offer gracious thanks and appreciation on behalf of Che Ju Do Police Department with whom 1st Lieutenant Leif Bangsbøll served as Military Advisor from June to October 1948. Without his help and advice, it would have been a much greater task of restoring peace and order to the island of Che Jo Du. Many times, 1st Lieutenant Bangsbøll risked his life, disregarding any personal safety to execute his mission and provide assistance to my police force. He showed great devotion and promoted good friendship and goodwill between America and South Korea.

With humble and grateful thanks,
Kim Bong Ho, Chief
Che Ju Do Police Department

Chapter 4

When Two Becomes Three

'If music be the food of love, play on.'
William Shakespeare, *Twelfth Night*

In late October 1948, shortly after Leif's return from his assignment in South Korea, Dorothy was involved in an incident that she and Leif would for years recall with fond humor and dramatic retelling. On this occasion, while Leif was at work at Camp McGill, Dorothy and Hiroshi were out doing errands and some local sightseeing. Dorothy insisted on driving, as she had quickly realized that Hiroshi, though well meaning, was a horrendously poor driver. Making driving an automobile more challenging, Japan's slow recovery from the war, the presence of horse or ox-drawn carts was still a routine event on city and country roadways. On one occasion, while driving along a dirt road adjacent to a rice paddy, heading back towards Yokohama, Dorothy and Hiroshi came by a farmer leading an ox, which was pulling a heavily laden cart. As Dorothy slowly attempted to pass the cart, the ox became spooked and lurched into the middle of the road towards the passing car. Fearing that she would hit the ox, Dorothy chose to steer into the ditch to avoid injuring the animal, the farmer or both. The soft, wet earth gave way beneath the vehicle and the car slide down to the bottom of the ditch.

After much frantic waving of hands in the air and much shouting in unintelligible Japanese by Hiroshi and the irate farmer, calmer heads prevailed, and apologies were eventually extended by all those involved. However, it was clear that the car was not going to get out of the ditch without some heavy-duty assistance. Initially the farmer offered to unhitch his ox from the cart to use it to extract the car, but this was met by serious opposition from the ox, who would have nothing to do with the offending automobile. Just as the farmer was re-hitching his ox to the cart, the unmistakable sound and rumbling ground vibrations of approaching heavy armored vehicles could be heard and felt, as several giant, steel behemoths traversed along the local country road. A column of American tanks was approaching.

Within minutes, six massive American M26 Pershing tanks of 5th Cavalry Regiment approached Dorothy's roadside situation. The commander of the lead tank was a sergeant whose torso was perched above his hatch observing the scene. With a brief radio call, he halted the tank column following behind him. Raising his goggles onto his helmet, he surveyed the situation and made an assessment:

> A pretty blonde women and her local chauffuer stuck in a ditch adjacent to a rice paddy. A large, and apparently unhappy oxen with an overloaded cart blocking the road. And a local farmer with a very concerned look on his face.

The sergeant / tank commander looked down at Dorothy as she carefully made her way to the side of the olive drab, iron war machine. The noise of the tank's engine made verbal communications difficult but following his command to put the tank into idle, the engine noise reduced enough so that Dorothy was able to shout sufficiently loud to make herself understood. As she explained her situation, the commander nodded, smiled and thought to himself, 'She's a Canadian woman, married to a lieutenant somebody or other of the 2nd Battalion, 5th Cavalry Regiment – an American infantry officer.' The fact that this stranded woman was a beautiful, young, blonde in need of assistance was all he needed to know. The lieutenant/tank platoon commander situated in the third tank, middle of the convoy, was advised of the situation and approved the sergeant's extraction plan. The convoy would proceed without delay and the last tank in the column would stop and assist with the stranded vehicle's recovery. 'Yes, sir, but the lady is concerned about the farmer and his ox… the ox and the cart are blocking the road.'

'Listen sergeant, I don't care how pretty the lady is, this column's gotta keep moving!' exclaimed the platoon commander. 'Get that damn ox cart out of the way now!'

The farmer and the ox did not need much encouragement. The revving of the tank engines was enough to send the ox, farmer and their loaded cart off at a good pace down the road and exiting on the first available path to make room for the tanks. The tank column lurched forward, each war machine belching gray smoke from their exhaust manifolds. As each tank passed, every tank crew commander smiled and waved at Dorothy who was stuck on the side of the road. Dorothy smiled enthusiastically back, while she waited patiently for the column to pass. Just as promised, the last tank in the column pulled up in front of the disabled car and within five minutes the tank crew had hooked up a steel towing cable and extracted the car from the ditch. Dorothy let Hiroshi sit behind the wheel for the vehicle extraction process, but quickly nudged him over once the car was back on the road so she could drive them home. Other than a minor dent in the front left fender and mud splattered along its side panel, the car was no worse for wear. Before thanking and bidding farewell to the tank crew that had assisted her, Dorothy made sure she obtained the name of the crew commander of the lead tank as well as the platoon commander's name. Dorothy was sure that Leif would want to thank them personally.

Later that evening, Leif, driving his army jeep, pulled into the driveway of their palatial residence. Dorothy had heard him arrive and moved onto the porch to greet her husband. As she prepared herself to tell him about her car accident earlier that day, out of the corner of her eye, she caught sight of Hiroshi, who was skulking nearby, just out of view from Leif – "the big bossy". Dorothy could tell by Hiroshi's body language that he was very worried that her husbanc would be angry with him for allowing the accident to happen. But as Leif came up the long walkway to the house, he could not contain the knowing smile on his face. As it turned out, within minutes of the roadside extraction, word had been radioed back to camp of a 'daring rescue' of a 'pretty, young Canadian women in distress.' It did not take long until Leif was given the gears by the entire battalion for letting an armored unit 'rescue' the wife of an infantry officer. And as expected, Leif sought out the tank platoon commander who had authorised and orchestrated Dorothy's rescue, thanked him and provided him with a case of Scotch whisky to pass on a bottle or two to each of the tank crews involved. The incident also made Dorothy quite popular at the Officers' Club Ladies' Association – known as the "Wives Club," where whispers could often be heard about 'that Canadian girl that got rescued by the United States cavalry.'

* * *

The year 1949 was busy for Leif, as the division had received new, replacement troops and was active with its new combat readiness training cycle. Dorothy too was busy running the household and entertaining the wives from the Officers' Club Ladies' Association. Ever since her car accident and cavalry rescue, Dorothy had become one of the most popular members of the association and her social calendar was always full. In June, Dorothy went for a medical check-up at the United States military hospital at Camp McGill and learned that she was pregnant. Leif was ecstatic when Dorothy shared the news! Their baby was expected in mid-January 1950.

In autumn 1949, a formal visit by members of the United States House of Representatives Arms Appropriations Committee was scheduled to assess the management of the United States' military occupation of Japan. Leif, along with the battalion adjutant, was tasked to organize and participate in a parade in honor of the visit. The parade, led by the 2nd Battalion, 5th Cavalry Regiment commander, Lieutenant Colonel R.L. Wadlington, took place on 18 November 1949 in front of the Japanese Imperial Palace with a great deal of pomp and circumstance and an impressive display of military might. The message was clear for all to see, including their distinguished visitors from the United States House of Representatives: the United States Army was present and still in control of the security and day to day management of the government and the population of Japan.

* * *

In late November 1949, Margaret Henry came to Japan to help her daughter through the last stages of her pregnancy and to be on hand for the arrival of her first grandchild. On 22 January 1950, Leif and Dorothy became parents to Leslie Margaret Bangsbøll. Born at the United States naval base in Yokosuka, Japan, to a Canadian mother and a Danish-born, now naturalized American citizen, Leslie would technically be a Japanese citizen until the administrative red tape could be sorted out almost two years later. With the arrival of their first born, both Leif and Dorothy knew life had changed dramatically. Having her mother with her to help with her new-born was a godsend for Dorothy. Margaret, the consummate host and socialite, helped Dorothy stay active within the Officers' Ladies' Club Association. Not long after arriving, Margaret's prowess in bridge playing became the envy of the association and known to Lieutenant General Walton Walker, the commander of the Eighth United States Army. Soon Margaret and General Walker were the bridge pair to beat, which few ever did.

Spring 1950 was busy for Leif. Aside from being a new father, the division had received new, replacement troops and he was kept active with its new combat readiness training cycle. Dorothy too was busy learning to be a mother and running the household while continuing to host wives from the Officers' Club Ladies' Association on a regular basis. Ever since her car accident and cavalry rescue, Dorothy had become one of the most popular members of the Officers' Wives' Club and her social calendar was always full.

In April 1950, Leif and Dorothy's exotic honeymoon adventure in Japan would come to an end when they received orders for Leif to join 11th Airborne Division at Fort Campbell, Kentucky. Both Dorothy and Hiroshi – her houseboy, translator and self-proclaimed guardian of Missy-San – wept when they bid farewell to each other.

Chapter 5

Rakkasans!

'Let Valor Not Fail.'
187th Airborne Regiment's motto

With his highly polished combat boots, bloused combat trousers and field jacket on, Lieutenant Bangsbøll walked towards the main entrance of the headquarters building of his new unit, the 187th Airborne Regiment with long, confident strides. As he approached the nerve center of his new assignment, he couldn't help but notice the large wooden sign mounted prominently above the doorway. On it, in bright gold lettering, was the word 'Rakkasans'. Leif smiled and laughed to himself. He had already done his homework on his new unit, and knew the unique and recent history of the term Rakkasan. With no actual word in the Japanese language for 'paratrooper', Rakkasans – which literally means 'falling down umbrella men' – was the closest possible, albeit quirky, translation. Leif's new unit, the 187th Airborne Regiment, had also just recently completed a three-year assignment in Japan as part of the post-Second World War occupation force and was now based out of Fort Campbell, Kentucky. During its time in Japan, the 187th Airborne Regiment had adopted the Japanese moniker of the Rakkasans and Leif loved this. Notwithstanding his brief, yet very intense counter-insurgency mission on the island of Che Ju Do, the recent assignment in Japan with his wife and new-born daughter had been the most tranquil and culturally interesting time that he'd had in a decade.

Leif, Dorothy and baby Leslie arrived at Fort Campbell in May 1950. Clearly, life at Fort Campbell would be far different from Dorothy's charmed life in Japan. The BOQs (base officers quarters) that they were assigned was small and old, and Dorothy no longer had four servants to look after her and manage her household; reality began to set in. As for Leif, he quickly and eagerly integrated himself into his new airborne assignment with 11th Airborne Division, 187th Airborne Regiment. Then everything changed.

On 25 June, 1950, after being at Fort Campbell for just five weeks, Leif and Dorothy's world would be turned upside down like so many other soldiers and their families. On that early morning in June 1950, 8 divisions of North Korean People's Army, known as Inmin'gun, composed of nearly 130,000 combat soldiers, poured across the entire length of 38th parallel into South Korea. South Korea and its United States ally had been completely caught by surprise. Years of minor border skirmishes between the North and South had dulled the South Korean and American leadership into a false sense of optimism that peace would be maintained. During those years, the North Korean leader, Kim Jong-il had been pressing hard with both Soviet Russia and communist China to support an invasion and the unification of North and South Korea. Finally, in May 1950, Russian leader Joseph Stalin and Mao agreed that it was time. Kim Jong-il would get his chance to 'touch the south with the point of a bayonet.' In response to this international crisis, the United Nations condemned the invasion of the Republic of Korea (South Korea) by the Democratic People's Republic of Korean (North Korea) and prepared to respond with an international military force.

At Fort Campbell, upon learning of the invasion of South Korea by the North, the 187th ARCT (Airborne Regimental Combat Team) was ordered to immediately begin assembling essential military assets and fine-tune its combat readiness to enable deployment in force to Korea as soon as practical. Leif's first action was to arrange to send both Dorothy, who was expecting their second child and Leslie to Oshawa, Canada to live with Dorothy's family – he could not leave for war and leave his pregnant wife and newborn daughter alone. Margaret and Clifford Henry would welcome their daughter and granddaughter home with open arms. Their son-in-law was going off to war again.

Leading up to the North Korean invasion of the South, and unbeknown to most Americans except senior military and political leaders, the Korean peninsula had been fraught with tension. There had been much political rhetoric and frequent, yet relatively minor military skirmishes all along the border of the 38th parallel separating North and South Korea throughout 1948 and 1949 and during the first half of 1950. North and South Korea were in a state of strained political tolerance. After two and a half years of minor, yet persistent political and military provocations by the North Korean government, the South Korean government had foolishly become desensitised to the growing threat from the North. As a result, both the South Korean government and the United States military command located in South Korea, along with their respective intelligence agencies, were caught completely off guard when, early in the morning of 25 June 1950, North Korea launched a massive surprise attack and full-scale military invasion on its neighbor to the south. The Korean War had begun, and the North Koreans were winning – rolling over South Korean and American military forces with overwhelming waves of zealous communist combat troops.

As the United States and the United Nations assembled their combat and support forces to engage the invading North Korean army, 187th ARCT, under the command of Brigadier General Frank Bowen, was busily finalizing its pre-combat mission preparations from its staging base just outside of Gimpo airfield (known to the Americans as Kimpo) in Seoul, South Korea. The 187th Airborne Infantry Regiment along with 674th Airborne Field Artillery Battalion, were detached from 11th Airborne Division and reformed as the 187th Airborne Regimental Combat Team, commonly referred to as the ARCT. Preparations of 187th ARCT deployment to South Korea were in high gear.

Most of the United States forces sent to Korea in the early stages of the war came from the Eighth United States Army, which was still performing occupation duties in Japan. Unfortunately, by 1950, many of the experienced combat veterans from the Second World War had been discharged or transferred stateside – like Leif. As a result, only 15 percent of the Eighth United States Army were seasoned Second World War combat veterans – the rest were green, untested soldiers. Major General Dean, Leif's former commander with 1st Cavalry Division, was now the commander of the 24th Infantry Division stationed in Japan and would lead his largely untested, inadequately equipped American troops against the North Korean army in an effort to save South Korea from being overrun. The valiant effort of the soldiers of the 24th Infantry Division in their delaying action against the advancing North Korean army was remarkable but extremely costly. The 24th Infantry Division would suffer over 2,400 casualties but would succeed in halting the North Korean advance on the outskirts of the southern port city of Busan. Regrettably, on 25 August 1950, Major General Dean would be captured by the North Koreans and would remain a PoW until its conclusion in September 1953.

By August 1950, the North Korean forces had pushed the Republic of Korea Army as well as the Eighth United States Army south to the outskirts of the coastal city of Busan. The North Koreans occupied over 90 per cent of South Korea. Elements of Leif's former unit, 1st Cavalry Division from Japan were airlifted into Busan to reinforce the defenses. In order to relieve the Busan perimeter, General Douglas MacArthur, the commander of all United Nations forces in Korea, ordered the remainder of 1st Cavalry Division from Japan to make a daring amphibious landing at Incheon on 15 September 1950 under the codename Operation Cromyte. Along with the Marines 1st Division and army's 7th Infantry Division, the massive Incheon landing came ashore deep behind the North Korean frontline forces. Planned and led by the infamous General MacArthur, the strategically brilliant and operationally daring seaborne landing virtually severed the Korean peninsula, striking the North Korean army in its vulnerable flank and thereby cutting the North Korean army and its supply lines in half and severing its lines of communications. The brilliantly executed counteroffensive immediately stopped the North Korean advance and trapped tens of thousands of North Korean troops in South Korea, sending the entire North Korean army into disarray.

Four weeks after the now famous Incheon landings that had caught the North Korean army by complete surprise, 187th ARCT was declared ready for combat operations. Despite the initial success of the Incheon-based counteroffensive, the North Koreans were not out of the fight. Knowing this, the United Nations and United States forces were preparing for another offensive action against the North Koreans amongst which the 187th ARCT would play a vital role. Lieutenant Bangsbøll oversaw the 187th's ARCT headquarters intelligence and reconnaissance platoon. Because of the special nature of the Int & Recon platoon's assignments, Colonel Aaron Bank, Ex-O (Executive Officer) of 187th ARCT and the regiment's S-3 operations officer, had to approve all missions deemed to fall into the 'special operations' category. The Int & Recon platoon would be the eyes and ears of the ARCT – their objective was to find the enemy and lead the ARCT to engage and destroy them.

On the morning of 20 October 1950, with more than 100 military troop-carrying aircraft parked before them, 3,000 Rakkasans of 187th ARCT assembled on the hot tarmac of Gimpo airfield, located just outside of Seoul, the capital of South Korea. The paratroopers moved in an orderly, yet awkwardly slow pace towards their waiting aircraft. Waddling much like overweight penguins under the heavy burden of their combat equipment, the airborne assault troops methodically lumbered towards their designated aircraft.

Like his fellow paratroopers of 187th ARCT stretched out before him and lined up behind him, Lieutenant Bangsbøll was laden with over 100 pounds of essential combat equipment. He wore a main parachute and helmet, carried a Thompson M1A1 submachine gun and Colt 45 pistol, and was loaded down with hundreds of rounds of ammunition packed into every available pocket and pouch. He carried a half dozen grenades, a bayonet, a folding entrenching tool, an army-issue flashlight, a map case, a week's worth of rations, two canteens of water, a first aid kit, a poncho and several pairs of spare socks. As an airborne infantry soldier, his primary mode of transportation was his feet; their care was essential for combat effectiveness. Clean, dry socks would keep the soldier moving, and mobility was essential in combat.

Though a reserve parachute was usually part of the paratrooper's kit, on a combat drop such as this, where the jump would be from an altitude of only 1,000 feet, a reserve parachute would not be needed; at that altitude there would not be sufficient time to activate a reserve parachute if the main one failed to deploy. That was just a fact of life in airborne combat operations.

Hot and uncomfortable, Leif waited patiently on the tarmac for his turn to board his aircraft. Climbing aboard and getting through the troop door of the

C-119 Boxcar aircraft was not an easy or elegant manoeuvre. It took the assistance of three other paratroopers to complete the task: two troopers standing in the doorway of the aircraft pulling the next paratrooper aboard by his outstretched arms and a third trooper, unceremoniously pushing from behind. The interior of the aircraft was stifling-hot and crammed with men and their weapons of war and felt like an oven. The weather on the Korean peninsula in autumn 1950 had been unusually hot and humid and was making these overladden soldiers miserable as they lumbered into their awaiting aircraft. Though still early in the morning, the sun had already heated the thin metal skin of the aircraft to a scorching temperature. The paratroopers were already soaked with sweat from simply walking across the tarmac, never mind the exertion required to climb aboard the aircraft. Once aboard, Leif made his way forward to his designated seat as platoon commander. As the platoon's leader, he was positioned in the middle of the row of sixteen paratroopers – known as a stick of paratroopers, on the portside of the aircraft's passenger/cargo compartment. His second-in-command, a first sergeant was similarly positioned on the starboard side of the aircraft, the logic being that they would land on the drop zone with their troops dispersed closely around them. This C-119 Boxcar would carry all thirty-two members of Leif's Int & Recon platoon into battle.

* * *

As Leif sat on the canvas webbing bench seat amongst the other Rakkasans waiting for the airborne armada to depart, he mentally reviewed his pre-jump checklist and drop zone assembly plan. As the minutes ticked by, he began to reflect on his one and only other combat jump. It was 6 October 1944, almost six years to the day from this, his second combat jump. But he knew that this mission was very different from his late night, clandestine parachute insertion into Denmark as an OSS agent. Then, alone, he was armed only with a pistol, was dressed in civilian clothing and had false identification to allow him to immediately integrate into the local society.

* * *

Today, he was with 3,000 fellow American paratroopers, heavily armed and ready for immediate combat engagement with the enemy. This combat mission would involve leading a platoon of soldiers and coordinating with other platoons within his company. His company commander would further coordinate with the regimental leadership, and the regiment's actions would be further coordinated with other supporting units assigned to the mission. Leif knew that this mission would require a different type of leadership than called for during his first combat missions in the Second World War.

The United Nations, through its lead nation – the United States – was about to launch its first airborne operation of the Korean War, and America's largest since Operation Market Garden during the Second World War. Seventy-one C-119s and forty C-47 aircraft would deliver Lieutenant Bangsbøll along with his paratrooper brothers of 187th ARCT to a drop zone near the towns of Sunchŏn and Sukchŏn, located 50 miles north of the capital city of Pyongyang in North Korea. The airborne assault was part of the United Nations offensive intended to drive the North Korean army back northward, out of South Korea. The communists were already retreating in the face of the overwhelming United Nations-United States offensive pushing northward. The objective of the Rakkasans' airborne assault was three-fold. Their primary objectives were to cut off the retreating North Korean army and capture members of the North Korean government and military leadership fleeing northward from the North Korean capital of Pyongyang. As well, they were to search for and free any American and United Nations prisoners of war believed to be in the hands of the North Korean army who were thought to be moving from Pyongyang towards the Manchurian border.

The one-hour flight from Gimpo airfield to the drop zones north of Pyongyang was rough, due to the air turbulence caused by the hot weather and further exacerbated by the turbulence generated by over 110 aircraft flying in formation. When the red jump light illuminated in the troop compartment indicating the drop zone was within five minutes, the paratroopers were relieved to be preparing to get out of the claustrophobic, gut-churning ride. The jumpmaster took up his position in the middle of the compartment, aft and between the two troop doors located on either side of the fuselage. All eyes looked aft towards him in anticipation of his next orders.

'PARATROOPERS STAND UP!' came the call from the jumpmaster. The thirty-two paratroopers strained to get to their feet and jostled to maintain their balance once they had. Then came the order 'CHECK YOUR EQUIPMENT!' and each trooper made sure that everything was secure – chin strap tightened, weapon straps tightened, static line free of tangles and static line connector in hand ready to attach to the static line cable. Once all the paratroops had completed their checks, they looked aft to the jumpmaster, which was his indication to continue. The jumpmaster then shouted, 'HOOK UP!' and each paratrooper attached their static line to the steel cable that ran down each side of the compartment just above their helmets. 'CHECK STATIC LINES!' and each paratrooper manually pulled on the static line connector of the paratrooper in front of themselves to verify the proper connection of the static line of their neighbor. The payload specialist opened the paratroop doors, and immediately, as though it were a physical blow, the noise level in the aircraft intensified. Despite the overwhelming vibrations and noise, the cool, fresh air that rushed in was a relief to the hot, stifling conditions in the cargo compartment.

Then came what they all knew would be the second to last pre-jump order from the jumpmaster, 'RAKKASANS READY!' Both sticks of sixteen paratroops on each side of the cargo compartment automatically shuffled aft towards the paratroop doors to minimize the space between each trooper and then each man gave a thumbs up signal to the jumpmaster – the Rakkasans were ready. Now they waited and tried to maintain their balance as the aircraft bucked and buffeted in the turbulent air as the pilot attempted to align the aircraft with both the drop zone and the aircraft in front while avoiding contact with the aircraft just off each wing tip.

For the first three troopers in line on each stick, the view out of the paratroop door was a blurred image of the ground below rushing by at 120 miles per hour a mere 1,000 feet below them. Leif, the eighth man on the left-hand stick of sixteen troopers could only see the parachute and the back of the helmet of the paratrooper immediately in front of him. Instinctively he was reviewing the priority of tasks he would give when they hit the ground. He leaned forward to speak to his radioman in front of him. The paratrooper turned his head to listen to his platoon commander, looking pale and nervous. The young radio operator was a 20-year-old private from Nebraska who had never seen combat before. As the young soldier was about to jump out of an aircraft from 1,000 foot altitude, directly into enemy-held territory, Leif thought to himself, 'He has reason to be frightened.' To be heard of the cacophony of noises from the open paratroop doors and the droning of the C-119 Boxcar's two powerful engines, Lieutenant Bangsboll shouted instructions to his radioman standing in line, in front of him,

> PROTECT THAT RADIO SON AND GET IT UP AND RUNNING AS SOON AS YOU GET ON THE GROUND. BE PREPARED TO RESPOND TO A REGIMENTAL POST-DROP RADIO CHECK ASAP. I'LL COME FIND YOU AND WE'LL HAVE THE PLATOON ASSEMBLE AROUND US. THE FIRST SERGEANT WILL DO A QUICK ASSESSMENT OF THE PLATOON TO SEE IF WE HAVE ANY INJURIES BEFORE WE MOVE OFF THE DROP ZONE TOGETHER. GOT IT?

The radioman nodded nervously. Leif then added,

> DON'T YOU WORRY, SON, YOU'VE GOT 3,000 BROTHERS JUMPING WITH YOU THIS MORNING… YOU'LL BE FINE. JUST FOLLOW YOUR BASIC JUMP TRAINING PROCEDURES. FOCUS ON YOUR BODY POSITION AS YOU HIT THE SLIP

> STREAM AND KEEP THOSE KNEES BENT AND TOGETHER WHEN YOU'RE ABOUT TO HIT THE GROUND.

Another nervous nod from the radioman and then Leif added,

> I'LL MEET YOU ON THE DROP ZONE AND WE'LL MAKE THOSE NORTH KOREAN BASTARDS WISH THEY'D STAYED ON THEIR SIDE OF THE BORDER.

The platoon's radioman looked back at his platoon commander, forced a smiled and despite the lack of moisture in his parched mouth, shouted: 'ROGER THAT SIR! AIRBORNE ALL THE WAY!' Leif looked back at the brave, scared soldier and smiled, giving him a wink and a friendly slap of encouragement on his helmet, as he silently wondered, 'How many of these brave young boys will die today?'

How the parachute drop and ensuing landing would actually unfold would depend on many factors, most of which were outside of Lieutenant Bangsbøll control at this point. The obvious and most critical factor was whether the enemy happened to be down there waiting for them in strength. The C-119's red jump light went out and the green jump light illuminated. 'GREEN GO!' shouted the jumpmaster as he slapped the shoulder of the paratrooper closest to the paratroop door. The next few seconds were a blur of motion as a methodical sequence of events repeated over and over again. Armed, heavily laden airborne warriors systematically shuffled forward into position, gripping the edges of the doorway with both hands and propelling themselves out into the slipstream as the next trooper moved into position behind them to do the same. The two lines of sixteen troops kept moving to the rear until only the payload specialist and the jumpmaster were left in the now cavernous, empty troop compartment. They each looked out their paratroop door, down and behind the aircraft to ensure there were no hung-up troopers and gave a thumbs up signal of all clear. Then the platoon's jumpmaster saluted the aircraft's payload specialist and jumped out the paratroop door shouting 'RAKKASANS!'

The United States Army intelligence experts and mission planners had been correct, the wide valley used as the drop zone was carpeted with mostly rice paddies and cabbage fields dotted with a few small villages. The only witnesses to the impressive sight of nearly 3,000 American paratroopers descending from the sky were a handful of astonished farmers and their frightened livestock. There were no North Korean soldiers to contend with, and the 'falling-down umbrella men' of the 187th ARCT landed unopposed. The 187th ARCT had landed behind enemy lines unscathed and were ready to find and destroy their enemy. Leif's Int & Recon platoon took the lead as the eyes and ears of the 187th ARCT.

Lieutenant Bangsbøll initial assessment was that the airborne assault was executed perfectly. Within hours of their landing, their objectives of the railway line and the main highway, which ran north, were cut off by the sudden and overwhelming arrival of the 187th ARCT airborne assault team. Though no United States or United Nations prisoners were located or freed by the airborne operation, thousands of enemy troops were killed or captured, and dozens of senior North Korean government officials and military leaders were taken prisoner and brought to South Korea for internment and interrogation. Over the next three weeks, 187th ARCT pressed forward with their assault and had subsequent major combat engagements against the North Korean army at the towns of Suan, Wonju, Kaesŏng, Munsan-ni and Inge. The surprise airborne assault behind enemy lines using modern, coordinated tactics, highly mobile armored units and precision air support overwhelmed the poorly equipped North Korean troops who were relying on outdated strategies, such as massed troop formations who made suicidal frontal charges without air support and only minimal, poorly coordinated artillery support. North Korean casualties were heavy: 6,000 soldiers were killed and over 10,000 captured during this 3-week offensive. The 187th ARCT suffered only minimal casualties in this heavy engagement: 28 killed and 105 wounded. For those twenty-eight dead Rakkasans and their grieving families, it was the ultimate sacrifice and the last full measure given for their country. The 187th ARCT had been re-baptized by fire and seen its first combat since the Second World War. Their performance was nothing short of outstanding.

During this first combat mission with 187th ARCT, Lieutenant Bangsbøll and his Int & Recon platoon acquitted themselves extremely well, adeptly leading the 187th ARCT into position to engage the larger, albeit retreating enemy. The sudden presence of American paratroopers in their rear echelon caught the North Korean commanders by surprise once again. The tenacity of the aggressive tactics of the Rakkasans unnerved the retreating North Korean army and turned the battle into a rout. As the lead element of the American assault, Leif's Int & Recon platoon engaged North Korean units at several vital transportation nodes, securing two bridges and a railway trestle. The Int & Recon platoon moved aggressively and operated with methodical efficiency and professionalism, suffering only a few minor injuries despite being one of the lead elements in the offensive.

Leif was proud of his platoon's performance in combat and was equally impressed with the entire 187th ARCT's conduct and capabilities in hostile conditions – they were a powerful and agile force that should be feared and respected. The first encounter with the enemy had certainly been an overwhelming success for the Rakkasans. Leif was optimistic about the future of their combat mission, but felt that this would be a long, tough struggle and was certain that the enemy was not yet beaten.

Chapter 6

The Danish Duke

'Though this be madness, yet there is method to it.'
William Shakespeare, *Hamlet*

With tracer bullets ripping through the air just inches over his head as well as impacting the ground just feet in front of him, Lieutenant Bangsbøll involuntarily flinched at each impact. Despite the onslaught, he continued to monitor and direct his platoons' response to the enemy's early morning assault on the 187th ARCT's position. In the pitch darkness, bookending the staccato of rifle and machine gun fire, was the incessant bugle calls of the enemy and their defiant, yet unintelligible war cries as their leaders tried to maneuver their assault forces amongst the chaos of battle. Ten minutes into the assault, Leif witnessed his M2, heavy machine gunner postioned to his right go down – hit in the shoulder by an enemy round. Knowing the vital importance of the heavy machine gun in their perimeter defence capabilities, Lieutenant Bangsbøll immediately ran towards and jumped into the gun pit. Assessing the wounded soldier briefly, he ripped open and placed a compression bandage onto the open shoulder wound, and smiled at the wounded paratrooper to reassure him, shouting over the cacophony of sounds from the firefight, 'JUST A SCRATCH – YOU'LL BE FINE SON! KEEP PRESSURE ON THAT WOUND UNTIL I COME BACK.' Leif winked at the prone soldier who was clearly in shock and just stared back with wide eyes at his platoon commander.

Leif immediately rolled over into the gun pit, grabbed the weapon's grip and pulled back on the cocking handle of the Browning M2 – known as the 'Ma Deuce' machine gun. The Ma Deuce could fire 600 rounds per minute. Leif's self-preservation instinct was to fight not flee. He aimed… aimed into the darkness in front of his position looking for a target. NOTHING – JUST DARKNESS! With only a black void in his gunsights, but fear in his heart, he knew that the enemy was out there and were getting closer. With adrenaline rushing through his veins, Leif squeezed the trigger far harder than necessary. Expecting the weapon to burst to life with fire and recoil – nothing. All he heard was the dull metallic 'clank' of the firing pin slamming forward. It was the sound of utter despair amongst the torrent of chaos of combat surrounding him.

Leif immediately went into a methodical series of muscle memory reactions. He re-cocked the weapon and looked to clear any stoppages. Seeing none, he yelled to himself, 'CLEAR!' Now focusing on the firing chamber which was clear – the ammo belt had run out. He shouted, 'NO AMMO!' and then looked to his left where the gun loader should be. Lieutenant Bangsbøll saw a soldier – not much more than a boy, with his hands frantically covering his ears and crying for his mother, and Leif thought, 'This soldier was out of the fight – at least for now.' Lieutenant Bangsbøll then scanned his immediate surroundings to his left and grabbed the loose end of an ammo belt which was thankfully protruding out of the half-empty ammo box. Forcing his shaking hands to do his bidding, he grabbed the loose end of the ammo belt into the firing chamber and slammed close the cover. Above the chaos and roar of combat around him – gunfire was emerging from all directions, accented with the shouts and war cries of the enemy which were getting louder – closer. It had only been twenty seconds since the machine gunner was hit and the weapon had stopped firing into the enemy.

Twenty seconds, during which the enemy would have noticed with satisfaction that the American gun position had been silenced. Leif thought to himself, 'Move towards the weakness in the line is what I would be telling my soldiers. Well, this will give them a surprise! It was too dark to see anything or anyone beyond a yard or two in front of his position, at least until the next illumination flare was launched. Fear of the darkness was as frightening as the sudden appearance from out of the darkness of the approaching enemy soldiers with death in their eyes – just steps away when the flare ignited and illuminated the battlefield once more. The flares helped to identify the enemy – their locations and direction of attack, but it also exposed him and his soldier. Eerily, the illumination flares also added a frightening and surreal aspect to the chaos of close-quarter combat – like watching a horror film's climax sequence with a strobe light flashing and the volume on an ear-splitting level.

Properly reloaded, this time, when Leif squeezed the trigger the M2/Ma Deuce barked to life – loud and lethal. He did not aim, he just began to rack back and forth through his field of fire, sending hundreds of hot metal projectiles into the darkness before him. The enemy were close and there were so many of them, packed shoulder to shoulder as they advanced up the hill – it would be impossible to miss them. From behind him an illumination flare was launched which revealed the battlefield before him. As Leif had expected many of the enemy had begun moving towards the silenced American machine gun position – his position. The enemy sensed weakness in the American line. But the machine gun wasn't silent anymore and the tight formation of North Koreans only 5 yards away were being obliterated by the hail of bullets being spat out by the Ma Deuce. Lieutenant Bangsbøll was mowing down the enemy by the dozen – reaping the enemy like a farmer's scythe. Stopping only to reload the next belt of ammunition, he continued his onslaught for what seemed like hours. In reality it had only been three minutes. But three minutes of constant firing had sent almost 2,000 rounds into the enemy – reaping carnage. This prolonged infalade of fire created an enormous amount of heat within the gun's barrel. Then, glowing red, the weapon's barrel said, 'No more'. But it had been long enough to stem the tide of the enemy's assault – dead in their tracks.

With the enemy assault repulsed, at least for the time being, Lieutenant Bangsbøll, roused the assistant gunner, the young private who had frozen up during the firefight and gave him the heat-resistant gloves and ordered him to replace the barrel on the machine gun. Leif needed everyman in the fight. He then called for a medic to take care of the wounded gunner and moved down his platoon's sector of the defensive line, checking on the wounded, ordering-up additional ammunition and generally ensuring his platoon's combat readiness – bruised but still fully mission capable. All along the defensive positions of 187th ARCT, squad and platoon leaders as well as company commanders were doing the same – expecting that the enemy would return in force.

That night, the 187th successfully repelled the North Korean counterattack. Reminding the Americans that though the enemy was withdrawing northward, they were still a very dangerous and determined foe. The North Koreans were also desperate, and desperate regimes will do desperate and despicable things.

It was only when the fighting had stopped and Leif had a moment to reflect on what had just transpired. "Dear God" Leif thought to himself, "how many men did I just kill…how many families I have just shattered?" Leif gazed across the battlefield as the first light of the day began to unveil the carnage. Leif felt like he could vomit - but he knew he must maintain his composure…the troops can't see their leader show weakness or vulnerability. The dramatic disparity of combat losses between the two warring sides was at times unsettling. Though 187th ARCT as well equipped and had a large percentage of soldiers and officers with Second World War combat experience, some United States Army units were composed of mostly green, untested troops, and were supported by an over-burdened and at times inept resupply system which resulted in unnecessary and in some cases, catastrophic losses and extreme hardship when in contact with the enemy. Clearly, the North Korean forces were woefully outclassed against the modern United States military and most of the other UN coalition partners when it came to the profession of arms, in terms of both tactics and modern weaponry. However, the one advantage the North Koreans – and subsequently the Chinese army – had over the UN forces in this conflict was the sheer numbers of soldiers that they could commit to the fight.

In many battles, the North Korean and Chinese commanders demonstrated little compassion or even common sense in the care and employment of their troops. The communist soldiers were often ordered to attack in massed, human waves, mindlessly assaulting well-fortified defensive positions that were manned with professional soldiers armed with state of the art weapons and supported by unmatched armored ground forces, coordinated artillery, as well as modern fighter bomber air support and massive naval firepower.

With the North Korean army reeling from the onslaught of the American-led UN offensive, disturbing intelligence reports began coming in through the UN command network indicating the discovery of acts of atrocity in the wake of the North Korean retreat. Oddly enough, the reported atrocities at the hands of the fleeing North Korean army, involving the murder of civilians, including women and children, was occurring in North Korea.

One particularly grim case was discovered on 22 October 1950, by elements of 187th ARCT. Following their parachute assault landing and two days of hard fighting, the 187th had taken control of the area around Highway 1, west of the town of Sunchŏn. This route was the main ground transport route from the capital, Pyongyang, straight north to the interior of North Korea and up to the border with China, upon which both the North Korean government and its army were retreating. As the main elements of 187th ARCT consolidated their position on the high ground overlooking Highway 1, Lieutenant Bangsbøll was tasked to lead the advance element of the battalion – his reconnaissance platoon beyond the highway towards the village of Sunchŏn to assess the enemy threat on the western flank of the 187th ARCT's position.

Leif's thirty-man unit moved cautiously but with speed and agility through the rough terrain of hills and ravines on their approach to Highway 1, north of the Capital city of Pyonyang. It was unseasonably hot for this time of year, and the heavily laden paratroopers were soaked in sweat. During their patrol they came across dozens of abandoned North Korean military vehicles, broken down and left on the side of the road, but saw no trace of any enemy troops. Through the day, the small American unit observed thousands of displaced civilians, including many families on the move. All were on foot, some with carts laden with all their meager possessions being pulled by exhausted, malnourished oxen or horses. Some were traveling north, following the North Korean army and away from the oncoming UN forces. Many others, however, were moving in a southern direction, towards the presumed safety of the UN forces. Then, late in the afternoon of the 22nd, on the outskirts of the village of Sunchŏn, Lieutenant Bangsbøll patrol came upon a horrific scene: two mass graves with hundreds of North Korean civilians dead and left unburied in large pits.

With two squads protecting their perimeter, Lieutenant Bangsbøll and the third ten-man squad stood at the edge of the first mass gravesite. There was silent disbelief at what they were seeing: the young and the elderly, men and women, piled on top of one another in an obscene and macabre mélange of bloated bodies. Even to the battle-hardened paratroops, the sight of such carnage was appalling and difficult to gaze upon.

The silence of the moment was broken by the sound of someone retching. Leif looked back and saw his young private, the radioman from Nebraska – not much more than a boy – bent over emptying the contents of his stomach onto the dusty ground. The sergeant squad leader went over and placed a comforting hand on the private's shoulder to try and reassure the young man. In between gut-wrenching spasms, the soldier, whose face was pale, spat to clear the foulness of his mouth, and forced out the questions that everyone present was asking themselves: 'Who did this? How could this happen?' The sergeant did not know what to say and looked to his lieutenant with questioning eyes. The lieutenant, too, was at a loss for words as his mind tried to process what he was observing. 'As a soldier in combat, you see some awful, unimaginable things that enemy soldiers do to one another in the heat of battle', Leif thought, 'but this deliberate act of barbarism, this massacre of so many defenceless civilians, is a whole other nightmare to try and process.'

Leif pulled his heavy ruck sack off his back, a welcome relief to his sore and tired shoulders and knees. He opened one of the side pouches and pulled out something metallic, black and silver. He walked over to his sergeant, who was still standing beside the young private, and handed the squad leader a small Kodak Rangefinder camera, the same camera he had used during his mission in Berlin. 'I want photographs of all of this – now!' were the only words he could muster. Photographs were taken of the two mass graves and the surrounding area, and a report of the grim discovery was immediately radioed to the commander of 187th ARCT for furtherance to General MacArthur's headquarters. American and UN intelligence agencies would later determine that in its haste to outrun the advancing UN forces, the North Korean government had ordered the execution of all political prisoners and any North Korean citizen suspected of having sympathies for South Korea. The prisons in Pyongyang had been emptied of all pro-Western/anti-communist prisoners and were now being summarily and systematically murdered as the North Korean army retreated northward.

By the end of October 1950, as the lopsided battle and overwhelming UN victories at Sunchŏn and Yongju were completed, 187th ARCT began to reconstitute itself while it dug in to establish a strong defensive position. They all knew that the North Koreans would surely initiate a counterattack, the only question was when? As Leif stood overseeing his troops digging their trenches and setting up their firing positions, he reflected upon his first major combat engagement since the Second World War, during which he had helped reclaim the city of Copenhagen from the Germans. Leif considered not only the 187th ARCT's achievements over the past two weeks, but also the series of violent events observed, and tactical lessons learned. The 187th ARCT had performed admirably, executing their combat mission with professional skill, precision, speed and agility. However, what stuck in Leif's mind was the enemy's strategically myopic and ultimately enormously costly and at times, mindless tactical decisions in terms of life and care of their troops and disregard for their own civilian population.

By mid-November, with the on-set of frigid winter weather, and as expected, North Korean and Chinese troops began to counterattack along a broad front of the UN lines. After a day of particularly hard fighting, fending off wave after wave of what seemed like mindless enemy assaults, Leif asked his tent mates a simple yet profound rhetorical question,

> What motivates our enemy's leadership to order such irresponsible, immoral, bordering on criminally negligent commands to their troops? At times they just keep coming at us, wave after wave, shouting fierce war cries and with those bugles blowing – it was ghastly to witness! And we just keep killing them, watching those poor devils pile up on the battlefield.

The reality was, that if the enemy happened to dislodge them from their defensive positions it would only be because they had run out of ammunition, or the barrels of their weapons had become too hot to fire anymore.

After a moment's reflection, Leif's close friend, Captain George Gormely, spoke up and made a profoundly true statement,

> Despite my deep fear and loathing of our enemy, I feel a degree of empathy for those communist bastards who are so fanatically following such blind, misguided leadership and are so determined to kill us. At times it feels like a massacre – meaningless. The only positive outcome might be the muted joy of still being alive after the battle.

As a result of the successes of the Int & Recon platoon, Lieutenant Bangsbøll had earned an impressive reputation within his company and within the regiment. At the completion of the airborne assault operation, during the commander's debrief of the mission's accomplishments, Brigadier General Bowen made a remark about Lieutenant Bangsbøll's conduct that would have long-lasting effects. Owing to Leif's family heritage and his panache and flair, Bowen, during his debrief with all his leadership cadre present, had fondly referred to Leif as 'The Danish Duke'. From that day forth, The Danish Duke was Leif's official nickname. Impressed with Lieutenant Bangsbøll's leadership skills and combat capabilities and being fully aware of his previous combat record with the OSS during the Second World War, Bowen relied on the junior officer's previous combat expertise and tested leadership skills for the toughest assignments. Though Bowen enjoyed referring to Leif by this newly established nickname, in more serious moments, Bowen had referred to him numerous times as an example of a soldier's soldier – an honor Leif would cherish for the rest of his life. This singular praise from his commander, a man he respected unreservedly, was more important to him than any of the medals that would adorn his uniform by the end of his career.

Autumn 1950 had seen the tide of the war change in favor of the UN forces. However, in early December 1950, aided now by 200,000 members of the Army of the People's Republic of China, the North Korean army drove their forces southward again, dislodging the UN forces and Eighth United States Army in the eastern sector, forcing another massive Allied retreat. A number of UN and American units had been overrun during the Chinese-North Korean offensive and in one particular case, 187th ARCT was assigned an impossibly challenging task: to infiltrate through enemy lines, and locate and return some abandoned, yet valuable United States Army property that had been hastily hidden and left behind as the Eighth United States Army retreated.

* * *

Lieutenant Colonel Aaron Bank called Lieutenant Bangsbøll into the operations tent to go over this new, special operation mission. Leif was one of the division's most experienced platoon commanders, especially in missions designed to infiltrate and operate behind enemy lines. And while he was eager to accept the assignment, he quickly realized that this would be a mission like none other he had undertaken before. An Eighth United States Army finance unit had a stockpile of gold they used for financing a multitude of logistical needs and purchasing supplies, as well as paying off local Koreans for information. About half of the gold had been brought back with the retreating American unit. However, fourteen crates containing gold bullion in 1- and 5-ounce bars had been left behind, hidden along with crates of ammunition, all sealed in a cave near their former encampment. The onslaught of the Chinese attack had been so swift that all the unit could do was blow up the entrance of the cave in the hopes the enemy would not notice it or care to investigate further.

With his new mission orders and the support plan in place, Leif and his Int & Recon platoon headed out the next day in six jeeps and two armored assault vehicles north-east towards the enemy lines to find the hidden cache of army gold. With the assistance of covering artillery and close air support from the USAAF, the eight-vehicle convoy – jeeps and armored cars – made its way 12 miles into enemy held territory. The vehicles were fast and highly mobile, something Leif needed if he were to get in and out of enemy territory as quickly as possible. With the navigational assistance of the division's finance officer from the Eighth United States Army, who had overseen the hasty concealment of the gold crates and in whose care the gold had been originally placed, the cave entrance was located. Four hours later, with ten men digging at a time and the remaining fifteen soldiers forming a defensive perimeter, the cave entrance was cleared. Miraculously, all fourteen crates of gold were found and extracted from their temporary tomb. Knowing that ammunition was almost as valuable as the gold they had just rescued, Leif ordered that each man was to grab at least one case of ammo from the cave.

Just as the last of the crates were loaded onto the jeeps, enemy artillery rounds began to impact the former American camp, within 100 yards of the cave entrance and the parked American vehicles. Evidently the enemy had spotted the American insertion team and wanted to destroy or at least deter them from remaining any longer. As the barrage slowly swept across the terrain towards them, Leif shouted over the defining noise of the explosions, 'MOUNT UP, RAKKASANS! IT'S TIME TO GET THE HELL OUTTA HERE!'

Needing no further instructions, the soldiers eagerly complied, and the convoy sped towards the American lines. Leif's jeep, with his driver and radioman was the last to depart – just as they did, Leif threw a satchel charge into the cave to destroy the stockpile of ammunition. The speeding convoy kicked up a cloud of dust from the dry dirt road. The dust cloud helped to mask their presence but made navigating at high speed a dangerous but necessary challenge. With the enemy now aware of their precise location and undoubtedly sending units to close in and pursue the fleeing Americans, the hasty retreat was a welcome relief to the American soldiers. Miraculously, the convoy of gold and all its rescuers returned unscathed to the 187th ACRT camp just before nightfall.

However, their safe return, though welcomed by their commander, was not the immediate concern. Over the previous twelve hours, the 187th ARCT camp had been under a sporadic enemy artillery barrage and harassing sniper fire. As Leif reported their safe return and the details of their successful mission, his first sergeant oversaw the unloading of the crates into a secure compound. The liberated gold would remain there until such time as the enemy ceased its current assault. Two days later, with the Chinese assault diminishing, Leif returned to the compound, located the canvas tarp under which the crates had been stacked and found fourteen wooden crates – twelve crates with gold bars and two crates of ammunition. Two crates of gold were missing. Leif and the finance officer signed over to the Eighth United States Army the twelve crates of gold worth over $1 million. The whereabouts of the two missing crates of gold bullion was never determined but explained as an accounting misunderstanding which occurred while under an enemy artillery barrage – two of the fourteen crates thought to be containing gold turned out to be ammunition. The finance officer attested to the commander that there were dozens of crates of ammunition also stored in the cave, and in their haste, while under enemy fire, two of the fourteen crates thought to contain gold were, in fact, ammunition. The finance office confirmed that Leif had ordered that as many of the ammunition crates be brought out as well as the gold. Despite this reasonable explanation, Lieutenant Bangsbøll fully expected the MP to show up at any time to begin an investigation, but they never did. Apparently, the Eighth United States Army was too busy defending against the Chinese and North Korean offensive and were satisfied, having recovered most of the lost gold.

* * *

With the gold recovery mission behind him, Lieutenant Bangsbøll refocused on the routine of caring for his platoon's needs, their training and daily duties in preparation for their next assignment. During winter 1950 to 1951 it was brutally cold and combat operations in the 187th ARCT's sector in early January 1951 was at a relatively low intensity. However, Lieutenant Bangsbøll and his Int & Recon platoon were kept as busy as ever – they were the eyes and ears of the unit and Brigadier General Bowen wanted to know what the enemy was up to in their sector. During the first week of January 1951, Leif was given orders to take one of his platoon's squads into North Korean-held territory to conduct a reconnaissance/intelligence gathering mission on enemy positions, assessing their strengths and weaknesses in the sector adjacent to the 187th ARCT's current position.

On the second day of the mission, Lieutenant Bangsbøll and his squad observed major construction activities on the shores of the Bukhan River, where Chinese military engineers and a large workforce of North Korean laborers were widening and reinforcing one bridge and just a mile upstream, were constructing another new bridge across the river. Leif said to his sergeant, 'This could be a prelude to another North Korean offensive.' After taking photographs and detailed map coordinates, Lieutenant Bangsbøll and his reconnaissance squad began their withdrawal towards their American/UN lines to report what they had discovered. However, that evening Leif and his squad of ten soldiers ran into a North Korean patrol, much larger than his and in a particularly unfavorable location for the Americans. During the ensuing firefight, Leif attempted to flank the enemy patrol to draw their attention and fire away from his men and allow his men to escape. In the chaos of the battle, Leif, under heavy enemy fire, became separated from his men and was trapped on the enemy's side of the ridge line. Thinking that he could follow the ridge down and double back to regroup with his men, Leif set out on his own. In the darkness, amongst the noise of diminishing gunfire, he made his way past dozens of enemy soldiers, both the dead and the wounded and some very much alive and eager to kill or capture him. The rest of Leif's squad took advantage of the opportunity to escape and moved quickly towards the safety of their lines.

Meanwhile, Leif realized that the route he had taken had led him further from his men and the safety of the Allied lines. Separated from and unable to communicate with his men, he was on his own in enemy territory. Deciding to continue to travel at night, and hide out and rest during the day, he began his solo journey southward, back through enemy-controlled territory towards the safety of the American and UN lines – hoping that the rest of his squad was doing the same.

On two separate occasions that first night, North Korean foot patrols came close enough to him that he could clearly hear them speaking. Fortunately, the enemy patrols moved on, and he was able to continue his trek southward. Though he could not understand their language, Leif knew he was in great danger and that they were actively searching for him and his patrol. Just before dawn, exhausted and hungry from his nocturnal ordeal, Leif had the good fortune to stumble on an ideal location to rest. Upon exiting a ravine from a mountain pass, Leif came upon a small, now abandoned North Korean village that had clearly been caught in heavy combat operations in the previous weeks. Artillery shell holes and debris were scattered about where the village had once stood. The smell of the decaying carcasses of a dog and several massive oxen that had been killed by the artillery barrage made it difficult to breath. But Leif knew that foulness of the air and the desolate state of the surroundings would likely keep North Korean patrols at a distance from what was left of the village. As he cautiously approached the only partially standing structure in the village, a small hut with two adjoining walls still standing and a portion of its thatched grass roof still intact, he noticed another odd smell and looked around and saw shards of brightly painted broken pottery containers strewn about the ground near a bomb crater. There was a new sour aroma, competing with the rotting carcasses.

The artillery explosions had unearthed and broken apart several kimchi pots. Kimchi is a traditional Korean dish made of salted and fermented cabbage and radishes and is a staple for Koreans in both North and South. In the summer months, the Koreans make and store the kimchi in porcelain pots with lids and bury them in the warm ground for weeks while the concoction ferments with the aid of the intense, Korean sun. In winter months, the cold earth acts as a refrigerator to store the kimchi for future consumption. It was now day three of Leif's impromptu escape and evasion mission, and his two days of rations had been consumed. He scanned the ground surrounding the bomb crater looking for any evidence of an unbroken kimchi pot and to his delight he found one, still partially buried in the ground. Thankful of his discovery, he unearthed the kimchi pot and nestled himself amongst the ruins in the corner of the half-standing hut. Scanning his surroundings once more, Leif thought to himself, 'This is as safe a spot as any.' He sat down facing the sun to collect its warmth and gently pried open the large porcelain jar.

The initial waft of vapour escaping the kimchi jar was so offensive it made his eyes water and stomach turn. Leif loved food but consuming the cold, sour kimchi was a challenge, even for him – a man who grew up eating raw pickled herring and raw steak tartare, adorned with a raw egg and capers. But he needed nourishment for the trek ahead of him, and after the first few forced mouthfuls, he ate contently. He covered himself with his poncho – his stressed body satisfied with some nutrition; he began to relax. He fell into a light sleep, keeping a wary ear for any approaching danger, but drifted off thinking of his wife and young daughter and the son who was due to be born any day. As the sun set and the temperature began to drop, he awoke and gathered his gear, verified his intended direction of travel with his compass and continued his trek southward.

Owing to his innate survival skills, the specialized training Leif had received over the years and a bit of good old Danish luck, he managed to evade the enemy for three long days and nights, enduring grueling hardship and applying effective escape and evasion tactics to outwit the Chinese and North Korean patrols. Late in the evening of the third day of his trek, Leif successfully made his way back to the base camp of the 187th ARCT. Leif went directly to the operations tent. He barged into the tent, scanned the room until he saw the operations officer and be said, 'Did the rest of my team make it back safely?' Stunned at the sudden appearance of the previously MIA platoon leader, the operations officer smiled and nodded, 'they all got back safely two days ago – scrapped up a bit, but alive and well.' Relieved at that news, Leif provided a quick summary of their observations of the North Korean activities, which confirmed what his sergeant had reported earlier, and then Leif handed over the camera with the photographs taken and map coordinates of the two North Korean bridges. 'If you'll excuse me, I'd like to go see my men.'

After a happy reunion with his sergeant, Lieutenant Bangsbøll assembled the whole platoon, reviewed what had happened during the reconnaissance patrol, and the intelligence they had gathered. Finally, Leif apologised for getting separated from the squad and congratulated the sergeant for getting the rest of the squad back to camp safely. As Leif left the gathering, his sergeant caught up to him and said,

> Sir, we all know what you did out there during that firefight – your actions saved us. Had you not flanked the enemy the way you did, I think we all would be still up-north – dead or prisoners.

'Thanks, sarg… couldn't have done it without you.' The two men shook hands and went their own ways.

Leif was hungry, sore and near physical and emotional exhaustion after his three-day ordeal. He headed straight for his quarters, thirsty for a real drink and keen for a hot shower. When he opened the flap to his four-man tent, he was dumbfounded to find his normally tranquil tent a bustle with a gathering of his airborne colleagues, including the Regimental Commander, Brigadier General Frank Bowen, the COS, Lieutenant Colonel Bank, his company commander Major Ron Speirs, along with Leif's three tent-mates, including his close friend Captain George Gormley. All totally inebriated. Believing that Leif had been killed or at the very least captured by the enemy, the word had quickly circulated around camp that The Danish Duke was MIA and presumed KIA.

It was well known that Leif always had an ample stock of Danish Akvavit and Scotch whisky at his disposal – mostly thanks to his fellow countrymen aboard the Danish hospital ship MS *Jutlandia*, which was supporting the UN mission in Korea. That evening, his American brothers-in-arms had gathered in his tent to grieve a lost comrade. Leif would never forget the greeting he received as he returned to camp unscathed but utterly exhausted from his unscheduled solo detour through enemy lines. When he lifted the tent flap, stood in the entrance to his quarters and caught sight of the six drunken officers, they all stopped mid-sentence and stared back at him. A second later, Lieutenant Colonel Bank jumped off Leif's bunk as if a fire had been lit under him, pointed at Leif, and with drunken disbelief in his eyes, and slurred speech said: 'Leif, you're supposed to be dead!' To which Leif replied, while looking around the tent with feigned concern, 'Well, Sir, if that's MY booze you're all drinking, it'll be YOU that are going to be dead!'

The next few hours were a blur of celebration by all and recounting the escape and evasion events of the past few days by Leif. As Brigadier General Bowen sat back on Leif's bed, with arms folded behind his head, feeling well over-served with alcohol, he enjoyed the ruckus of the moment and thought

> We so rarely have cause to celebrate anything in this God-forsaken war – losing the Danish Duke would have been very bad for morale... having him resurrected from the MIA list was worth celebrating... especially now that he's a father again...

'Hey Leif', Bowen said, 'I've got some news from home for you...'

In war, the veil between life and death can be just seconds apart – one moment you're alive and the next you're dead – it's as simple as that. In this case, it was happily the opposite... one moment Leif was presumed dead and suddenly he was alive and the life of the party as the proud father of a son named Leif Christian Bangsbøll.

* * *

Though Brigadier General Bowen certainly was the genesis of Leif's Danish Duke moniker, Leif duly earned the honor of his nickname over time through a variety of unique situations he was involved in during the Korean War. First and foremost, it was Leif's Danish heritage and unmistakable accent that earned him a reputation. But what was most alluring about him and endeared him to many of his military colleagues was his ability to wheel and deal to get things done where others could not – things that others would not even attempt to try but somehow Leif would pull it off.

A stunning example of this was his ability to scrounge supplies that were, understandably, in short supply in a combat zone. For instance, North American alcohol and cigarettes were always in high demand and oftentimes a challenge to obtain for frontline units. However, with Leif's connections with the *Jutlandia* – assigned to the UN forces and at anchor off the coast from Seoul, Leif worked his magic and developed a reliable supply line of class six – military supply code for luxury items, such as alcohol and cigarette products. On a regular basis he would show up at camp with a jeep full of booze and cigarettes for the appreciative troops and his colleagues at the 187th ARCT.

According to his close friends and tent mates, the manner in which Leif had established his unique 'working relationship' with the Danish hospital ship helped affirm how they had come to endorse his nickname. Shortly after arriving to support the UN mission, Lieutenant Commander Kai Hammerich, commander of the *Jutlandia*, received a radio communication from the United States Army's 187th Infantry Regiment:

> *Hej, dette er Lieutenant Leif Bangsbøll fra den Amerikanske hær, der er stationeret her i Sydkore. Må jeg tale med kaptajnen i Jyllandia?* [Hello, this

is Lieutenant Leif Bangsbøll of the American army stationed here in South Korea. May I speak to the captain of the Jutlandia?]

Surprised to hear Danish spoken to him from an American unit, Lieutenant-Commander Hammerich immediately recognized the name Bangsbøll. 'Leif, are you a family relation of Commodore Frederik Bangsbøll of the Royal Danish Navy?' he asked. 'Why of course I am – I'm his long-lost son!' replied Leif. Once the introductions and appropriate social exchanges had been completed, Leif made his pitch to Lieutenant-Commander Hammerich. Two days later, with a day's furlough approved by Major Spiers, his CO, and with one of the regiment's jeeps at his disposal, Leif drove to the port of Incheon, just west of Seoul. There, he was ferried out to the *Jutlandia* where he met Lieutenant-Commander Hammerich in person. The two Danes immediately became friends. After getting caught up on the news of the war from the perspective of the young Danish paratrooper in exchange for news from Denmark, the ship's captain, demonstrating how proud the Danish naval officer was to be part of the UN contributing force, gave Leif a tour of the ship. During the tour and prior to heading back to shore, Leif was introduced to the ship's supply officer with clear instructions from the ship's captain to provide the young Danish paratrooper with 'anything he might need and could fit into his jeep.' And so, Leif had established his vital supply line for non-combat, class-six stores.

That evening, Leif arrived back on camp with a jeep full of highly sought-after luxury supplies. His first stop was to deliver a case of Johnny Walker Scotch whisky to his company's CO, Major Speirs, to thank him for the day off and the use of the jeep. From there Leif delivered a case of Scotch and several cartons of cigarettes to his platoon and then went back to his quarters to share the rest of his bounty with his tent mates. It was like Christmas, with gifts of Scotch and cigarettes all around. However, Leif's prized possessions were a case of genuine Aalborg Akvavit and a few jars of his favorite pickled herrings, which he kept for himself – nobody else was interested in either of these Danish 'luxury items'.

The Danish hospital ship, *Jutlandia*, whose captain and crew Leif had befriended would provide tremendous medical care for tens of thousands of UN troops and South Korean civilians throughout the Korean War. It also provided Leif with a venue to visit and speak with fellow Danes in addition to accessing the luxury supplies for his regiment. During one such visit to *Jutlandia* in late January 1951, a reporter from the Danish newspaper *Nationaltidende* was aboard the ship, writing an article on the lifesaving work the *Jutlandia*'s crew and medical staff were performing in support of the UN mission. When introduced to Leif by Lieutenant Commander Hammerich, the reporter immediately took an interest in this unique Danish-American angle to the Korean War. The resulting article

'Danish Born Soldier Fights Alongside American Paratroopers' appeared in the Danish press in early February and in the United States Military's publication, *Stars and Stripes*, several weeks later. It included some of the paratrooper's earlier life and career history:

> Leif Bangsbøll at just six weeks of age was transported into the North Sea, along with his mother by a [Royal] Danish Navy submarine for his christening aboard a Danish naval cruiser in the North Atlantic and as a result has forty-two Godfathers (the entire crew of the cruiser). Leif served with the Royal Danish Navy and the Danish Merchant Navy, and at the outbreak of World War II qualified as a Norwegian Air Force pilot under the British Commonwealth Air Training Program in Canada. He became an American Army Officer and fought with the Danish Underground/Resistance in occupied Denmark in 1944–45 and was part of the liberation force in Copenhagen in the final days of the war. First Lieutenant Leif Bangsbøll is now a member of the American 11th Airborne Division fighting alongside other United Nations countries in Korea.

The publication of the article in the *Stars and Stripes* gave 11th Airborne Division and the 187th ARCT some great publicity and did much to reinforce Leif's flamboyant reputation and nickname. He had become a celebrity among United States Army colleagues within his current unit, 11th Airborne Division, and his former unit, 1st Calvary Division, which was also in combat operations in Korea.

A couple of weeks after the publication of the *Stars and Stripes* article, Leif was relaxing in his quarters, lying on his bed and looking up at the tent ceiling with his hands folded behind his head, while listening contently to his tent mate, Captain Gormely, read a letter from home. Domestic news about their children's homework and sports accomplishments were the focus of Gormely's most recent letter from his wife. According to the letter and despite being at war, America seemed to be moving along with routine sameness. Then, suddenly came a voice from just outside the tent entrance. 'Lieutenant Bangsbøll, sir, are you in there?' A corporal from the 187th ARCT headquarters orderly room had been sent to find Lieutenant Bangsbøll to advise him that 'the Old Man' – the CO – wanted to see him immediately. Leif put on his combat shirt, donned his helmet and walked over to the headquarters tent. The dark interior of the large tent, relative to the bright sunshine outside, at first made it difficult for Leif to see well. Once his eyes adjusted to the dim light, he could make out that Brigadier General Bowen, the commander, and Lieutenant Colonel Bank, the regiment's S-3 operations officer, were speaking to a man in civilian clothes. The three men were smiling and seemed to know each other. As Leif approached the three men, he suddenly recognized the civilian guest. It was his old friend Agent Hans Tofte, a fellow Dane who, like Leif, had also been recruited into the OSS during the Second World War. The two had met and worked together in London during the war. They embraced each other as long-lost brothers.

Though Lieutenant Colonel Bank and Tofte had never met each other before, the fact that they were affiliated as former members of their beloved OSS and knew each other by reputation made them kindred spirits, and immediate bonds of trust were established between these two men. Leif asked Hans what had brought him to the 187th. Tofte laughed and said that he was working with the CIA and had read the article about the Danish warrior in the recent issue of the *Stars and Stripes* and knew he had to find his old friend to say hello. Bowen and Bank acknowledged that the publicity had made Leif quite a celebrity within the regiment and even further afield. Brigadier General Bowen then shook Tofte's hand and thanked him for the visit and the CIA's intelligence report he provided and departed, nodding to both Leif and Bank as he left.

Bank then invited both Leif and Hans back to his quarters, where they reminisced about events and missions from the previous war and their former lives as secret agents. The evening was spent depleting the better part of a bottle of Scotch and reliving their old war stories. The three former OSS agents and comrades-in-arms revelled in a few hours recounting war stories in the good old days.

Though Hans was aware that Leif, the former OSS agent codenamed Jorgen Bech, had suddenly left the OSS service soon after its transition to the CIA had begun, he was not aware of the details of his sudden disappearance. However, in that line of work, agents often just disappear as a result of mission secrecy requirements. Tofte had heard rumors of some 'sensitive activities' within the Soviet Zone of Berlin soon after the end of the Second World War – nothing more. Bank, on the other hand, had read the OSS report of the KGB incident in Berlin that was the cause of Leif's sudden career transition. But Bank had never heard the details of the events from Leif's perspective until that evening in his tent in Korea. As Leif recalled salient facts and outlined his mission and the dire situation he and his OSS team were facing in East Berlin back in autumn 1945, his two colleagues listened intently to the drama-filled account of Leif's final OSS mission. When Leif was finished retelling the story of how he had eliminated a KGB agent in a quasi-peacetime situation to save his two OSS colleagues and lead their escape from East to West Germany, he looked to his two colleagues – for what, he wasn't sure. Approval, maybe. A degree of understanding – most assuredly. Maybe he just needed to tell the story to two former agents who might just accept it at face value. After hearing the end of Leif's account of the events and following a moment of uncomfortable silence, Bank got up from his chair, refilled their three glasses with Scotch and proposed a toast, 'To the orginal shadow warriors of the OSS. And Leif added: 'To those and them like us...damn few left.' And Hans added: ... 'Most of whom are dead or soon will be.' Their glasses clinked, not gently. Some of the clear, amber liquid spilled over their fingers and dripped to the tent's dirt floor. They laughed and then their glasses came up in unison and they tilted their heads back and swallowed the liquid. The alcohol warmed their throats as they looked at each other knowingly. They knew that they had each done things in the line of duty that would stay with them for the rest of their lives. Nothing more needed to be said.

After that somber moment, Leif asked: 'Hans, tell me what happened to you after the war?' Tofte refilled their glasses and went on to tell his story.

> The sudden demise of the OSS back in September 1945 caught us all off guard. I was back in Washington at the time and was able to make the transition from the OSS and briefly with the SSU and eventually became part of the CIA. I'm here in Korea on their dime.

With a smile, he added, 'But today I'm here strictly for personal reasons. To meet up with old friends.'

The surprise encounter with his former OSS colleague Hans Tofte, now a CIA agent, was a welcome but emotional reunion for Leif. It was comforting to retell the details of his last OSS mission in Berlin to two of his most trusted colleagues, yet somewhat disturbing to revisit such memories. That evening of drinking and reminiscing in Bank's tent would be the last time that Leif and Tofte would see each other for years. However, just a few weeks after this impromptu reunion, Leif would be given a dangerous and daring assignment under orders from Brigadier General Bowen and overseen by Bank. A mission which, unbeknownst to Leif at the time, was based upon secret intelligence gathered and provided by his friend and colleague, Hans Tofte.

Chapter 7

The Devil's Harvest

'A day of battle is a day of harvest for the devil.'
William Hooke, 1640

Leif's second combat parachute mission in Korea with the 187th ARCT came when his unit conducted an airborne assault on 23 March 1951. The air assault was part of a larger UN offensive known as Operation Courageous, and the187th ARCT airborne portion of the mission was designated Operation Tomahawk.

This operation was slightly smaller in scale than their first combat jump six months earlier. This time, 187th ARCT's mission objective was to cut off and eliminate Chinese and North Korean troops at Munsan-ni as they fled north to the safety of China in the wake of the new UN offensive. Once again, the Americans' use of airborne combat troops inserted behind enemy lines proved to be enormously effective. The 187th ARCT inflicted over 2,500 enemy casualties and captured over 1,000 enemy soldiers while sustaining less than 50 casualties themselves. As a result of this highly successful mission, 187th ARCT would earn its second Presidential Citation of the Korean War.

By the end of April 1951, 187th ARCT was pulled off the frontline and placed as a reserve unit for a fifteen-day period. The battalion relocated 20 miles south, collocated with several support units in the rear echelon area. There, 187th ARCT would recover from its prolonged combat assignment, and their most recent high intensity fighting as part of Operation Tomahawk. They would get three hot meals per day, be reissued equipment and uniforms and conduct low intensity training exercises to ensure the troops maintained their physical fitness and battle-readiness. It was also time to remember those members of 187th ARCT who had fallen in battle and recognize those who had distinguished themselves in the face of the enemy.

On the morning of 4 May 1951, a parade was held during which the entire 187th ARCT and complements of other reserve units assembled on an open field adjacent to their camp. Following the commander's inspection of the troops on parade, the chaplain performed a solemn memorial service to recognize the sacrifice of those injured and killed in action over the past six months of

187th ARCT's combat tour. Then the battalion adjutant called out names of medal recipients one after another. Each soldier marched forward to receive various medals from the commander in recognition of their outstanding service and bravery. Dozens of Purple Hearts were presented in recognition of being wounded in combat. Several Bronze Stars and citations for heroism in the face of the enemy were announced and pinned upon combat uniforms of proud soldiers and officers.

The final medal presented that morning, the Silver Star – third only to the Medal of Honor – was bestowed with special attention. In a loud, clear voice, the adjutant called out one recipient: '01997738, FIRST LIEUTENANT L. BANGSBØLL, INT AND RECCON PLATOON'. Coming to attention, Leif replied in an equally clear voice, 'SIR!' and marched forward. He came to halt and stood at attention in front of his commander. The adjutant then announced, 'ATTENTION TO ORDERS'. He then read aloud the full citation of the Silver Star medal.

> Lieutenant Leif Bangsbøll, 0-1997738, a member of Headquarters Company, 187th Airborne Infantry Regiment, is cited for gallantry in action against an armed enemy at Pyongwon-ni, North Korea on 16 November 1950. While on a reconnaissance mission deep in enemy territory, Lieutenant Bangsbøll and his platoon entered the village of Pyongwon-ni where he located a large warehouse of enemy supplies and provisions. In a successful effort to gain control of this warehouse, he engaged a numerically superior enemy force, three of which were killed, seven wounded, two captured unharmed and the remainder dispersed. A search of the enemy dead and captured resulted in intelligence data being obtained which later proved of great value to his Command. Later, Lieutenant Bangsbøll was given the subsequent mission of returning to Pyongwon-ni and destroying the warehouse. In a brilliantly executed attack in which he again engaged and dispersed a larger enemy force he seized the village and destroyed the warehouse and the military supplies therein. He planned and executed all phases of this mission so skillfully that his platoon suffered no casualties due to enemy action. His cool, capable leadership was a constant inspiration to his men and was responsible for the success of his daring achievements. The gallantry displayed by Lieutenant Bangsbøll reflects great credit on himself, his unit and the military service.
>
> By the order of Lieutenant General Ridgway, Commanding General of the Eighth United States Army (Korea), dated 6 March 1951.

The medal was pinned on Leif's combat jacket, above his left chest pocket. The commander then shook his hand and congratulated him on his outstanding leadership and inspiring conduct in combat. Leif saluted smartly, and following his commander's return salute, executed an about turn and marched back towards his place in formation. As the applause rose from the assembled troops, a lone voice from somewhere in the back of the parade called out: 'CAN'T WAIT TO SEE WHAT THE DANISH DUKE'S GONNA DO NEXT!' A mixture of good-nature laughter and cheers spread amongst the battalion.

Upon dismissal from parade, the troops dispersed, many of whom sought out the medal recipients to congratulate them with a hearty handshake or a slap on the back. Leif, embarrassed at the attention being drawn to him, could not contain his pride – he beamed with a broad smile and thanked his comrades for their support and recognition.

A week later, well rested, the 187th ARCT was ordered back to the frontline. It was time to get back to work. Apparently, the devil's harvest had not been fully reaped. Two weeks following the 187th ARCT's medals parade, Lieutenant Bangsbøll was told to report to the operations tent. Lieutenant Colonel Bank, with the dual responsibilities as the Ex-O and S-3 operations officer for the 187th ARCT reread the CIA intelligence report and handed it over to Leif. The report had originated from the CIA, its author, Agent Hans Tofte. The CIA report indicated that several separate and reliable sources of intelligence had indicated with a high level of confidence that there was a temporary North Korean PoW camp where a dozen UN/American PoWs were suspected of being held captive. This PoW camp was located just 12 miles behind the current North Korean lines.

It had been determined that these United Nations/United States prisoners had been captured during the recent Chinese offensive which was in response to the bold American attacks, codenamed Operation Courageous and Operation Tomahawk in late March 1951. The Chinese had regrouped and subsequently counterattacked in mid-April 1951 with a massive offensive, pushing the UN line back – south to the 38th parallel. Despite being completely outclassed by modern American and UN weaponry and the allies' far superior air power, the enemy – North Korean and Chinese troops – had overwhelmed the UN lines with their sheer numbers.

By 20 April 1951, the UN forces had halted the enemy's counterattack which created a new frontline – designated as the Kansas Line – situated along the 38th parallel, the original North-South Korean border. The UN losses were relatively light, given the magnitude of the Chinese offensive. However, a number of UN units, including some American units, had been overrun and in the confusion – bordering on chaos – of the general retreat, a number of

American and other UN troops had been taken prisoner by the tidal waves of the advancing enemy forces.

The question posed to the S-3 section was, 'Could these UN prisoners of war be located and rescued?' That was the question conveyed to Bank by Tofte who had driven out to the 187th ARCT camp to hand deliver the CIA's intelligence report.

Bank, Bangsbøll and Tofte surrounded the table and stared down at the map. Bank looked up at Tofte and said,

> If I were to ask the average American or United Nations infantry officer serving in this theater of war, 'Would you be willing to lead your platoon, without supporting units on such a mission, through and behind the enemy's line and operate within enemy territory, would you take this mission?' the likely – and the correct and sane – answer to that question would be, 'No thank you, sir.'

Leif saw that question differently. As the leader of the regiment's headquarters, Int & Recon platoon, that was his duty, and he had built a reputation of being an outstanding leader with innate combat skills who seemed to thrive on the adrenaline that such challenging and clandestine missions generated and was always eager to meet the unique challenges inherent in such assignments. After considering all the facts presented to him by Bank and Tofte, Leif paused and looked up from the map before them and said, 'Yes, we can do it. But it must be a small unit, a night airborne insertion.'

After discussing details of the mission with Bank, Tofte and the regiment's operations officer about the concept of the mission execution, combat and logistical support he would need, Leif returned to his platoon, located his sergeant to discuss which of their platoon members should be selected for this mission. Following his meeting with his sergeant, Leif returned to his tent, where he was met by his friend, colleague and tent mate, Captain Gormely. After describing the mission he had just accepted to Gormely, his friend shook his head and said, 'Leif, it's like you actually want to conduct those types of absurdly dangerous missions.'

'George', Leif replied, 'there is no greater thrill than to be sneaking around in your enemy's back yard undetected and causing mayhem.' Leif knew that these types of missions provided valuable information, and when such opportunities arose, he welcomed the chance to attack and create havoc amongst an unsuspecting foe, but this mission truly was unique – a rescue mission. Leif thought, nothing could be more important than that. George knew that with Leif's previous experience in occupied Denmark, operating virtually right under the noses of the Nazis, that his friend had refined his ability to remain calm, cool and collected in the face of imminent danger and great uncertainties and was the best suited officer for this task.

Leif had also worked hard to pass along these unique lessons and skills to his platoon members, which emboldened their confidence and ultimately improved their combat effectiveness. As a result of all of this, and despite the disproportionate number of high-risk missions Leif and his platoon had been assigned relative to the other platoons within the 187th ARCT, his platoon had the lowest sustained casualty rate in the entire regiment. All these facts were not lost on the commander or his operations and intelligence section. So, when an assignment to verify the existence and possible rescue of UN PoWs held captive by the enemy at a location within striking distance, the task fell naturally to Lieutenant Bangsbøll and his platoon.

Later that afternoon, Lieutenant Bangsbøll, with supporting briefs from the S-3 staff, outlined to Agent Tofte, Major Spiers and Lieutenant Colonel Bank the proposed insertion plan. Leif stressed that parachuting in with even a platoon of thirty paratroopers would be too large a force to maintain secrecy for long. He knew that they had to get into the area of operation unobserved and move quickly and quietly to maintain the element of surprise to give themselves any chance of finding and freeing the prisoners. Leif outlined that the terrain in the area of operation would be extremely rugged, consisting of steep, rocky hills mostly covered in scrub bushes, along with deep ravines. Local farming was limited to the narrow valley floors, but some of the gentler hills had agricultural terracing, which increased the arable land available for farming. All of this was positive information as it meant less likelihood of encountering local, unfriendly North Korean inhabitants or any large enemy units. As part of the plan, a suitable drop zone had been identified by the division's intelligence section. The selected drop zone was in an area that had not seen any persistent presence of the enemy and was located 12 miles north of the Kansas Line. It was a remote area with little strategic value and did not have a railway or main highways nearby. The drop zone itself appeared to be a long, narrow series of agricultural fields, most likely rice paddies, running along a valley floor with 2,000-foot hills bracketing them on either side. The drop zone was located approximately 10 miles from the suspected North Korean PoW camp – close enough for the rescuers to traverse the rugged terrain relatively quickly to their objective and far enough away that the aircraft and the parachute drop would not be observed by the enemy at or near the PoW camp.

The plan for getting back out to the safety of the UN lines would have to be decided later, however, contingency plans for extracting the rescue force and the PoWs were being developed by the intelligence and operations staff.

Later that evening, with the insertion plan approved by Bank, Lieutenant Bangsbøll gathered his platoon, outlined the mission and then announced the selected two squads that would participate in the mission – sixteen of his best and most experienced soldiers. The following day, weapons were cleaned, extra ammunition and four days of rations were issued. Then, after a hot meal, the small airborne special operations team loaded up their gear and boarded two troop trucks and departed the 187th ARCT's camp. Two hours later they arrived at Gimpo airfield. The insertion team immediately drew their parachutes from the 187th ARCT's para-rigger's storeroom and walked single-file out to their awaiting aircraft. They would take main parachutes only as this would be another combat jump at minimum altitude to minimize detection, making reserve parachutes superfluous.

There had been several days of rain, and more was expected. The sky over Gimpo airfield was overcast with no moon. These were all good factors for supporting this clandestine mission, but not ideal for flying and parachuting at such low altitudes in a mountainous region. The plan was to be inserted at night, and Leif and his two squads would maneuver through the mountainous terrain at night, avoiding villages and North Korean and/or Chinese patrols at all costs. It was estimated that by traveling only at night, it would take them thirty-six hours to make their way to a point where they could observe the PoW camp and determine the best assault approach. This time frame was dependent on many factors and variables, including the weather, the presence of local inhabitants and, of course, the enemy's current disposition and troop movements in that region. Though Leif, the soldier, relied on timely, accurate intelligence and methodical planning to improve the likelihood of success of any mission, Leif the man knew that there were many unknown factors and variables outside of his control and that a little bit of good luck would be welcome. And to date, Loki, the Norse God of Mischief and Good Fortune, had been a good ally to Leif, who was counting on Loki's favor once more.

Lieutenant Bangsbøll and his sixteen paratroopers boarded the Douglas C-47 'Dakota' or 'Dak'. The C-47 was designed to airlift up to twenty-six combat soldiers or twenty combat-equipped paratroopers. That night's flight was relatively comfortable for the seventeen Rakkasans. The aircraft took off at 2130 hours and if everything went as planned, by 2330 hours they would be floating silently to earth – like falling-down umbrella men. Though the drop zone was only a forty-minute flight north-east of their current location at Gimpo airfield, the pilot had been instructed by the operations officer to mask their destination by flying the aircraft westward, out over the Yellow Sea and then turn north and backtrack towards the North Korean coast and their true destination. This route, if picked up by enemy radar, would only indicate a single aircraft coming in from the sea and would be less likely to be considered by the enemy as a threat, let alone a parachute assault threat. Ninety minutes after take-off, the single C-47 flight approached the western shore of North Korea at an altitude of 9,000 feet. Only a sporadic few, aimed anti-aircraft shells were sent up into the overcast sky, in their general direction by the enemy's shore defenses. As a single aircraft, not a formation of bombers or fighter bombers on a bombardment mission, this was not assessed as a significant threat to the enemy. To further mask this insertion flight, several UN artillery units were providing heavy shelling far to the east and west of the intended drop zone which further drew the enemy's attention away. Within a minute of encountering the ineffective anti-aircraft shells, the enemy's shore batteries went silent. No alerts were sent out by the North Korean command. The Dak was flying over North Korea anonymously and unmolested, just as planned.

With the heavy cloud-cover, the pilot was flying virtually blind as he descended into the valley towards the designated drop zone approach altitude of 1,500 feet and finally descending to the risky, but effective combat jump altitude of 1,000 feet for the drop. With the drop zone 15 miles ahead, five minutes out from the projected release point, the red jump light illuminated the troop compartment and Lieutenant Bangsbøll, acting as the jumpmaster, stood up and shouted out in sequential order the instructions that every one of his paratroopers knew by heart: 'STAND UP! HOOK UP! CHECK YOUR EQUIPMENT!'

The jumpmaster received thumbs-up from all sixteen of his troopers – the Rakkasans were ready. As the Dakota aircraft descended through 2,500-feet altitude, it broke through the cloud cover. Only the vague, dark shapes of the mountains on either side of the valley could be seen by the pilot and co-pilot; the drop zone should be just ahead.

At the thirty second warning, the co-pilot activated the switch to illuminate the cargo compartment in red lights, which was the signal for the air dispatcher to open the paratroop doors on both sides of the fuselage. Time seemed to move slowly for both the pilots and the paratroopers. The sixteen paratroopers looked aft towards their platoon leader and jumpmaster – fear and eager anticipation were contrasting emotions running through each man's mind. Then, the green jump light illuminated, and Leif immediately shouted the command, 'GO, GO, GO!' The only words he heard in reply was a succession of 'GERONIMO!' and 'RAKKASANS!' as the paratroopers shuffled past him and jumped through the open doors and disappeared into the black void of the night. A second after the last paratrooper had exited the aircraft, Leif made a quick inspection to confirm with the air dispatcher that none of his troopers were fouled up in the static lines streaming behind the aircraft from the open para doors. A second later, Leif was falling through space following his men into the darkness and the danger below.

At that moment in time, Leif felt so alive – he was once again doing what he loved and what he did best: airborne, special operations. And in this instance, he had a specific assignment and was bound and determined that they would locate and rescue those PoWs – or die trying. In the few seconds it took to descend to the earth under his parachute's canopy, he thought how very different this combat jump was to the last two airborne assaults with the entire 187th ARCT earlier in the year. Tonight, he was with just 16 soldiers in support of his mission, not 3,000!

The 187th ARCT usually practise their parachute jumps between 2,000 and 1,500 feet. Parachuting from an altitude of 1,000 feet was riskier, but minimized the time in the air, which reduced the opportunity they might be observed or heard by the enemy. But this tactic also ensured that they were falling at the highest, most dangerous rate allowable. Fortunately, the ground was mercifully soft from the previous days of rain. Once the small task force had assembled around their leader, the first sergeant counted heads, checked for injuries and confirmed the order of march. All seventeen paratroopers landed hard but safely, with only minor bumps, bruises and scrapes. The radioman sent the message '17 Moving Out' to their aircraft – confirming their safe landing. The aircraft had already turned south-west and was heading back towards Gimpo airfield. The co-pilot relayed the message to the 187th ACRT – the paratroopers had landed safely and were moving off the drop zone. With a confirming nod from his lieutenant, the first sergeant got the small task force to move into line and silently move north-east towards the ridge of mountains and towards their objective beyond. Each man carried their parachutes and harnesses with them from the drop zone to conceal them once they got into the hills. Leaving those items in the rice paddy would be a dead giveaway to any enemy patrols.

Moving with stealth, relying on the cover of darkness, Lieutenant Bangsbøll and his two squads traversed up and down a series of ridges and ravines – it was very slow going. As dawn approached, the rescue team made camp on the top of a ridge which provided good observation of all approach routes. There they would spend the day resting and preparing to continue their trek when night fell. They had not seen nor heard anyone during their night trek. Given the objective of their mission, it was essential to avoid any contact with the enemy if they were to reach the PoW camp unobserved and unopposed – Leif looked at his map, they had traveled 4 miles – 6 to go – so far, so good.

On the second evening behind enemy lines, heavy rain began to fall. Though the rain helped to mask their presence from the enemy, it also prevented the Americans from detecting any enemy movement in their vicinity. The circumstances were perfect for an unwanted encounter. At approximately 2200 hours, after traversing steep and narrow mountain trails for only two hours, the lead squad's scout and point man came running back along the narrow mountain path that the Americans were following and indicated that a small enemy force, possible a platoon size unit, was moving in their direction, along the same mountain path where the Rakkasans now stood. Considering his options, Leif chose to avoid contact: he would have to quickly and quietly get his team to move up the slope to the high ground above the path, in hopes that the enemy patrol would continue past them and then he and his team could continue on their way. Keeping in mind that if contact was made with the oncoming enemy patrol, Leif wanted to be in an advantageous position – above the enemy.

With a few quick, silent hand signals from their platoon leader, the Rakkasans silently disappeared into the scrub brush and proceeded up the muddy hillside with determined purpose. The rain was still falling, which masked much of the noise made by the soldier's ascent, but the ground was slippery – Leif was sure they would be heard by the enemy. Within two minutes they had reached a plateau above the path that provided excellent cover and concealment. The Rakkasans lay prone at the top of the plateau and aimed their weapons back down the slope from where they had come. They were situated on a rice paddy about the size of a tennis court on a terraced slope. The outline of another terrace could be just seen through the darkness, 20 yards further up the hillside. Though it was a good defensive position relative to where the enemy was located, it left the Americans completely exposed to the elements. Owing to the heavy rain, the rice paddy was brimming with knee deep water. There, the Rakkasans, wet, cold and hungry waited – ready to fight.

Five minutes later, the enemy patrol could be heard traversing the trail below the small band of Americans, but it was too dark and the rain too heavy to see their foe. As bad luck would have it, the enemy commander chose the same portion of the mountain path that the Americans had just vacated to make their camp for the night. Leif quickly deduced that the enemy commander would send out pickets (sentries) in all directions to protect the perimeter of their overnight encampment. That meant that an enemy soldier or two would soon be making their way up the same hillside that he and his paratroopers had just traversed. Within a minute, Leif could hear the sounds of several enemy soldiers struggling up the slippery slope towards them. Realizing that there was not enough time to move to the next higher terrace, Leif instructed his two squad leaders to gather their men and ease themselves down into the edges of the rice paddy. In the darkness, with this rain, their forms might not be visible against the mud and the water-filled field and the bordering vegetation. Leif gave his squad leaders their final instructions. 'Maintain absolute silence', he stated,

> and nobody starts shooting unless I do. And if I start firing, squad No. 1 will immediately move forward to join me at the top of this ridge and rain fire onto our visitors below while squad No. 2 will move back and up to establish another defensive position at the next terrace above, where squad Number 1 will withdraw to if needed.

He motioned with his eyes and head in the direction.

> Once we've put the fear of God into our visitors below, squad No. 1 and I will displace and rejoin squad No. 2 at the new defensive position up top. Got it?

The two squad leaders whispered in unison, 'Affirmative.' With nods from both squad leaders, the troops silently dispersed to position themselves as instructed. Leif remained at the edge of the terrace and peered down into the darkness and listened. He could clearly make out the sounds of two or three enemy soldiers who continued to progress up the muddy hillside, though by the sounds of it, with some difficulty.

'Based on the amount of noise they're making, they certainly don't know we are here', Leif thought, 'and that's to our advantage.' Leif slowly moved back 6 feet from the ridge of the terrace and slid his lower torso into the water-filled rice paddy to conceal himself. He then scanned the ridgeline for the appearance of enemy intruders and thought, 'This could be a long, cold, wet night or it might become quite hot, very soon.'

Frustrated with their slow climb up the muddy slopes and tired from their full day of patrolling the mountain trails, the two enemy soldiers that had been sent up for sentry duty stopped their ascent about 20 feet below the ridge line of the terrace, just beneath where Leif and his small task force lay silently waiting. After an hour had passed and the sounds of the enemy camp preparations began to diminish, Leif passed the word to his squad leaders that they would be staying in position where they were for the night. No smoking and no eating were permitted. Noise discipline – absolute silence – would be the difference between life and death at this point. The instructions were passed along to all the platoon members to quietly make themselves as comfortable as possible but stay alert. Sentry assignments were given by the squad leaders. The rain kept falling.

Unable to sleep given the current situation, Lieutenant Bangsbøll passed the night alternating between two trains of thought. Firstly, what courses of action could be taken the following day depending upon what the enemy below did next? And secondly, how were Dorothy, little Leslie and young Christian doing back in Oshawa? His son was already 4 months old, and he had not yet laid eyes on him.

'How cruel is this?' Leif thought. 'And speaking of cruel', he mused, his distracted mind wandering down a third train of thought,

> the stench emanating from this rice paddy is unbelievable! The farmers must have just spread a heavy load of fresh fertilizer onto the rice paddy... Christ, it reeks!

Sometime in the early morning, the rain finally stopped. Just before sunrise, the enemy force below packed up and continued their patrol in a southerly direction, completely unaware of the close proximity of the seventeen American paratroopers. As the sun came up over the ridgeline, the welcome warmth of its rays eased into the Rakkasans' cold, stiff bodies. But the light of day also brought the horrid realization that the stench of the rice paddy was not animal manure and human excrement used as fertilizer by the local farmers as they had thought. To their dismay, scattered amongst the rice paddy were the rotting, putrefied corpses of what appeared to be half a dozen North Korean soldiers.

Without much fuss, and with only a few vile expletives being spoken in hushed tones, Leif and his sixteen paratroopers cautiously moved higher up the hillside, found a reasonably protected and dry area, and made camp for the day. The sun was up, the sky clear, so the paratroopers dried their uniforms and equipment, ate their rations and took turns sleeping. Leif instructed his radioman to send an encrypted transmission to let regimental headquarters know their position and status. Last night's encounter with the enemy had delayed their progress, so tonight's travel would have to be more productive if they were to keep to his plan and reach their objective by first light, the next morning.

From their hilltop vantage point, the small group of Rakkasans passed a leisurely day, enjoying the warmth of the sun, and the relative safety of their location. From their vantage point, the sounds of enemy vehicle movement a few miles off to the west could be heard reverberating through the valley. As well, some distant artillery from the UN lines echoed through the hills, and the occasional white contrails of United States bomber aircraft heading north to deliver death and destruction could be seen across the cloudless blue sky. Only once he had verified that all his men had eaten and that their weapons had been cleaned and oiled after the night's rain soaking did Leif finally sit down, lean against a tree to enjoy the warmth of the sun and eat his first meal in twenty-four hours.

The tired platoon leader took in his surroundings. 'Other than the war all around us, and those rotting corpses below us, this is quite a nice little spot.' Once again, the ever-optimistic Leif took whatever bit of peace and tranquility he could out of a bad situation. Hours later, as the sun began to set behind the adjacent hills, the rescue team began to ready itself for the night's march. They only had 6 miles to go, but it was some of the most rugged terrain on earth and would be doing so in the darkness within enemy territory. Leif estimated that their objective was at least a seven-hour trek from their present position. Ideally, he wanted to be in position to observe the PoW camp early the next morning, just before sunrise. This was possible, but only if they could move swiftly and did not run into any more enemy patrols.

Loki was on their side that night. Their march through the mountains passed without incident. And as hoped, just as the eastern sky began to lighten, the two squads took up a position on a hilltop overlooking a North Korean village, and what appeared to be a large compound that appeared to be some-sort of factory or warehouse complex – possibly the PoW camp they sought. Leif, his radioman and his two squad leaders watched their objective for several hours. There was the usual, expected day to day activity in the village – smoke rising from cooking fires, villagers moving about tending to their business, oxen being herded, dogs barking and children playing. However, there did not appear to be any signs of activity in the adjacent compound. Several small buildings and one larger warehouse-like structure could be seen within its perimeter fence, but no vehicles, no people, no movement – nothing. Leif considered that either they had the wrong location, or the PoWs were no longer there. But he knew that he had to get down there to confirm his conjectures.

About an hour before sunset, the small task force moved forward. A portion of squad No. 1 entered the North Korean village with weapons at the ready, while the rest of the squad approached the expected PoW compound. The remainder of the troops of the second squad positioned themselves as the ready reserve at the edge of the village, in case either of the troops of squad No. 1 ran into trouble.

The village elder immediately came out to engage the trespassing Americans and was clearly agitated to have these foreign intruders come through his village again. Apparently, this village had been occupied by American/UN forces at least once during the ongoing conflict and had probably changed hands several times during the course of the war. The mere presence of the Americans could prove disastrous to the North Korean villagers, who, when later confronted by the Chinese or North Korean forces, could be executed for aiding the enemy. As a result, the Americans were treated with fear and disdain. But the Americans had a job to do and made it clear that they would not allow the villagers to interfere. With the village secure, Leif took two additional troopers with him to inspect the suspected PoW compound. What they found horrified and infuriated them. Behind the large warehouse they discovered the remains of eight American soldiers lying in the adjacent field, their bodies lined up roughly in a row. Their hands were bound with cords behind their backs, and they were blindfolded. Each had been shot in the back of the head.

Inspecting each of the murdered soldiers for evidence of their personal identity and unit affiliation, Leif carefully and respectfully assessed them all. All the personal affects and identification had been taken by the captors, rings, watches, and wallets However, several letters from family members were found and one soldier's field jacket with his name tag was found as well as two of soldiers had attached a spare dog tag / US Army identity plate to their boots – a common practice amongst veteran soldiers. This information would help the graves registration team identify their bodies. It was a gruesome, heart wrenching task but it had to be done. Leif noticed that some of the dead had what appeared to be chemical burns around their eyes, nose and mouth. He surmised that these American prisoners had undergone biological or chemical experimentation and torture at the hands of their captors before being executed – murdered. Leif selected one of the dead Americans with evidence of chemical burns to be wrapped in a body bag and taken back with them so that he could be examined by medical staff for possible chemical agent poisoning. The rest of the dead Americans would be buried respectfully in place where they had fallen.

Leif, along with the radioman and the reserve squad moved back to the top of the overlooking hill to improve radio transmission and provided their regimental headquarters with a report of their mission. They were ordered to photograph everything, bring back any evidence and then destroy the village. The village elder along with a dozen men from the village were brought over at gunpoint and ordered to dig seven proper graves for the slain American soldiers. Meanwhile, Leif and one of the sergeants photographed and recorded the names of the murdered soldiers that could be identified, and searched for evidence of what chemical or biological agents the PoWs might have been exposed to by their enemy captors.

The Eighth United States Army and the 187th ARCT had developed various extraction plans on how to get the rescue team and the prisoners out of enemy territory, all of which were contingent on finding prisoners to be rescued. As such, four Sikorsky H-19 Chickasaw utility helicopters that had only come into service with the USAAC and Marines in 1950 had been placed on standby in the event of a successful rescue of the prisoners. With a capacity of twelve combat troops or eight medical litters, two of the helicopters were configured for transport of litter patients and two were ready to pick up Lieutenant Bangsbøll and his sixteen rescue team members. One H-19 would go in first with ten combat-ready troops to secure the landing zone, assist with the extraction and lay down covering fire for the evacuees if needed. The helicopters would allow for surprise and a swift extraction, but there was one major drawback. In the confined valley that surrounded the village, the helicopters would be easy targets to enemy fire. The alternate extraction plan was to have the 187th ARCT with supporting UN artillery and American fighter-bomber cover break through the enemy line in a narrow but deliberate path of assault and rapidly push straight to the prisoners' location and withdraw them under close artillery and air support protection. This course of action was riskier and would take longer to execute, so the helicopter airlift was selected as the primary option.

If Lieutenant Bangsbøll and his rescue team were either intercepted by the enemy or if they were unable to locate the PoWs they would be expected to make their retreat back to friendly lines on foot, in the cover of darkness, with only Allied artillery and air support if the situation deemed it necessary. If the rescuers could get in and out without risking the helicopters or an enemy engagement, all the better. Given their circumstances, Leif sent the coded message that indicated to regimental headquarters that he and his two squads would be returning on foot, with one dead American PoW. Night was falling and Leif now considered the helicopter extraction too risky given the waning light and the heavy concentration of enemy forces in the vicinity. Those whirly-birds would be easy targets for the enemy who would be soon blanketing the hillsides in pursuit, thought Leif.

Night had fallen, and the American rescue team slipped back into the mountains. Behind them was the billowing smoke and orange glow of the village, engulfed in flames. The villagers were allowed to flee. Leif and his squad leaders knew they had to put as much distance as possible between themselves and the village before sunrise. Fueled by their rage at the evidence of atrocities, the two squads moved quickly and silently southward towards the safety of the UN frontlines. To help mask their withdrawal and the conflagration of the burning village, a heavy UN artillery barrage was unleashed to the north, east and west of their current location. Leif and his team marched all night, stopping every two hours for no more than ten minutes. Leif knew, as did the rest of his team, that the Chinese and North Korean forces would undoubtedly be pursuing them by now. Speed and agility were essential to their survival. The burden of carrying their dead comrade was never an issue. The rescue team was adamant that they would get this one American hero home, as a token of respect for him and his fellow comrades, and as evidence of chemical poisoning and murder – war crimes the enemy had committed.

By sunrise the next morning, both squads were exhausted, having traversed 10 miles of mountain trails in the darkness at a grueling forced march pace. Again, miraculously, they had not encountered any enemy units during their night's trek. Soon their luck would run out. After daybreak they came upon an abandoned farm and used it as their base camp for a few hours. They were about 3 miles from the American/UN lines. There, they set up a defensive perimeter to allow them to eat a meal and get some rest. After an hour of quiet recovery, the rear guard came running into their makeshift camp and reported that a company-sized enemy force, probably Chinese, was less than a mile behind them and moving fast up the trail towards their current position. With the Allied lines still 3 miles ahead of them, Leif knew they would need some covering support. He radioed the regiment's headquarters and gave the estimated grid reference of the oncoming enemy force, requesting an artillery fire mission. Within three minutes a barrage of high-explosive shells from a Turkish artillery battery pulverised the valley behind the Americans and decimated the forward echelon of the enemy company that had been pursuing them.

As Lieutenant Bangsbøll completed his radio report, the radio being carried on the back of his radioman exploded right in front of his face, knocking the radioman to the ground and ripping the radio handset out of the platoon commander's hand. 'SNIPER!' someone yelled, and everyone scattered for a place of concealment. Leif dove on top of his radioman to shield him from further fire and then dragged him towards the farmhouse wall where they would be protected from the sniper fire. He quickly removed the damaged radio from the radioman's back and inspected him for injuries. Remarkably, the radioman was shaken but not seriously injured. The radio had taken the full impact of the sniper round and only minor shrapnel wounds were inflicted on the radioman's back and neck. It was not surprising that the sniper had taken aim at the radioman and officer using the radio. The enemy would always prioritise killing medics, radiomen or officers first.

After two or three minutes of sporadic fire from the adjacent hills, the two squads replied with enough return fire to convince the enemy sniper to cease fire and withdraw. 'That was a close call', thought Leif, 'We have to get moving.' Sensing a wetness on his chin, Leif lifted his hand to inspect his face. Fragments of metal from the radio had made several small lacerations of his chin and cheek, but other than the loss of the radio and these minor injuries, the team was unscathed and ready to continue its dash for safety of friendly lines.

With their position compromised, Lieutenant Bangsbøll ordered his two squads to move out at a fast pace. Without radio communications, they would have to rely on the regimental headquarters staff to track their anticipated movement back towards the UN lines. Leif thought to himself, 'I sure hope the

S-3 staff were paying attention to my planned return route and crossing point when I briefed them earlier in the week.'

Over the next two hours, the small rescue team made its way along their planned route back towards friendly, American lines, running most of the way, except over the steepest and narrowest parts of the paths – mostly near the crest of each ridge they crossed. At one point, as the Rakkasans were just reaching the top of a ridgeline and were therefore more exposed to the enemy, a hail of bullets fired from a distance of 600 yards struck the rocks and bushes around them. Two paratroopers were hit and sustained serious but non-life-threatening wounds. As the American paratroopers laid down heavy return fire to slow down the enemy's advance, it gave time for the medic to stabilise his two wounded soldiers.

Despite his disdain for the enemy, at one level, Leif recognized and admired their courage and stamina. 'They are pursuing us with great vigor and military skill', he thought,

> and are clearly prepared to fight and die for their cause – though a maniacal and misguided cause that it is. But they or those like them just murdered eight American soldiers. That's it! Enough of this running with our tails between our legs! Let's give those bastards something to think about!

Lieutenant Bangsbøll then ordered one squad, including the medic to assist the wounded and those carrying their dead colleague, over the ridge, while he and the second squad provided covering fire. The withdrawing squad was also ordered to hand over half of their remaining ammunition and all of the ammo of the two injured soldiers. Once the ammo was redistributed amongst the squad that was preparing to engage the enemy, Leif gave the signal and he and his squad provided a well measured, prolonged cover fire, which allowed his second squad to cross the exposed ridge safely.

Now it was time to confront their pursuers. It was absolutely essential that the squad he was leading retain sufficient ammo for the next phase of his plan. Once their barrage of cover fire ended, they would now remain silent, reload their weapons and prepare to unload every bullet and all the hand grenades they had remaining in one final assault against the pursuing enemy. 'Let them come close… really close… too close for comfort… and wait for me to open up.' Bangsbøll instructed. Silent acknowledgement from his squad confirmed their understanding of the gravity of the situation. Leif thought, 'The last thing our friends from the north will expect is a full-frontal charge from a bunch of retreating Yankee Imperialists.'

Moving 20 yards above and adjacent to the mountain trail that they had just used and along which the enemy was now traveling towards them, Leif and his eight squad members concealed themselves behind the boulders and bushes that carpeted the mountainside. There they waited for their prey.

Major Kim, the pursuing North Korean company commander, estimated that there were fewer than twenty American soldiers in retreat and, with the UN line less than 2 miles further, that they would be scared and eager to get to safety. The last burst of fire from the Americans was clearly their dash over the exposed ridge and they must be in full flight down the opposite side of the mountain. The North Korean major had underestimated his American imperialist foe. As such, his company-sized pursuit force of North Korean regulars moved with aggressive speed up their side of the mountain trail with reckless abandon. The North Korean infantry commander knew that failure to capture or kill this small force of Americans who had dared to venture deep into his country would be an embarrassment to his commander – and as a result, it would be detrimental to his own well-being. And so, the North Koreans pressed forward with enthusiastic and ill-advised, undisciplined vigor, as Major Kim shouted orders to his troops: '*JEONBANG GONG*! *GYEOG*! [FORWARD! ATTACK!]'

With the Americans appearing to be in full retreat, Leif's counterassault came with such surprise, swiftness and ferocity and from a tactically ideal location, that it swept the much larger North Korean force off the mountain trail and sent those who were not immediately killed or wounded fleeing down onto the steep, rugged slopes below. Major Kim, at the lead of the North Korean column, had momentarily stood his ground, but before he could give any further orders, he had all but disintegrated as two American fragmentation grenades detonated simultaneously within just a few feet of his position. Several other North Korean soldiers near their leader were hit with shrapnel and went down as well. At a disadvantageous position as a result of the sudden and overwhelming and unexpected American assault from the high-ground and with their company commander killed, the remainder of the North Koreans soldiers scattered and ceased to be an effective fighting force. The enemy had had enough and withdrew into the valley below to regroup – in short, abandoning their pursuit of the Americans.

Following their successful ambush, and sure that the North Koreans were now out of action for at least the immediate future, Lieutenant Bangsbøll and his squad rejoined the first squad, which had progressed a full mile down the trail to the valley below. They were now a mile closer to friendly UN lines.

During the final stage of their escape, a flight of four F-86 Super-Sabre fighter-bombers took turns flying at low level up and down the valley that the American paratroopers were now traversing. The screaming fighter aircraft strafed the trail and hillside behind the small American unit to eliminate or deter any further enemy encroachment. The sight and sound of those aircraft overhead gave the small American force great confidence that the 187th ARCT knew where they were and that the USAAF was there to provide top-cover and make the enemy think twice about pursuing them any further.

Leif and his small band of would-be rescuers arrived at their designated re-entry point mid-afternoon, three and a half days after they had parachuted into North Korea. Waiting for them at the crossing point were two American 5-ton troop trucks and two jeeps. As well, Lieutenant Colonel Bank had sent two Sherman tanks as heavy muscle to deter the enemy if they had continued their pursuit as far as the American lines.

Thankful for not have to march the remaining mile back to the 187th ARCT camp, the exhausted paratroopers climbed aboard the trucks as Leif and his radioman jumped aboard the jeep. And there, freshly painted in bright yellow letters on the hood of the lead jeep were the words: 'The Danish Duke'. With a grin on his face and a wink to the jeep driver, Leif quietly let out an indiscernible sigh of relief. He and his men had completed their mission and had returned once more with only three minor casualties. Leif settled in for the short ride back to camp and began formulating the after-action report in his mind. The fact that their rescue mission had arrived too late to save the American soldiers would be something to think about later – and it would be something he would think about for years to come.

Upon his return to camp, Lieutenant Bangsbøll went directly to the S-3 operations and intelligence tent to report his platoon's safe return and to provide an initial, verbal report of the events of the past four days. He also handed over the camera to the duty intelligence officer, emphasizing that the film contained photographs of a war crime scene against American soldiers. The body of the lone American soldier who had been tortured and executed was taken to the mortuary tent to be examined by divisional doctors. Meanwhile, the two squad leaders took their three wounded soldiers to the medical tent and saw to it that the rest of their men ate, rearmed their ammunition pouches and cleaned their weapons before they were allowed some well-deserved rest. Both sergeants knew that their platoon commander, the affable but always vigilant 'Danish Duke' would soon come by to verify that his team members, despite their exhaustion, had cleaned their weapons, restocked their ammunition, were fed and watered and back to mission-ready status before he would let them rest. Once he had verified that all those things were completed to his satisfaction and only then would he himself go to his own quarters to rest or have a meal for himself.

In May 1951, the 187th ARCT, transferred to the command of Brigadier General Trapnell, and received orders to redeploy the entire unit to Japan as a strategic reserve unit. That same week, Lieutenant Bangsbøll received separate orders, reassigning him immediately to Fort Bragg with 82nd Airborne Division to work again for recently promoted Colonel Bank who had already left Korea for Washington where he would work on the Special Forces Warfare Center's staff under Brigadier General Robert McClure. Soon afterward, he would be heading-up a new army initiative – the creation of the first United States Army Special Forces unit – the 10th Special Forces Group.

Though thankful that his combat tour was at an end, Leif was apprehensive to leave his platoon while it was still in the thick of things in North Korea. Having completed three combat assaults, dozens of patrols and firefights with the enemy and several special operations missions behind enemy lines, now, recently promoted to Captain, Leif Bangsbøll did not have a single casualty in his platoon – lots of wounded soldiers, but no one killed. Leif was proud of this. His soldiers had been the eyes and ears of the 187th ARCT, been given some of the toughest missions and performed admirably. However, it was time to go – orders are orders. Leif was honored and excited to learn that he would be working again with his good friend and colleague, Colonel Bank on a very special assignment State-side.

The Korean War would continue until its ceasefire was signed on 27 July 1953. The final toll: 178,405 UN forces dead, 33,000 missing and 566,434 wounded. The Chinese and North Korean losses are estimated at between 500,000 and 750,000 dead and somewhere between 700,000 and 800,000 wounded. Civilian casualties are estimated at 400,000. The cost of the Korean War in terms of lives lost and human suffering is unimaginable. The Korean War is technically not over. To this day, seventy years later, only tenuous ceasefire separates North and South Korea.

The United States would sustain 34,515 military personnel killed in action during the Korean War. During their assignment in Korea, 11th Airborne Division's 187th ARCT would suffer 2,115 casualties of which 442 were KIA and 17 MIA, presumed killed. Like many other wars, the Korean War was marked by both victories and defeats, from the overwhelming surprise attack by the North Koreans, which started the conflict, to the daring American amphibious invasion at Incheon, which turned the tide of the war in the UN forces' favor. The Battle of Yongju and the successes of the massive American airborne assaults on Sunchŏn and Sukchŏn that Leif participated in and the incredibly heroic stand the Australians, Canadians and New Zealanders made at the Battle of Kapyong to the disastrous, yet heroic defence of the Chosin Reservoir by the United States' 1st Marine Division when the Chinese entered the war and flooded south through the Korean peninsula. The Korean War was a roller coaster of victories and defeats for both sides, all of which took a gruesome toll on all those involved.

The Korean War took a terrible personal toll on Leif. His former unit, 1st Cavalry Division, from his previous assignment in Japan would suffer horrific losses during the conflict, suffering 12,053 wounded, 3,355 KIA and 448 MIA, presumed killed. Many of Leif's close friends and colleagues were among those lost, including Second Lieutenant John McGuire of 9th Infantry Regiment, Leif's close friend and best man at his wedding. The most senior American officer to die in the Korean War was Lieutenant General Walton Walker, commander of the Eighth United States Army, Leif's commander and Margaret Henry's new friend and admired bridge partner. The devil had surely taken his due – it had been the devil's harvest.

* * *

Twenty-five years after the end of the Korean hostilities, and almost thirteen years after Leif had retired from military service, an unexpected and most welcome event occurred that would forge a special bond between a son and his father. It was summer 1977 when Leif's son, Mark, a West Point cadet going into his senior year at the academy, was temporarily assigned to 8th Infantry Division in West Germany, close to the East-West German border. Mark Bangsbøll was assigned to this operational, frontline combat division for what is known as 'summer semester contact training'. The West Point Cadet Summer Contact Program was designed to give the cadets practical exposure to operational units prior to graduation.

The commanding general of 8th Infantry Division at the time was Major General John Cleland. On a particular morning that summer, Major General Cleland had scheduled a professional development briefing for the division's leadership. There were more than 250 officers and senior non-commissioned officers present, along with a dozen visiting West Point cadets gathered in the camp auditorium. Upon the commander's arrival, Mark, who was the senior cadet in attendance was introduced to Major General Cleland and reported with a smart salute, 'Cadet Bangsbøll reports all cadets present or accounted for, sir.'

Cleland returned the salute, shook Mark's hand and lingered for a moment as he looked at the cadet's name tag with an air of recognition. 'Would you be a family relation to Leif Bangsbøll?' asked the commander. After a moment's hesitation at the unexpected question, Mark replied, 'Yes sir, he's my father.' The general smiled and responded with one word, 'Rakkasans'. He placed his hand on Mark's shoulder and gave it a squeeze and before ascending the steps to the stage said, 'I'm proud to meet you, son.'

In a booming voice, the commander – who was dressed in immaculately fitted, starched combat fatigues and highly polished jump boots – gave his opening address to the gathering of American warriors. Cleland spoke about their collective burden of responsibility, and the importance of strong, innovative leadership, and the great obligation that all those gathered together that morning had in providing the most effective leadership possible, especially given the menacingly close proximity and lethal threat posed by the Soviet and Warsaw Pact forces.

Major General Cleland stated,

> A modern, well-equipped adversary is massed just a few miles from where we sit. An enemy that is poised to invade the ground we occupy with massive, mechanised ground and air forces.

Cleland paused, looking down into the gathered audience and making direct eye contact with Mark who was seated in the front row of the auditorium. Cleland had prepared his comments the previous night and had several cue cards in his breast pocket that he had intended to use to keep his address on point. But in that moment, instead of relying on his notes, he began to improvise. 'During the Korean War', he recalled, with a noticeable shift and in a voice somewhat gentler than that with which he had started,

> I had the honor to be part of a hardened combat unit known as the 187th Airborne, Regimental Combat Team. Today they are still affectionately known as the Rakkasans. Back in 1950, despite overwhelming numbers of enemy forces – North Korean and Chinese – the 187th stood their ground and confronted and consistently defeated the enemy in a multitude of small, medium- and large-scale combat engagements. On two occasions we conducted massive combat parachute assaults behind the enemy lines, cutting off their retreat, and killing or capturing thousands. I witnessed outstanding leadership and incredible bravery, and observed American forces using innovative tactics, guile and audacity to outmaneuver the enemy both physically and intellectually on the field of battle. One of the finest, bravest and most dynamic combat leaders I have ever had the honor to serve with was a Rakkasan named Captain Leif Bangsbøll. He was Danish by birth and fought like a Viking. His conduct in the face of the enemy was dynamic and as cold and strong as steel. His care and devotion to his troops was unparalleled. Leif Bangsbøll was the epitome of a soldier's soldier.

Major General Cleland then outstretched his arm and pointed to the front row of the auditorium. 'That young West Point Cadet is Lieutenant Colonel Leif Bangsbøll's son, carrying on the tradition of service.' And then added, 'Son, you have some big jump boots to fill.' Mark was dumbfounded by this unexpected and public pronouncement about his father from such a senior leader about events that had taken place so long ago. But Cleland was not quite finished,

> Captain Bangsbøll and I were platoon commanders with the 187th ARCT and I still begrudge the fact that Bangsbøll had the advantage over me back there in Korea, because his mentor was the famous Colonel Aaron Bank, arguably one of the greatest special operations officers the United States Army has ever produced. Many of you know that Colonel Aaron Bank was instrumental in leading the creation of the United States Army Special Forces, and under the direct orders of President Eisenhower built the first Green Beret special forces unit along with a select few other combat-tested experts such as Cadet Bangsbøll's father.

'Those men were hard-charging leaders.' Cleland emphasized, his voice once again rising towards booming.

> Combat-hardened, war fighting, forward-thinking officers who were able to motivate and lead their troops under the most arduous conditions and hone their combat skills to create the finest, most lethal fighting force this nation has ever produced. They were men who did not accept the concept of defeat. They were simply and ultimately America's Best.

He paused then concluded,

> I say to you now that you should all strive in your chosen careers as war fighters to reach those levels of technical expertise, dedication and sense of duty.

With that, Major General Cleland handed over the stage to the adjutant to continue with the morning's briefings.

Up to that moment, Mark knew that his father had had a fascinating and impressive military career. The war stories alone that his father would on occasion tell made that obvious. However, thanks to that experience in the auditorium with the commander of 8th Infantry Division and under the looming shadow of the Soviet military threat, Mark began to fully appreciate the impact his father had during his career and the truly remarkable reputation that his father had earned as a United States Army officer. Mark was astounded that even twenty-five years after the Korean War and over thirty years since the end of the Second World War, the simple mention of his father's name amongst many of the most senior officers of the United States Army evoked an immediate sense of pride and fond memories of their past affiliation with 'The Danish Duke' – the soldier's soldier.

* * *

In August of 2024, 72 years after the end of the Korean War, Lieutenant Colonel (Retired) Leif Bangsboll, United States Army was postumously awarded the South Korean Government's Peace Medal in recognition of his heroic actions in the defence of South Korea during the Korean War. The author had the honour to accept this medal on his father's behalf.

Chapter 8

Sine Pari – Veritas et Libertas

> 'Guerrilla warfare is not dependent for success on the efficient operation of complex military devices, highly organized logistical systems, or the accuracy of computers. It can be conducted in any terrain, in any climate, in any weather; in swamps, in mountains, in farmed fields; its basic element is man, and man is more complex and dynamic than any of his machines.'
>
> General S.B. Griffith, USMC, 1961

Two weeks before Leif received his orders sending him State-side, the Korean combat tour of Lieutenant Colonel Bank, the 187th ARCT's Ex-O, came to an end when he received orders promoting him to full colonel and reassigning him to an important, and unique leadership opportunity back in the States. Colonel Bank was tasked to create the United States Army's first special operations force: commandos. The initial unit members would be hand selected and specially trained and equipped, and would be called the 10th Special Forces Group (SFG), the first unit of this kind in the United States Army's history. The 10th SFG traced its origins back to the Second World War and the famous American-Canadian joint commando unit known as the Devil's Brigade, which served with distinction in Italy and France, often and effectively engaging the enemy well behind their frontlines. The 10th SFG could also trace its origins the the highly successful, yet short-lived time of the OSS.

By mid-May 1951, Colonel Bank had settled into his new assignment and went to work overseeing the building of 10th SFG infrastructure at Fort Bragg, creating the essential tables of organization and their associated equipment and weapons inventory. But most importantly, assembling the list of desired instructors and command staff for their new United States Army Special Forces' unit. Colonel Bank personally ensured that one of the officers near the top of the list was newly promoted Captain Leif Bangsbøll, who was just completing his combat tour in Korea with 187th ARCT.

By late May 1951, a few weeks after Colonel Bank's departure, Leif bid farewell to the 187th ARCT and Korea – destined for Fort Campbell, Kentucky, in order to clear out administratively from the 187th ARCT and then report to Fort Bragg. Bragg, as it is affectionately known by many in the American military, is the home of the airborne and Lieutenant Bangsbøll's new and intriguing assignment with the newly created 10th Special Forces Group. Once Leif had cleared in at United States Army Special Forces' headquarters and secured his on base family living quarters, his first order of business was to take a month of post-combat leave to reunite with his family before commencing his new assignment.

* * *

With his signed leave pass in his pocket and a substantial amount of cash from his accumulated back pay in his wallet, Leif drove north, up Interstate 85 once again, to Oshawa, Ontario Canada – a route he had become very familiar with over the past few years. Leif parked the car on the gravel driveway and as he walked up the path towards 231 King Street East, he looked up and saw his wife beaming in all her beauty, with a smile from ear to ear. Standing beside Dorothy was her father, Clifford, who was holding Leslie – now one-and-one-half year old. On her other side was her mother, Margaret, who was holding Christian – now 6 months old. Dorothy, wearing her best Sunday dress and high-heeled shoes, with tears welling in her eyes ran down the wooden stairs from the veranda and leapt into the arms of her returning soldier. There, they embraced for the longest, most sole-calming, joyous moment that both Leif and Dorothy had ever experienced. Upon their slow, loving release of their welcoming embrace, Leif turned his attention to the blonde little girl in his mother-in-law's arms. At first Leslie played coy and clung tightly to her grandmother, but soon enough she reached out to be held by this handsome uniformed man. Clifford then approached and smiled with pride and held out the bundle he was holding – Leif then laid eyes on his son, Leif Christian Bangsbøll, for the very first time. In addition to the overwhelming joy and thoughts of parental obligations flooding through his very soul, Leif realized at that moment that this child was the first-male descendant of his father Frederik and mother Rigmor and represented the continued bloodline of the Sorensen-Bangsbøll clan – linking him to Denmark's ancient Viking King Harald Gorm 'Bluetooth' – the Great Communicator and his son, King Svein Haraldson 'Forkbeard', the first Viking king of England.

* * *

While Leif was on his post-combat leave in Oshawa, Colonel Bank was busy, splitting his time between setting-up the United States Army Special Forces headquarters at Fort Bragg and meetings in Washington, at The Pentagon.

Bank, along with a small cadre of selected, and very experienced combat veterans, including Captain Bangsbøll, Lieutenant Colonel Russell Volckmann, Lieutenant Colonel Wendel Fertig and Captain John Hemingway, would chart new territory for the United States Army. They were tasked to implement President Dwight D. Eisenhower's order to create an elite special combat force within the army. In summer 1951, a small select group of army officers and NCOs began to assemble at Fort Bragg, to create the Special Operations Force and Psychological Warfare Center. This unit would soon be renamed the United States Army Special Forces' Warfare Center under 10th SFG, commanded by Brigadier General Charles Karlstad.

* * *

By the end of July 1951, the Bangsbøll family – Leif, Dorothy, Leslie and Chris – took up residence in the married officer housing section on the sprawling, 250 square miles, pine tree covered expanses of Fort Bragg, North Carolina. As a member of 82nd Airborne Division – 'All Americans' again – and now as a member of the first elite United States Army Special Forces unit, Leif felt like he was truly home. The initial year with Colonel Bank under the new special forces banner was spent expanding and redesigning aspects of the Fort Bragg training area as well as traveling between North Carolina and Washington DC, to develop the new special forces doctrine and training syllabi, securing the funding and personnel resources and equipment to set up the new United States Army Special Forces Group infrastructure.

Based closely upon the OSS' foundations from the Second World War, Lieutenant Bangsbøll helped develop the special forces doctrine, which laid out this fundamental guidance:

> The special forces soldier can expect to operate in areas within enemy territory or within regions where the 'frontline of battle' was not distinct and where distinguishing friend from foe would not necessarily be evident. The special forces soldier should expect to operate in a high-threat environment for prolonged periods of time. The special forces soldier will not only need to be an elite combat soldier, familiar with a wide range of foreign weaponry, but also be a teacher, mentor and negotiator. The special forces soldier should be proficient in multiple languages and have the physical and psychological strength to operate independently for prolonged periods of time in stressful conditions without direct support from his unit. The special forces soldier must be able to improvise and operate in austere and hostile territory for prolonged periods of time. Finally, the special

Lieutenant Leif Bangsbøll, OSS Agent with Sergeant Alfred Keller (Agent Bjorn Toller) in background, following the defeat of Nazi Germany. Photo taken in Copenhagen Denmark, mid-May 1945. Note both American soldiers are wearing the Danish Resistance arm band on their left sleeves. (*Courtesy of the Bangsbøll family photo collection*)

Commodore Frederik Bangsbøll, Royal Danish Navy and son, Leif Bangsbøll, First Lieutenant United States Army, reunion after the liberation of Denmark from five years of Nazi occupation, Copenhagen Denmark, May 1945. (*Courtesy of the Bangsbøll family photo collection*)

Lieutenant Leif Bangsbøll, receiving United States Distinguished Service Cross medal from Commander SOE / OSS, Major-General Gubbins, July 1945. (*Courtesy of the Bangsbøll family photo collection*)

From left to right, OSS / SSU agents Carl Vestegaard, William Jacobsen and Jorgen Bech (AKA Lieutenant Leif Bangsbøll) in East Germany (Soviet Zone), fall of 1945. The Russian sign reads: "Access forbidden to all foreign mission personnel." (*Courtesy of the Bangsbøll family photo collection*)

Captain Leif Bangsbøll, 82nd Airborne Division, Fort Bragg North Carolina, 1947. (*Courtesy of the Bangsbøll family photo collection*)

The bride, Dorothy Jean Henry with mother Margaret, the Maid of Honor, San Francisco, December 10th 1947. (*Courtesy of the Bangsbøll family photo collection*)

Lieutenant Leif Bangsbøll with wife Dorothy in front of their official residence, Hayama Japan, May 1948. (*Courtesy of the Bangsbøll family photo collection*)

Lieutenant Leif Bangsbøll (seated, fourth from the left) with Police Agent Han Joon Dak (seated, third from the left) with their South Korean Police staff on the island of Che Ju Do, August 1948. (*Courtesy of the Bangsbøll family photo collection*)

Lieutenant Leif Bangsbøll (third from left) with his mother-in-law Margaret Henry (far right) along with local house staff Hayama Japan. Hiroshi, their translator and head of the household staff is standing to the right of Leif, 1948. (*Courtesy of the Bangsbøll family photo collection*)

Lieutenant Leif Bangsbøll with wife Dorothy and mother-in-law Margaret Henry in front the grand statue of Buda, 1948. (*Courtesy of the Bangsbøll family photo collection*)

Lieutenant Bangsbøll (third from the left) marching with 2nd Battalion, 5th Infantry Division in front of the Imperial Japanese Palace, 18 November 1949. (*Courtesy of the Bangsbøll family photo collection*)

Paratroopers of the 187th ARCT known as the "Rakkasans" board a C-119 Boxcar, Operation TOMAHAWK, Kimpo airfield, South Korea, March 1951. (*Achieve photo obtained from internet*)

Paratroopers of the 187th ARCT a board a C-119 Boxcar, Operation TOMAHAWK, Kimpo airfield, South Korea, March 1951. (*Archive photo obtained from internet*)

One of seventy-one C-119 Boxcars and forty-seven C-47 Dakotas used in the airborne assault by 3,000 members of the U.S. 187th ARCT (Airborne Regiment Combat Team) dropped into North Korea as part of Operation COURAGEOUS, 20 October 1950. (*Courtesy of the Bangsbøll family photo collection*)

View from the paratroop door of three members of the 187th ARCT jumping into North Korea near the town of Sunch'on. (*Courtesy of the Bangsbøll family photo collection*)

View of five of the forty-seven C-119 Boxcars involved in the mass para-assault by the 187th ARCT in October 1950. The surprise insertion of 3,000 American paratroopers behind enemy lines disrupted the retreat of the North Korean Army and its Government officials. (*Courtesy of the Bangsbøll family photo collection*)

Mass graves of North Korean civilians discovered by Lieutenant Bangsbøll's reconnaissance patrol near the village of Suckchon, North Korea on 22 October 1950. North Korean Government had ordered the murder of any pro-western / anti-Communist citizens. (*Courtesy of the Bangsbøll family photo collection*)

Mass graves of North Korean civilians discovered by Lieutenant Bangsbøll's reconnaissance patrol near the village of Suckchon, North Korea on 22 October 1950. North Korean Government had ordered the murder of any pro-western / anti-Communist citizens. (*Courtesy of the Bangsbøll family photo collection*)

Lieutenant Leif Bangsbøll "The Danish Duke" and commander of the 187th ARCT Headquarters Intelligence and Reconnaissance platoon, leans against armoured patrol vehicle, Korea 1950–51. (*Courtesy of the Bangsbøll family photo collection*)

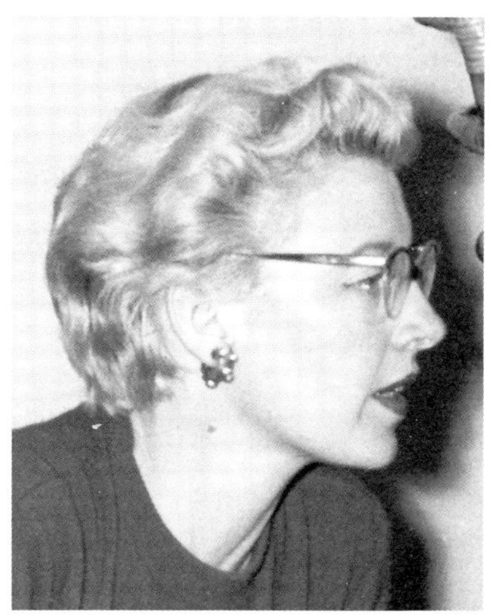

Dorothy Jean Bangsbøll, Bad Tolz Germany, 1955. (*Courtesy of the Bangsbøll family photo collection*)

U.S. Persing Tank as part of the "Red / Enemy Force" during NATO exercise near Bad Tolz Germany. Photographed by Dorothy Bangsbøll. (*Courtesy of the Bangsbøll family photo collection*)

U.S. Persing Tank as part of the "Red / Enemy Force" during NATO exercise near Bad Tolz Germany. Photographed by Dorothy Bangsbøll after being rescued. (*Courtesy of the Bangsbøll family photo collection*)

U.S. armored personnel carrier as part of the "Red / Enemy Force" during NATO exercise near Bad Tolz Germany. Photographed by Dorothy Bangsbøll. (*Courtesy of the Bangsbøll family photo collection*)

Captain Leif Bangsbøll, (facing camera) at wreath laying ceremony, Ryvangen / Copenhagen Denmark, 5th of May 1955, marking the 10th Anniversary of the end of World War II. (*Courtesy of the Bangsbøll family photo collection*)

Captain Leif Bangsbøll, (leading the Honor Guard of 82nd Airborne troops) at wreath laying ceremony, Aalborg Denmark, 9th of May 1955, marking the 10th Anniversary of the end of World War II. (*Courtesy of the Bangsbøll family photo collection*)

Members of the 302nd TAC RECCON Squadron on survival training exercise "Feebier '57", Palatinate Forest, West Germany, March 1957. Captain "The Danish Duke" Bangsbøll standing center with hands in jacket pockets. Captain Audrey "Rabbit" Hare standing for left. Lieutenant Don Breedlove seated, second from left and Sergeant Beemer, kneeling front row, right. (*Courtesy of the Bangsbøll family photo collection*)

Captain Bangsbøll receiving award, Fort Bragg North Carolina, 1959. (*Courtesy of the Bangsbøll family photo collection*)

Colonel Sonnek, West German Army presents Major Bangsbøll with German Second Corps Commander's Commendation, 1960. Leif's father Frederik looking on from behind. (*Courtesy of the Bangsbøll family photo collection*)

Bangsbøll family Christmas card, December 1962, Oberammergau, West Germany. (*Courtesy of the Bangsbøll family photo collection*)

Medal presentation at Lieutenant-Colonel Leif Bangsbøll's retirement parade, Oberammergau, West Germany, 30th of April, 1963. (*Courtesy of the Bangsbøll family photo collection*)

Marching past the colors during Lieutenant-Colonel Leif Bangsbøll's retirement parade, Oberammergau, West Germany, 30th of April, 1963. (*Courtesy of the Bangsbøll family photo collection*)

Bangsbøll family photo, Toronto Canada, 1967. (*Courtesy of the Bangsbøll family photo collection*)

The Bangsbøll children – Mark, Leslie, Chris, Wendy and Brook at Mom's 70th birthday, October 1992, Bradenton Florida. (*Courtesy of the Bangsbøll family photo collection*)

Dorothy and Leif enjoying their retirement together in Bradenton Florida, 1992. (*Courtesy of the Bangsbøll family photo collection*)

General Clarke, Commander of U.S. Special Operations Command and his Sergeant-Major present U.S. Special Forces Commando Hall of Honor award to Lieutenant-Colonel Leif Bangsbøll (posthumously). Receiving the award on his behalf are his sons, Lieutenant-Colonel Brook Bangsbøll and Lieutenant (Navy Retired) Chris Bangsbøll, April 2019. (*Courtesy of the Bangsbøll family photo collection*)

Lieutenant-Colonel Brook Bangsbøll and Lieutenant (Navy Retired) Chris Bangsbøll, pose next to the LTC Leif Bangsbøll display in the Special Forces Operations Command's Commando Hall of Honor, April 2029. (*Courtesy of the Bangsbøll family photo collection*)

Centre – seated: Leif Bangsbøll, U.S. Army (retired), back row, from left: Chris Bangsbøll (son), Canadian Navy (retired), Brook Bangsbøll (son), Royal Canadian Air Force, Bryce Morawiec (grandson), Canadian Army, Erika Henry (niece) Canadian Army, Mark Bangsbøll, U.S. Army, Garrett Morawiec (grandson) Canadian Army, Elliot "Chip" Grey (nephew), U.S. Army. (14 August, 2000). (*Courtesy of the Bangsbøll family photo collection*)

Sketch of Leif Bangsbøll, 2000. Artist – Nancy Bangsbøll. (*Courtesy of the Bangsbøll family photo collection*)

> forces soldier must be prepared to make critical decisions without precise direction from his commander – make difficult choices, which will put others in harm's way and accept the consequences of those decisions in order to achieve the objective. (US Army Special Forces Field Manual)

Officially, the Special Forces' Warfare Center stood up the 10th SFG(A) on 19 June 1952. Of the original 1,000 members of the first United States Army Special Forces unit, fourteen were combat tested, core leaders and former OSS agents, including Captain Leif Bangsbøll. The intent of this unit was to create specially trained, combat ready forces with advanced and specialised skills that would provide the American president and the United States military with a more flexible and dynamic option to respond to and deal with the growing communist inspired conflicts around the world. The American president wanted a force that was unconventional in its methods and lethal in its effect. The force needed to be able to operate in small and medium-sized units on short notice and to be independent of many of the conventional army constructs and reporting protocols. And that is just what they created. The United States Special Forces, famously known as the Green Berets, due to their distinctive service headgear would be responsible for five primary missions: unconventional warfare, foreign internal defense, special reconnaissance, direct combat actions and counterterrorism. The motto of the Special Operations Group was '*Sine Pari* [Without Equal]'. The Green Beret special forces insignia bore the motto: '*De Oppresso Liber* [Free the Oppressed]'.

* * *

By early July 1951, Leif and Dorothy had their assigned married quarters at Fort Bragg set up and feeling very much like a family home, complete with a swing and sandbox in the back yard. With his family settled in, just a ten-minute walk from his office at the new United States Army Special Forces headquarters and Special Forces Warfare Center, Leif was a happy man. With his family taken care of, Leif immersed himself in his assignment.

* * *

Leif was in his element; all the clandestine tactics and tricks of the trade, the knowledge of human behavior under stressful, combat and counterinsurgency operations were his to develop and teach to the new breed of America's elite warriors. Though Leif relished this new, unique assignment, his true, personal contentment came by knowing that at the end of each long day of training and instructing he had his loving, growing family to come home to… every night.

The newly created Special Forces Warfare Centere, to which Captain Bangsbøll now belonged to, adopted the motto '*Veritas et Libertas* [Truth and Freedom]'. Ironically, the motto was in stark contrast to the clandestine nature of their mission. At the Special Forces Warfare Center, Lieutenant Bangsbøll became the lead instructor for special operations, counterinsurgency and guerrilla warfare tactics. He, along with a handful of other former OSS agents, now United States Army Special Forces, Green Berets, would teach eager, hand-picked soldiers, who had been identified by their parent units as the toughest, best and brightest they had to offer. The training was challenging and based on their OSS experiences, which called for intense language and cultural fluency along with unconventional training in sabotage and espionage. They were taught that a small unit of well-trained special forces could equal or exceed the effectiveness of a vastly larger force, and by employing stealthy maneuverability and unpredictability, generate a combat effect far beyond its size and scope.

Leif and his fellow 10th SFG personnel, including Captain John Hemingway, the son of the famous American author Ernest Hemingway, would convey their combat experiences – much of which was learned behind enemy lines as OSS agents during the Second World War and with frontline combat units during the Korean War – into formalised doctrine, training manuals and tactical lesson plans. Their lessons would not be limited to historical accounts of previous military achievements, but rather would place a new focus on an array of factors along the spectrum of war and the human psyche – physical, technical and psychological aspects of combat that could be taught, tested and refined, designed to create a lethal and dynamic instrument of war.

The instructors were also looking to the future at emerging technologies to anticipate how new strategies and technological developments could be harnessed and integrated into the special forces' toolkit of capabilities. The use of helicopters for troop insertion was recognized early on as an essential mode of conveyance, and the innovative use of SCUBA diving technologies for secret insertion or sabotage missions, as well as leading edge airborne technology, known as HALO (high altitude, low opening) parachuting and skydiving techniques using oxygen assist, were all new assets for the special forces to use and integrate into their operations manuals and training objectives.

One of the most important factors that the special forces leadership needed to develop was the psycho-sociological skills required to aid the Green Beret soldiers to win the hearts and minds of oppressed foreign populations to rally them to help fight their oppressors. This psychological aspect of their mission was essential to help create upheaval within an enemy regime and to promote and foster internal political and military dissension and eventual influence over electoral or revolutionary regime change. Their training also included the fundamentals of unobtrusive insertion into the enemy's vulnerable points and effective sabotage techniques of vital points, all of which was intended to create havoc within the enemy's society and promote uncertainty, fear and distrust amongst its population and the regime's soldiers. The theory suggested that ultimately, such activities would degrade both the political and military will and confidence and eventually lead to the enemy's defeat or the government's downfall.

In early 1953, the 10th SFG/Green Berets began to see their first combat assignments as individuals and as small special forces units deployed to Korea during the final stages of the war. Working with the United States Army regular force units as well as with the South Korean army and partisans, the United States Army Special Forces conducted operations behind enemy lines with remarkable success until the end of the war in July 1953. Intercepted enemy communications described encounters with these new United States Army Special Forces units as being decidedly unpleasant and costly. In addition, the enemy's assessment and estimation of the size of the American elite force being encountered were consistently reported as far larger than they were. Clearly, the United States Army Special Forces were having the desired impact on the battlefield.

* * *

In late October 1953, Leif received a troubling telegram from his father indicating that Frederik had been diagnosed with lung cancer and needed surgery. The following week, Leif returned to Copenhagen to help his father with his post-surgical convalescence. Upon arrival at the Royal Danish Veterans' Hospital, two days after his father's surgery, Leif found his father, much to his happy surprise, sitting up in his hospital bed chatting playfully with a nurse. His father had a large bandage wrapped around his chest and intravenous tubes in his arm but appeared to be in good spirits. Judging from his father's appearance, Leif assumed the operation had been a success. 'I see Father, you are well enough to flirt and regale the nurses with your charms', he joked. 'Ah, Leif, how wonderful for you to come!' exclaimed Frederik. The nurse smiled at Leif and assured Frederik she would return shortly with his medications and left father and son to themselves.

After gently embracing his father, Leif asked how he was feeling and what the prognosis was. Again, judging by his father's current demeanor, Leif was sure the news must surely be good.

'Jocom, I've always been honest with you, and I won't begin misleading you now.' Frederik continued,

> The surgery was over quickly, I mean, once the doctor opened up my chest and had a look at my tired, smoke-ridden lungs, they just sewed me back up – the cancer is everywhere. They tell me that there is nothing more they can do for me except supply me with painkillers to ease my discomfort – my time is nigh.

Leif was taken aback and stared speechlessly at his father. Frederick, in his stoic as ever nature, shrugged his shoulders, reached out his hand and placed it on his son's hand. 'I've had a good life, son', he said. 'There's nothing left for me here on earth; I will join your mother and sisters soon.'

On 6 March 1954, less than six months after his surgery, Frederik Christian Sørensen Bangsbøll succumbed to his condition. Leif, who was still stationed at Fort Bragg had returned to Denmark a month earlier to bid farewell, one last time to his father and to help, in his own way, usher his father and mentor into Odin's great hall of Valhalla.

Though devastated at the loss of his father, the one true compass of his life, Leif knew he had obligations, both professionally and personally that he needed to tend to – Leif knew his father would expect nothing less.

* * *

The Army Commander and the War Department, pleased with the capabilities of the first 1,000 special forces soldiers trained at the Special Forces Warfare Center (SFWC), authorized Colonel Bank to form the 77th SFG which would be manned with the next 1,000 graduates of the SFWC – trained under the watchful eye of Captain Bangsbøll. These elite troops of 77th SFG were immediately deployed to West Germany to bolster regular army troops facing the growing Soviet threat in central Europe.

As the newly trained troops of 77th SFG moved into central Europe, back at Fort Bragg, Captain Bangsbøll had ambitious plans to further the special forces capabilities. Always cognisant of the need to put into practice the application of new, developing special forces techniques while testing the security capabilities of existing and well-established defense facilities, Leif became the driving force within the Special Forces Warfare Center's evaluation team. Leif began to organize and run realistic exercises during which such training could be conducted, observed, evaluated and improved upon. The Special Forces' Warfare Center had been in operation nearly a year and Leif thought it was time to expand their practical training beyond the confines of the Fort Bragg training area.

Early one morning in April 1954, Captain Bangsbøll, in his role of special forces training coordinator and senior instructor, had an appointment with the commander of the Special Forces Warfare Center. After waiting a few minutes in the commander's outer office, Captain Bangsbøll was advised by the commander's adjutant that Colonel Bank was ready to see him. Coming to a halt at the office doorway, Captain Bangsbøll stomped his heavy jump boot down hard on the wooden floor and brought his right hand up in a smart, military salute. Looking up from his large oak desk, covered in papers and file jackets, many of which were marked secret, Bank smiled and gave a casual, half effort salute in return.

'Hello, Leif. What kind of trouble are you into now?' inquired Bank as he pushed back from his desk and came over to properly greet his old friend with a firm handshake. 'I haven't seen you around the headquarters much these past few weeks… what have you been up to?'

Leif replied,

> Sir, I've been spending most of my time with the new trainees out in the training area, the obstacle course, ordnance and firing range, and with the occasional parachute jump to keep the rust off my skills.

Bank shot back, 'You – The Danish Duke – get rusty? I doubt that very much, Leif!'

Leif smiled and asked, 'Sir, shall I get right to the point of my visit?'

'Why don't you Leif,…subtleties and protocol have never been your strong suit!' Bank retorted with a grin.

> Sir, I'd like your permission to take our training out to the real world… conduct some infiltration missions with mock sabotage training at one or two of the larger commercial and naval ports here on the east coast.

Leif continued, 'Our trainees need to practise their skills and test their capability outside of the Bragg training area, in more realistic environments.'

Leif outlined his plans in detail, demonstrating to his commander that he had thoroughly researched everything, including the state authorities that would need to be contacted in advance and the logistics support he would require to conduct such peacetime training in active seaports and vital installations. After considering the proposal for a moment, Bank looked his old friend straight in the eye and said, 'Approved. But don't expect me or Brigadier General Karlstad to come bail you out of jail if you get caught.' And with a wry smile, Leif replied,

> Don't worry, sir, you know that The Danish Duke never gets caught – and if he did, he would never divulge a word of the Warfare Center's or your involvement.

Leif saluted, and the two men shook hands and bid farewell. As Leif turned to leave, Bank slapped him on the back and shouted so his whole office staff could hear, 'Why do you get to have all the fun, while I'm stuck here behind this damn desk pushing papers?' Leif waited until he was down the hallway and out of sight – but still within earshot – to respond equally loudly, 'Because you're the damn colonel and I'm just a goddamn airborne soldier, sir!' Amused at first with Leif's response, Bank's suddenly took on a more serious tone as he looked over to his adjutant and said,

> See that I get some face time with the trainees tomorrow while they're out in the training area… I feel I'm losing touch with the real work that's going on around here.

Bank returned to his file-covered desk with a renewed motivation to get through this deluge of paperwork so he could get out and see his troops in action.

* * *

After several successful mock sabotage missions and training assaults on an electrical generating station in Raleigh, Norfolk Naval Base and the commercial port of Baltimore, in which small groups of United States Army Special Forces trainees used various clandestine techniques to gain entry, Captain Bangsbøll decided to demonstrate to his eager trainees an alternate approach to saboteur operations. He would show his trainees a more subtle, yet brazenly bold method of infiltration of a secure facility using no small measure of guile and effective subterfuge.

In order for Lieutenant Bangsbøll and the special forces to conduct such training on another federal agency's establishment, the proper, high-level authorities and coordination were arranged. Once that long and arduous administrative process was accomplished, Leif and one of his trainees proceeded to meet with the base commander and the port authority officer who were co-responsible for the Charleston Naval Base to ensure that approval of the planned security exercise was acknowledged, and the rules of engagement were understood. The 'why' was straightforward: to test the routine security protocols of the naval base to ensure that important naval resources were protected from possible enemy/communist saboteurs and to provide realistic training for the United States Army Special Forces. However, Captain Bangsbøll did not provide the base commander or port authority with any details of 'who, what, when or where' exactly the test would occur. Those facts would have to be learned the hard way. Now it was time to watch and enjoy how their plan would unveil itself. At the end of the day, with all the prearrangements in place and confirmed, Leif and his trainees headed back to Fort Bragg. Leif decided that they would execute the plan three weeks later. That would give him time to arrange for the appropriate documents to be forged and more importantly, give him time to convince his wife to participate in his clandestine scheme.

* * *

It was Thursday, 4 June 1954, a hot, humid and sunny afternoon in Charleston, South Carolina. The pretty, blonde 26-year-old woman from Raleigh, North Carolina, stepped into the prisoner's cell as instructed by the large, serious looking Military Police (MP) officer. The young homemaker, pretending to be a school teacher, had never seen a jail cell before, and her body flinched when the distinctive sound of heavy metal on metal resonated off the cement walls of the cell as the iron door clanged shut behind her. The jarring, metallic reverberation made her stomach turn.

Dorothy Bangsbøll scanned her surroundings: three gray cement walls, one with a small window about 8 feet off the floor protected by iron bars. The fourth wall was made of iron bars that ran floor to ceiling and contained the iron door that had just been shut and locked behind her. Dorothy, who had spent the last two hours under the blazing sun, walking on the hot steel decks of a naval destroyer moored in the dockyard, thought 'Well, at least it's cool in here.' As she surveyed her stark surroundings, she pondered her situation. A series of questions began to tumble through her mind as she reviewed the events of the past few hours. 'What have I got myself into?' Dorothy wondered or more appropriately, 'What has my husband got me into?' Then the more practical and analytical part of her brain took over.

> Where did I go wrong?' she speculated. 'Did someone find the bomb on the ship? Did I inadvertently say or do something that gave me away? It all seemed to be going so well. My request to get a tour of a navy ship here in Charleston Harbor was formally approved by the base commander thanks to the kind base public affairs officer. My escort officer seemed

very accommodating to my needs and did not seem suspicious of me. I'm sure they did not suspect anything was out of the ordinary – so why have I been arrested?

Dorothy sat down on the steel bench to think. The bench was cold and hard and was bolted to the floor in the holding cell, there in the Charleston Naval Base military police station. The Brig, as it is called in the navy, was staffed by MPs, known as Navy Shore Patrol, who despite their orders to apprehend this young school teacher as a possible saboteur, were polite and professional, offering her the privacy of her own cell and a cup of coffee while they waited for the provost marshal, the senior local MP officer, to arrive and begin the interrogation. And many questions needed to be answered.

In 1954, the naval dockyards, and the navy in general, were still almost exclusively a man's world, with few women aside from clerical office workers. Dorothy was quite sure that she was the first female prisoner to set foot inside the Brig. This fact – though she was proudly amused – brought Dorothy back to the real question at hand.

How do I get out of this mess? Surely Leif will explain the situation to the Navy Shore Patrol. He'll explain to them that it was just an exercise to test the navy's security. And yes, we planted a fake bomb on one of their ships and sort of blew it up, and now all those involved will be angry and embarrassed. But it was, after all, just a military exercise – a practical lesson to make them aware of their security vulnerabilities. The whole point of the exercise was to make America safer… right?

Dorothy began to go over in her mind the sequence of events that led her to this predicament. Her fake credentials as a high school history teacher from Raleigh, provided to her by her husband and co-conspirator, had been accepted at face value by the Charleston Naval Base public affairs officer, as well as the base security officer and even the base commander. In fact, Dorothy even had the admiral's signature on her visit request approval letter to prove it. Her story was that she was teaching tenth grade American history, and would, in a few weeks' time, be bringing her class to visit Fort Sumter, the site of the first salvos of the American Civil War, arguing that a tour of a modern navy ship might bring together nicely the experience of American Civil War history and the modern age navy for the students. The naval officials had accepted her story and fake credentials and began making arrangements for the class visit and Dorothy's pre-visit.

During today's pre-visit, Dorothy had learned some historical facts that she genuinely thought were interesting. She learned that the destroyer that she had toured, the USS *Conner*, had actually been built in Charleston in 1941 and was currently back alongside undergoing a 'refit' or overhaul. As such, there was only a skeleton naval crew onboard the *Conner*, along with a dozen or so civilian contractors; primarily engineers, mechanics and steamfitters conducting repairs. Dorothy also learned that the Charleston Naval Base currently employed over 8,000 civilians – far fewer than the 25,000 workers that were employed here to maintain many of the United States Navy and United States Merchant Navy ships during the war years of 1942 to 1945.

Dorothy's thoughts returned to her capture. She figured that she must have said or done something during that morning's pre-visit tour to raise their suspicions. But what it was, she was not sure. She recalled that when she had asked to use the restroom during the tour of the ship, the escort officer was exceedingly gallant and offered to stand outside 'the head [the naval term for toilet]' to ensure her privacy, as there were no female-designated restrooms aboard military ships. Armed with a pocketknife, a textbook sized package wrapped in brown paper and bound with electrical wire, and a small battery-operated alarm clock safely tucked into her handbag, Dorothy, the innocent looking high school teacher had excused herself from her escort. Once inside the restroom, she located and unscrewed a ventilation screen using the pocket knife her husband had given her and then placed the fake explosive device in the air ventilation duct, set the alarm clock timer and reattached the screen. When she emerged, the tour continued without interruption.

Dorothy realized that how she got caught was not important, but rather, it was the fact that she had been caught and was now in custody that was really the issue at hand. How could she explain to the police why she had placed a fake bomb aboard a United States Navy destroyer without implicating her husband and by extension, implicating the Special Forces' Warfare Center back at Fort Bragg?

Dorothy looked at her wristwatch and realized that the alarm clock was set to activate in just under thirty minutes. She made a pledge to herself that she would not tell them (the shore patrol officer or anyone else for that matter) anything until at least 1330 hours, at which time the fake bomb would have detonated – mission accomplished. 'I can hold out until then', she assured herself. 'Leif will come save me – he always does.'

Once she decided that she would not spill the beans on her co-conspirators – Leif and the four United States Army Special Forces trainees Leif had brought along to observe – Dorothy was content with going back over the day's events to see where she had mis-stepped. She and the escort officer had completed the tour of the *Conner* less than an hour ago. She had just called a taxi from the office at the main gate and planned to go back to the hotel located on the outskirts of Charleston where she was to meet up with her husband and the four trainees to brief them on how the fake bomb delivery went and discuss what she had learned about the naval base's security protocols. As she stood near the main gate of the naval base, a military jeep with the large, white letters 'SP' stenciled on the hood pulled up and stopped abruptly in front of her. Two burley Navy Shore Patrol MPs stepped out of the jeep to confront her and subsequently escorted her to the Brig.

Maybe someone had found the bomb she had planted on the ship. If the truth be told – the fake bomb. Or possibly she had said something that gave away her fake identity. Or perhaps someone from the navy department questioned why a high school teacher from Raleigh wanted a tour of the Charleston Naval Base, which might, in turn, have raised suspicions at the base that uncovered her ruse. She honestly did not know which, if any, of these possibilities were the true cause of her arrest.

In fact, Dorothy's mission had been executed with precision and without a single false step or questionable act on her part. An hour after her arrest, at precisely 14:30 hours, several sailors and a civilian steelworker aboard the *Conner*, designated DD-582, heard the sound of an alarm clock ringing. A few minutes later, after a brief search that traced the sound of the alarm to its source, a ship's crew member found the fake bomb located in the air vent in the lower deck toilet, adjacent to the engine room and fuel bunker of the ship.

The sabotage training mission was a complete success – from the viewpoint of the saboteurs. Though Dorothy had executed her task flawlessly, she had been apprehended because of an anonymous call that had been received by the Charleston Naval Base operator. According to the operator, the caller was a man with some sort of foreign accent who had indicated that a young blonde school teacher was part of a radical communist sympathiser organization and had on her person an explosive device that she intended to place onboard a ship in the Charleston Naval Base. The caller had hung up before the operator could ask any questions.

The caller with the foreign accent was Leif Bangsbøll – the young blonde woman's husband and the leader of this clandestine exercise that was unfolding in Charleston Naval Yard. Leif had complete confidence that his wife would be able to pull off the clandestine act of a saboteur with relative ease, which was why he had asked her to help him with this mission in the first place. Dorothy was an excellent actress, loved theatrics, but above all, she understood Leif's explanation of the importance of such training exercises – exercises that would identify vulnerabilities and ultimately save American lives. Over the years as a secret agent and special forces expert, Leif had become fascinated with the psychology of the subterfuge of his profession and was interested to see how Dorothy would react if she were caught by the authorities. That uncertainty about his wife's resolve intrigued Leif and was the main reason for his last minute amendment to the plan. He also considered that allowing Dorothy – the high school teacher/imposter/saboteur – to be caught would provide a modicum of face-saving success for the security personnel of the naval base while allowing Leif to get a sense of just how tough and resourceful his wife really was when confronted by real police who were pissed off at her brazen and successful intrusion into their area of responsibility. It seemed like a win-win situation to Leif: he and his trainees would win by completing an effective infiltration of a secure and vital point of the United States Department of Defense; the naval yard security personnel would learn a good lesson about their vulnerability while still getting credit for capturing the bad guy (gal); Dorothy would get another feather in her cap as an effective agent (albeit an agent that had to spend some time incarcerated for her efforts); and finally, Leif would get to learn a bit more about his lovely bride's mental agility, maybe even get a glimpse of those inner strengths one has, but that often remain unseen until a person finds themself in a suddenly stressful situation… the type of skills that are essential in the special forces line of work.

For two hours the provost marshal sat across from his young, blonde, communist captive, repeatedly asking questions pertaining to her identity and her reason for being on the Charleston Naval Base property. And for two hours, his prisoner assured him that she was a schoolteacher, repeatedly referring to the letter authorizing her presence on the installation. Midway through the interrogation, which was going nowhere, a Navy Shore Patrol officer knocked on the interview room door and placed what appeared to be a time bomb on the desk in front of his boss. Initially startled at the sudden appearance of an explosive device, the provost marshal quickly realized that it was a fake. The six sticks of dynamite were, in fact, 1 inch dowels of wood, 8 inches long, which had been painted red. The wires wrapping around the dynamite were just that, wrapped around the red wooden dowels, securing a standard, battery operated alarm clock to the device. 'Sir, this was found with the alarm going off aboard the destroyer *Conner*.' The provost marshal brought his attention back to his prisoner and asked for an explanation. The schoolteacher come prisoner looked at the device and said, 'Oh my!' and nothing more. Realizing that further inquiries with this suspect would be fruitless, the provost marshal got up from the table. 'Miss', he said, 'I don't know what would possess you to go to all the trouble to access this military facility and plant a fake bomb on a war ship, but what I do know is that you've committed a federal offence, and tomorrow, I'll be speaking with the FBI.' The provost marshal left the interrogation room, and Dorothy was escorted by a Navy Shore Patrol officer back to her cell. There she would remain overnight.

The morning after the successful sabotage training mission, Captain Bangsbøll, wearing his Class A dress uniform, entered the provost marshal's office at Charleston Naval Base. He was accompanied by the Charleston Naval Base Commander, also wearing his Class A uniform and the Director of the Charleston Port Authority in a business suit. At first the provost marshal looked bewildered at the unexpected presence of two senior authorities in his chain of command, standing in his office. Without much discussion, the Charleston Port Authority director handed him the letter signed by the governor of the state of South Carolina, which indicated that a Mrs Dorothy J. Bangsbøll of Fort Bragg, North Carolina, was part of an authorised security evaluation team working under the joint authority of both North and South Carolina's state attorney general's office and the War Department. The 'light went on', and the provost marshal immediately realized something significant had just transpired on his watch. Without hesitation, the base commander signed the release form for the prisoner and handed it back to the provost marshal who stood speechless, feeling violated and vulnerable. Stumbling as he stated, 'I'll… I'll have the prisoner, ah …,' looking back down at the letter, 'umh… Mrs Bangsbøll brought out immediately, sir.' This was the only sensible thing the provost marshal could think to say before he walked out of his office to arrange the release of his prisoner. Five minutes later, Dorothy was free and walked out of the MP station, bracketed by her three saviors – only one of whom was mildly nervous about her state of mind over her overnight stay in the Brig.

Dorothy had spent an afternoon and evening in a navy jail cell under suspicion of having committed a federal offense – a premeditated act of sabotage against a United States Federal Defense establishment facility; she was released by the governor's orders, and hand delivered by the two most senior men at Charleston Naval Base into the custody of one of the instructors from the Special Forces Warfare Center. According to the provost marshal, Dorothy gave him and his interrogators absolutely no information other than that of her cover story. She maintained that she was a tenth grade history teacher from Raleigh, North Carolina. She appeared calm and collected and not too concerned about her predicament, despite threats of a longer prison term if she did not cooperate. Dorothy did not cooperate.

In response to the successful mock sabotage attack on the base he was charged to protect, the provost marshal thoroughly examined the chain of events that had unfolded on 5 June 1954. He learned, among other things, that being unfamiliar with security protocols concerning a bomb threat notification call, the naval base operator/receptionist had sought out her supervisor for guidance. However, her supervisor was on lunch at the time, which further delayed the security response. By the time the bomb threat information reached the Navy Shore Patrol office and subsequently the commander, it was too late to initiate a search of the *Conner* let alone warn the crew and civilian workers aboard the vessel. A report from the duty officer aboard the *Conner* notifying the Navy Shore Patrol of the presence of the fake explosive device – after it had 'detonated' – had already been received. Had it been a real bomb, the damage to the ship and the injuries inflicted would have been significant. The lessons learned by the security personnel and the commander were clear: improvements to the security of the naval base had to be made – and quickly. The Department of the Navy and the Department of Defense were also put on notice that security measures currently in place across the country needed to be reviewed at all sensitive or vital military and industrial sites.

Due to the secretive nature of their work, the United States Army Special Forces did not advertise their activities, be they successes or failures. However, as a result of her participation in the field exercise, Dorothy Bangsbøll received the following letter from 10th SFG, Special Forces Warfare Center:

Mrs Dorothy J. Bangsbøll
211 Slagel Place
Wherry Housing Project
Fort Bragg, North Carolina

10 June 1954

Dear Mrs Bangsbøll,
On behalf of the members of the 10th Special Forces Group Airborne who participated in the important, covert field exercise during the period 3–5 June 1954, I wish to extend my sincere thanks and appreciation for your cooperation, generosity and skills.

By placing your services at our disposal, you added immeasurably to not only the successes but the realism of our field training, from which our trainees gained many valuable insights into the nature of special operations.

Again, please accept my sincere appreciation for your wholehearted assistance and cooperation in this unique and valuable training exercise.

De Oppresso Liber.

Robert L. Milan
Lieutenant Colonel, Infantry Commanding

Exactly how the post-incarceration reunion went between Dorothy and Leif and the conversations thereafter remains their secret. One can assume that their exchange was quite dynamic and colorful in nature but have come to understand over the years through Dorothy's account of those events in Charleston became more focused on the successful execution of an important security training mission and how fun it was to be involved in such a scheme and less about Leif's treachery. However, as Dorothy retold the story, it was always evident in Leif's eyes just how proud he was of Dorothy for not only her willingness to participate in such a challenging, clandestine training mission, but in her cool, calm execution of her role in the mission and her wonderful ability to put on the charm and act her way through any tight situation. One thing is certain, the evening of her release from jail, Leif took Dorothy out for an expensive dinner at one of the nicest restaurants in Charleston. The results of that bold training mission not only gave all those involved an appreciation for Dorothy's character, but it also demonstrated to the United States Army Special Forces trainees and instructors that they should not limit their mission planning efforts to standard military practices and that they should keep an open mind to less orthodox methods of achieving their mission objectives.

* * *

The remainder of Leif's tour with 10th SFG/Green Berets was spent running exercises and evaluating unit readiness while completing hundreds of training parachute jumps from a variety of fixed-wing and rotary-wing aircraft. On one particular day, Leif got in six training jumps from a helicopter – a divisional record that stood for many years. During this time at Fort Bragg, he also earned his Master Parachutist Wings – a demanding and highly coveted achievement, especially for a 35-year-old. The physical demands of such airborne operations dictated that the strength, stamina and flexibility of youth were essential assets for success. It appears that no one ever told Leif this fact.

Colonel Bank, as the architect and inspiration for the United States Army Special Forces, would ultimately be recognized for his unparalleled leadership in this effort, and be recognized by a Congressional Resolution that named him the 'Father of Special Forces'.

Leif was immensely proud of his affiliation with the United States Army Special Forces and though modest to a fault, he truly loved the notion that he and his Green Beret colleagues were affectionately known within the United States armed forces as 'America's Best'. Today, owing to the groundbreaking work, skills, dedication and leadership of warriors of the likes of Colonel Bank, Lieutenant Colonels Volckmann and Fertig, as well as Leif Bangsbøll himself, this focal point of United States special forces expertise remains strong and is a critical component within the United States Department of War's inventory of capabilities.

Chapter 9

The Return of Mata Hari

'Drama is very important in life:
You have to come on with a bang.
You never want to go out with a whimper.'

Julia Child,
Chef and former OSS employee

Dieter Gruber, the former Wehrmacht sergeant, stood in the middle of the hillside path, halfway up the slope, smoking another cigarette. His gaze was fixed on the far side slope of a valley freshly covered in a blanket of pristine snow. From his vantage point he could see the distant end of the wide pasture where the dirt road he stood upon, used mostly to shepherd cattle from one pasture to another, entered the thick Bavarian forest. In the distance he could hear the chimes of a church bell echoing softly through the pastoral valley. He inhaled deeply and quietly lamented to himself '*wunderbar* [wonderful]'. Then his thoughts turned to the reason he was there: this is where the American armored column is expected to emerge and cross into the Fulda Valley.

The Fulda gap, as it was known by military personnel in Europe, was one of the most likely approach routes of a Soviet invasion force into the heart of West Germany. As such, NATO forces had taken to conducting large scale training exercises in this area to ensure their personnel were familiar with the Fulda Valley's terrain. 'Know your battle space.' Dieter tossed the nearly spent cigarette onto the snowy ground, where it joined the three cigarette butts that he had consumed previously. He then walked back down the road 100 yards towards the car. The Bangsbøll family car – an Opel Sedan – remained awkwardly positioned in the ditch at the intersection of two dirt roads below, more like wide, well-worn paths than roads in reality. An hour earlier, Dieter had watched while his female companion maneuvered the car slowly, but purposefully, into the ditch. It had snowed several inches the previous night, which allowed the car to slide down easily without much effort on the part of its driver. The driver, a young woman, still sat behind the steering wheel. She, too, was waiting and looking towards the far side of the valley. She was anxious but outwardly calm.

From his current vantage point, Dieter could see only her profile: the woman wore a bright red chiffon scarf over her blonde hair, secured under her chin with a bow. She was smoking a cigarette as well, but hers was held in a stylish 6-inch-long, ebony cigarette holder with silver trim. Dieter thought, 'She looks like a Hollywood actress – a movie star.' The downward sloping angle of the car allowed the woman to sit comfortably in the driver's seat and stretch out her legs onto the front passenger seat. She was careful not to allow her stylish boar hide hiking boots to soil the upholstery. She wore slim black ski pants that disappeared into the top of her hiking boots, and a white Bavarian-style jacket with colorful embroidered trim along its upturned collar and sleeve cuffs. The jacket had intricately designed deer antler buttons secured by fine leather cord which fastened through leather loops. Her husband had recently bought her this traditional German outfit during a family outing to Garmisch-Partenkirchen. Garmisch, as it is known to locals, is a beautiful Tyrolean town at the foot of the spectacular Zugspitze mountain and just an hour's drive through the Bavarian Alps from the Bangsbøll home at the Bad Tölz Kaserne.

The Bavarian sky was deep blue, and the eastern horizon was glowing beautifully orange behind the mountain peaks as the new day was dawning. The mountain air was cool and damp. As Dieter approached the car, the woman in the front seat pronounced, 'Don't you just love the smell of these mountain pastures, Dieter?' 'Frau Bangsbøll', Dieter replied in a sarcastic tone, 'it is just cow manure.'

'Yes and isn't it wonderful though!' replied Dorothy.

Dieter now stood beside the car and asked, 'Frau Bangsbøll, are you sure this is where your husband wanted us to wait?'

'Yes, Dieter', Dorothy replied, 'this intersection of mountain roads is exactly where Leif showed me to put the car into the ditch and wait for the convoy to pass.'

'Yes, of course, forgive me for questioning you or your husband's plan.'

From where they had positioned themselves, they could both clearly see the far side of the pasture where the winding dirt road disappeared into the forest and from where the American armored column was expected to emerge. They just had to be patient and wait. Based upon Leif's pre-NATO exercise intelligence gathering, his tactical threat assessment and his personal intuition – gut feelings, he expected an American armored column – consisting of 80 to 100 tanks, armored personnel carriers and artillery pieces were expected to pass. This armored column, designated as the Red Force, or Enemy Force – represented attacking Soviet forces. Dorothy's husband, Captain Leif Bangsbøll, the 77th SFG intelligence officer, had surmised through his own intelligence gathering network, that the Red Force had four probable transit routes into the massive Grafenwöhr military training area, one of NATO's largest live fire training areas in central Europe. This mountain approach was far more challenging to maneuver the wide, heavy armored vehicles than the other three possible access points to the vast training area, all of which were further north from this location. Leif's instincts had told him, 'This is the route the enemy would take – it's the route I would take.' And this is the theory that he had emphasized to his special forces intelligence staff in the weeks preceding the exercise commencement.

Dieter and Dorothy, meanwhile, watched, listened and waited. A few minutes later, using only his functional right hand, Dieter pulled a cigarette case from his left breast pocket, adeptly opened it, and offered Dorothy another cigarette. She politely took two and said, '*Danke* [Thank you]'.

Dieter closed the case, returned it to his pocket and withdrew a silver lighter; with an agile hand he ignited it and carefully lit the two cigarettes now held between Dorothy's lips. Dorothy inhaled to ensure they were lit, then handed one back to Dieter with a smile and inserted the other into her cigarette holder. Dieter nodded his appreciation, noticing a smudge of red lipstick adorning his cigarette, then took a drag and inhaled the American tobacco deeply. Since the end of the Second World War, Dieter had learned to enjoy many things American – their jazz music, their Bourbon, but most of all, their cigarettes.

Dieter Gruber was the proud owner of a *Gasthof* [restaurant] in Bad Tölz that Leif and Dorothy had happened upon soon after moving to the quaint German town and of which they were now regular patrons. The restaurant was located close to the United States Army base where Leif and Dorothy lived with their young family. It was on Leif and Dorothy's fourth or fifth dinner with their four children at Dieter's *Gasthof* that they had learned that Sergeant Dieter Gruber had been a member of a Panzergrenadier division and part of the 4th Panzer Army, and that he had lost his left arm during the war. His unit had faced the ferocity of the Russian army on the Eastern Front and suffered tremendous losses. He had been severely wounded in September 1943, shortly after the infamous and bloody Battle of Kursk – the largest tank battle in history. Dieter considered himself extremely fortunate to have survived the carnage of the ill-fated war with only the loss of an arm. Months later, after recovering from his injuries, and then with only one arm, he had been reassigned to a homeland defense unit as part of the Volkssturm national militia and was sent to a unit that had been ordered to defend Munich. The one-armed sergeant would teach the 14- and 15-year-old boys and aging old men how to handle weapons and how to defend their country in a time of utter madness and unadulterated brutality. Dieter knew the war was lost, but much of Germany and the German leadership were in a state of denial. But he continued to do his duty to the best of his abilities. When Munich was liberated by the United States Army, Dieter surrendered his small band of misfit soldiers and was treated humanely by his captors. He was thankful that he had not be sent to defend Berlin in the final days of the war – he would probably be dead or, worse yet, still rotting in a Russian gulag somewhere in Siberia. He had fought for the Fatherland because it was his duty. He was not a Nazi and reviled those who were. As a result, he was always polite to Americans and the other Allied soldiers who occupied his country – out of respect, not out of humiliation or fear. He was a proud and honest man. When he first met him, Leif immediately saw these qualities in Dieter and admired him for it. The fact that his kitchen produced an exquisite array of traditional Bavarian food, including Leif's favorite – *wiener schnitzel* – also made Leif fond of him. Dorothy thought he was a charming man who ran a wonderful restaurant.

As he stood beside the immobile car, Dieter noticed that in this early morning light, the dark green Bavarian jacket he wore was almost the same hue as his former Wehrmacht uniform. His jacket's left sleeve was neatly folded under and had been securely stitched by his wife to keep the sleeve in place and out of the way. Now, Dieter stood in the tranquil morning hours on the expanses of a wide Bavarian valley, assisting a young Canadian woman, who was playing espionage for her American army officer husband. This unanticipated foray into a NATO exercise was a welcome relief from the day-to-day labors of running the restaurant and brought back memories of his military service. Some fond memories but most were unpleasant and suppressed deep-down in his soul.

Leif and Dorothy, along with their four children, ranging in age from 1 to 7, had been posted from Fort Bragg, and Leif's Special Forces Training Center assignment to Bad Tölz, Germany, in summer 1956. Assigned to 77th SFG under Colonel William Ekman, where Leif's unique combat experience and recent affiliation with the heart and soul of the United States Army Special Forces at Fort Bragg were ideal for the frontline combat units facing and deterring the ominous Soviet threat. The 77th SFG had deployed from Fort Bragg to Bad Tölz as a result of violent uprisings in East Germany in 1953, which had been brutally crushed by Soviet forces. The Bad Tölz location put the elite combat unit in a better position to respond rapidly should the Russians decide to invade West Germany or any other European NATO country. The 77th SFG was trained and prepared to conduct unconventional warfare, special reconnaissance and counterinsurgency operations against their aggressive, battle-ready foe. As the brigade's intelligence officer, Leif brought his extensive combat experience and a vibrant enthusiasm, which included unabashedly using all resources at his disposal to improve his unit's operational readiness. To Leif, that meant involving not only his wife and mother of his four young children in a large-scale NATO military exercise, but also the services of a former Second World War German soldier as a special agent for 77th SFG. Not surprisingly, Leif's favorite Danish proverb was: 'The Gods favor the bold.'

Dorothy was aware of her husband's unique military skills and Leif, in return, knew that Dorothy could be relied upon to remain composed in any challenging situation – she could be the consummate actress when needed. That is why he had asked her to play a major role in this clandestine mission. Their adventures in Japan – when Dorothy had been rescued by an American armored cavalry unit when she and her faithful houseboy, Huroshi, got their car stuck in a rice paddy – was the inspiration for today's Bavarian adventure with 77th SFG. Recalling how willing the American 5th Cavalry Regiment tank convoy had been to assist a pretty young lady in distress a the side of the road in Japan, Leif arranged to have Dorothy and their new friend, Dieter, get the Bangsbøll family car stuck in a ditch along a German country road, a road that Leif surmised would be used by the enemy Red Force at any moment. 'No red-blooded soldier could resist rescuing a beautiful young lady in distress?' thought Leif.

Dorothy heard the sound first. It seemed to be muffled by the snow blanketing the valley, but she knew she had heard something unnatural in this beautiful Bavarian setting. And whatever it was, it was approaching them. She leaned forward and locked her gaze on the far hillside where the valley road entered the forest and where they anticipated the convoy would appear. Dieter, whose hearing was marred from the damage caused by the prolonged auditory assault of combat, did not hear it, but noticed Dorothy's change in demeanor. He looked and listened intently at the same spot Dorothy now stared. The former Panzergrenadier soldier felt the unmistakable vibrations of tanks on the move, but then, despite the passage of years and the auditory damage he had suffered, he heard it too: the rumbling sounds of metal tracks turning on metal wheels and sprockets and of squeaking axles gave away the approaching armored vehicles. It was unmistakable, and it momentarily and quite without warning shot a surge of excitement through his body. But just as suddenly, the sounds brought back frightening memories of the ravages of war. Dieter flinched and shook his head to clear his mind of those dark thoughts.

Two minutes later, the lead American combat tank, the M-47 Patton, at the head of a long, armored column emerged from the forest on the far side of the valley. Five minutes later the first tank had reached the intersection where the Bangsbøll family car lay partially in the ditch and partially blocking the road. The lead tank stopped abruptly as did the succession of tanks and armored vehicles, which now stretched out across the valley floor. The turret hatch opened, and the crew commander extracted himself, jumping to the ground, and approached Dorothy and Dieter who now both stood beside the stricken car. Assuming this was a German couple, possibly a father and daughter, the United States Army captain instinctively directed his first question in English towards the man. 'Good morning', he said, 'I'm Captain Stedman. What seems to be the problem here?' Not waiting for a reply, he continued in passable German, '*Was ist los*? [What's going on?]'. He then made an associated gesture with his gloved hands, palms up. Immediately Dorothy stepped forward and introduced herself as the dependant wife of Captain Leif Bangsbøll, United States Army, who was stationed in nearby Bad Tölz. She handed over her United States Army-issued dependant ID card. As the captain's eyes scanned over the laminated document, Dorothy continued.

> I believe this gentleman is named Peter Grudder or Grupper, I'm really not sure. I think he's the farmer who owns this land – he does not seem to speak English.

Without being asked, Dorothy continued to describe her situation. 'I drove out here this morning to paint some landscapes and take photographs of these beautiful mountains…' gesturing towards the box of art supplies and camera bag in the back seat of the car, '…and was marvelling at the beauty of this valley, but not paying attention to the road, when my car slid into this ditch.' She then added, 'The snow is very slick, it could have happened to anyone.' Dorothy then continued, 'This gentleman, just a moment ago came along to assist, but as you can see, I've got my husband's car pretty much stuck and probably ruined.'

At that, and as if on cue, Dorothy's eyes began to well up and tears began to trickle down her cheeks. The captain craned his neck to see the front end of the car. 'Now, now, ma'am', he reassured her, 'you're lucky. It doesn't look like you've damaged the car at all!'

'Oh, really?' feigned Dorthy in her reply. 'Thank goodness! Otherwise, my husband would be furious with me if I damaged it.'

'Don't worry ma'am we'll get your car outta there in no time and your husband will be none the wiser.'

Then, to the surprise of both Dorothy and Dieter, the captain looked to Dieter – 'the farmer' – and said, 'Do you have a tractor to pull this car out of the ditch?' Pretending that he could not understand English, Dieter shrugged his shoulders and replied to the soldier, '*Ich kann dich nicht verstehen* [I cannot understand you]' and threw his one good arm up in frustration.

Dieter then turned and walked away in the direction of the farmhouse in the distance – 'his' farmhouse, while waving his hand above his head in feigned frustration. Dorothy turned her back on the young officer, bowed her head, and began to quietly sob into her handkerchief, saying,

'He's not going to help.' The young captain looked back and forth between the visibly upset woman, the car in the ditch, the farmer walking away and his immobile tank column.

Ten minutes later, now with an audience of twenty or so participating and onlooking United States soldiers from the armored column, the captain's 44-ton tank easily pulled the light Opel out of the ditch. Thrilled that at her rescue, Dorothy insisted on getting the names of the tank crew members who had orchestrated the vehicle recovery. She pulled a notepad from her purse and the naïve soldiers sprang forth with all the details. Dorothy wrote down as much information as possible. 'And who should I address my thank-you letter to?' inquired Dorothy innocently. After obtaining the name of the armored unit and its home location, along with the name and rank of its COs, Dorothy pulled out Leif's Kodak Rangefinder from the camera bag in the car and began to have photographs taken of herself with her rescuers, their armored equipment in the background. Acknowledging that they had an important time schedule to keep, the soldiers promptly remounted their M47 tanks and M113 armored personnel carriers and trucks towing artillery pieces and rumbled past, one after another. As they did, the young Canadian-American woman they had just rescued waved enthusiastically and continued taking photographs of them passing by – click, click, click.

No sooner had the armored column disappeared from view than Dieter came running back up the sloping path to the four-way intersection where Dorothy stood beside her car. Both of them sported wide grins. Overtaken by the excitement of the moment, Dorothy threw herself into Dieter. His one, strong, right arm grasped her about the waist, and they spun around 360° with joy and relief at the success of their mission. Now, with her two, stylish Bavarian Boar-hide boots back on the ground and with adrenaline rushing through her veins, Dorothy said, 'Quickly, Dieter! We must get my notes and this film to my husband as soon as we can!'

When all was said and done, Dorothy and Dieter had dutifully recorded the number of Red Force tanks, APCs, trucks and artillery pieces in the convoy, in addition to their direction of travel – and they had the photographs to prove it. With this invaluable intelligence in hand, 77th SFG's intelligence officer reported to the Blue Force commander, in great detail, the movements of the large enemy Red Force through the Bavarian countryside approaching the Grafenwöhr training area. The information was received in time for their Blue Force commander to take the necessary counter-maneuver action to repel the Red Force just as it began to maneuver itself into position in the training ground. This small but critical clandestine intelligence gathering mission during this large-scale military exercise earned both Leif and Dorothy the admiration of many colleagues within the Blue Force and in 77th SFG, as well as the distain of a few armored officers, namely the Red Force convoy commander and the CO of the armored battalion that had been duped along the Bavarian roadside by a young woman and a former Wehrmacht sergeant. Leif's teachable moment from that experience for his special forces troops and anyone else who cared to learn, was to

> expect the unexpected, use those resources at your disposal to the maximum extent possible, and think beyond the imposed restrictions of a given situation. Be bold. And finally, if you ever come across a young, blonde woman stranded on the roadside – beware! Looks can be deceiving.

* * *

A week later, after the NATO exercise was over, Leif returned to Bad Tölz. Upon his arrival at their married quarters apartment, Leif found Dorothy feeding supper to their four children. As their father entered the apartment, the three oldest children rushed from the kitchen table and jumped into their father's waiting, loving arms shouting 'Daddy! Daddy!' Once the commotion was over, Dorothy stepped in a gave her husband a kiss. 'Welcome home, dear.' Leif replied with, 'It's good to be home, honey. How's my Mata Hari doing?' They smiled and kissed again – life was good in the Bangsbøll home. As Leif walked down the hall towards their bedroom and the hot shower he longed for, he made a detour into the kitchen to give his (at that time) youngest son, Mark, now just over 1 year old and sitting in a highchair, a kiss on his head. With his combat jacket already off and slung over his shoulder, Leif entered the bedroom and called back to Dorothy,

> Dottie, do you think you could get us a babysitter for a few hours tonight so we can go down to have a drink at Heir Gruber's? I think I owe you two a beer!

The Bangsbøll family's first year in Bad Tölz in Germany was wonderfully enjoyable and interesting as the children adapted to the international, on base school system and explored their new, exciting European surroundings. However, the following year, growing friction between NATO and the Warsaw Pact alliance stemming from Soviet President Nikita Khrushchev's threats to close Berlin to the United States, Britain and France created a new focus on NATO's ability to deter the Warsaw Pact threat, which made life more stressful, especially for those standing to in the defence of Western Europe. At that time, a unique opening for an Army Liaison Officer (ALO) was created with a frontline USAF unit at the 66th Tactical Recognisance Wing, stationed at Sembach Air Base in West Germany. The wing commander thought Leif was ideally suited for this assignment, as the recent rotation of pilots had seen a dramatic decrease in operational experience.

As a result, in June 1956, Leif and Dorothy packed up the family and moved 80 miles north from the Bad Tölz Kaserne to Sembach Air Base, near the beautiful town of Kaiserslautern. The Bangsbøll clan immediately fell in love with Sembach and their new air force friends. Their new neighbourhood was full of young American military families and the skies overhead were full of loud, fast moving fighter jets. In the apartment below the Bangsbølls were fellow 302nd Tactical Recconaissance Squadron (TRS) member and soon to be best friends, Captain Audrey 'Rabbit' Hare and his lovely wife Virginia 'Ginny' and their three children: daughter, Bunni, son, Allen, and daughter, Rhonda, ranging from 8 weeks to 4 years old. With the new-found air force association and camaraderie, particularly with the Hare, Breedlove and Zartman families, the Bangsbølls' recent assignments at Bad Tölz and even Fort Bragg were quickly fading to distant but fond memories.

Chapter 10

The Danish Duke and Rabbit

'Screw your courage to the sticking point and we'll not fail.'
William Shakespeare, *Macbeth*

The Allison J33-A-35 turbojet engine screamed with ear shattering and bone rattling intensity that shook the aircraft to its core. As the engine spewed out over 5,000 pounds of thrust, a surge of adrenaline pulsed through the pilot's veins, creating a mixture of sensations. Experiencing both exhilaration and defiance, as well as a modest degree of fear induced by self-preservation instincts, the American aviator jammed the aircraft's throttle to the wall – maximum power!

The aircraft was in a rapid, steep decent. The structural and engine specifications of the Lockheed T-33 Shooting Star, a tactical fighter currently being used in a photograph reconnaissance capacity, were approaching their design limits. Like a thoroughbred racehorse that will run until its heart bursts if its rider does not hold back the reigns, the aircraft was at the mercy of its pilot and both the engineering limitations and the aerodynamic forces of nature being acted on it. Just as the adrenaline surges through the endocrine system of the pilot and the racehorse, the jet fuel, air intakes and the hydraulic fluids feed the aircraft with the necessities of life. The exhilaration of the race overrides the defiance of the creature's physical limitations. With a maximum designed speed of 520 knots or 600 miles per hour, this Shooting Star was now traveling at 655 miles per hour and accelerating in an almost vertical dive. Departing their original, planned cruise and photograph reconnaissance mission altitude of 10,000 feet, their current rate of descent of 500 feet per second gave Captain Audrey Hare, the aircraft's pilot (call sign Rabbit) about ten seconds to live if his aircraft did not pull out of the dive.

Thirty seconds earlier, Rabbit, the fighter pilot, and his passenger/observer Captain Leif Bangsbøll, the squadron's army liaison officer (ALO) – call sign: The Danish Duke had been cruising straight and level at 10,000 feet at 250 knots – just under 300 miles per hour. They had been flying just below the cloud ceiling with all ten of the aircraft's high-resolution reconnaissance cameras running, ten photographs being taken every second. Both men were members of the 302nd Tactical Reconnaissance Squadron (TRS), which was part of 66th Tactical Reconnaissance Wing, stationed out of Sembach Air Base, located near Kaiserslautern, West Germany. That morning, they were flying a routine, yet always risky, photograph reconnaissance mission along, and at times, several miles over, the border above communist East Germany. The 302nd TRS was outfitted with fifteen RF-84-F tactical reconnaissance fighters, known as the Thunderflash, which were single seat aircraft. However, that morning's mission required a pilot and an observer and as such, Captain Hare had been assigned one of 66th Tactical Reconnaissance Wing's four T-33 Shooting Star fighter reconnaissance aircraft, affectionately referred to as the T-Bird, which were dual-seat aircraft and used for training and special operations missions. Today's mission was both. The T-Bird was a subsonic jet whose design was based on the specifications of the F-80 Shooting Star, the first American, mass produced, frontline fighter aircraft.

Their mission, on that December morning in 1956, was designed to give the squadron's ALO the opportunity to observe a subtle, not overt penetration reconnaissance mission over hostile territory and the associated aviation protocols and photo reconnaissance procedures. It was also an opportunity for the ALO to experience the physical and mental stressors that the pilots regularly endured as part of flying tactical reconnaissance missions. That morning, they were flying straight and level over enemy territory, photographing Soviet and East German troop activity and military installations. Their pre-planned mission route vectored them across the south-east border of East Germany, over the region called Karl-Marx-Stadt (modern day Chemnitz), adjacent to the Czechoslovakian boarder. For years these type of USAAF/NATO tactical reconnaissance missions had been relatively routine in nature. Juxtaposing the technically superior American aircraft against the inferior aircraft in the Soviet Air Force. However, during the past few years, soviet radar, communications, and tactical aircraft technologies had begun to close the capability gap with the Americans and their NATO allies.

On this day, two new, state of the art Soviet Mikoyan-Gurevich MiG 17, fighter interceptors, known by the NATO identifier as Frescos, had just bounced – intercepted the slower, less maneuverable American T-33. Captain 'Rabbit' Hare, a consummate professional, combat hardened aviator and veteran of the Second World War and the Korean War, was not startled by the sudden appearance of two hostile fighter interceptors. The two enemy fighters had appeared several hundred yards off and slightly behind his starboard wing, descending out of the heavy, gray cloud cover that is prevalent in central Europe in autumn. The possibility of being intercepted by enemy aircraft was an assumption of every American pilot's pre-mission plan, especially when operating this close to the East German border. Rabbit was prepared and gave a simple but absolutely clear warning to his back-seater. 'BANDITS – FOUR O'CLOCK, LEVEL – EVASIVE ACTION!'

Even though Leif was a former pilot himself, he did not have time to mentally process the transmission coming through his helmet's headphones. Instinctively, he turned his head to the right towards the unseen threat when the T-33 abruptly nosed up into the protection of the thick gray clouds. Now invisible to the two MiGs, Rabbit waited in the dense clouds for ten seconds, predicting that the MIGs would follow him and would expect him to appear above the cloud layer momentarily. After ten seconds, streaking blindly through the cloud bank, Rabbit jerked the control stick violently to the left and forward, rolling the nose of the aircraft down and accelerating aggressively. Reappearing back under the cloud cover, he began racing towards the earth in the hopes that his maneuver would trick the MiGs long enough that if they followed in the steep dive down, his aircraft might create enough distance from the Russians and be visually lost from view in the background of the green and brown patchwork of the countryside below them.

As expected, the two MiGs had followed the American aircraft up into the clouds. The subsequent evasive maneuver by the American aircraft probably would have been successful had the Soviet pilot in the lead aircraft not noticed a flash of movement and color in the cloud bank as the right auxiliary full tank on the wing tip of the American T-33 Shooting Star, which was painted red, sliced through the clouds as the aircraft rolled to the left and gave the American's position away. Realizing the American pilot's intentions to evade them by sneaking back under the cloud cover, the two Soviet MiGs quickly followed suit, and rolled left and dove back under the clouds in hot pursuit of the American intruder.

The sudden roll and onslaught of negative G-force made every loose item in the T-33's cockpit take on a life of its own. Leif's map, notepad and grease pencil flew out of his lap and stuck to the Plexiglas canopy above him as the aircraft plummeted towards earth. His oxygen mask hose stretched up and to the right as the aircraft moved at an incredible rate down and to the left. Pressed back into his ejection seat by the invisible force, which felt as if a giant hand was pulling him back into his seat, Leif's heart rate climbed rapidly, and he struggled to breathe as his lungs compressed with the increasing G-forces being exerted on his body. The blood rushed to his upper extremities, and he felt as if his head and helmet might explode.

Within seconds, the American with the two Soviet aircraft in pursuit had broken through the lower level of the clouds in a near vertical dive. The American aircraft was now only 8,000 feet above the rolling green hills of East Germany with the two Soviet MiGs closing-in. Leif craned his neck to the right to look for their pursuers. In a calm, clear voice Leif advised the pilot, 'TWO BOGGIES STILL ON OUR TAIL – 500 HUNDRED YARDS AND CLOSING.' Several seconds passed with only the sounds of their labored breathing coming through their earphones, adding to the background noise of the screaming jet engine. Ack" [acknowledged] came Rabbit's reply…. "We'll loose them when we pull out of this dive - hold on Duke. Directly in front and below them, the East-German villages and their houses splayed out before them were getting larger and larger with each passing second. The altimeter was spinning down… 4,000… 3,500… 3,000… 2,500… 2,000… Instinctively, and as a former pilot, Leif wanted to shout a warning to his friend and colleague, but stifled the reflex, knowing that Rabbit was a tremendously experienced fighter pilot, and did not need the frantic advice of a back seater, let alone a lowly army officer, during a mid-air crisis in a fighter aircraft.

A second later, as The Danish Duke closed his eyes for the impending and surely lethal impact of their machine with the German countryside, an incredible sensation suddenly overtook his entire body. Despite being a former pilot, admittedly of a far less powerful aircraft, the sensation he felt was like nothing he had experienced before. Leif felt the G-forces build as if an invisible hand were grasping his entire body and trying to pull him out of the aircraft through the Plexiglas canopy. In addition to the blood saturation occurring in his brain, the straps on his four-point seat harness, across lap and shoulders began to tighten as the G-forces squeezed his torso into the back of the ejection seat as the aircraft continued its high-G dive – it was as if the aircraft had taken on a life of its own and was crushing him. Leif sucked hard to draw oxygen through his mask as his lungs compressed. As he gasped for breath, his vision grayed and narrowed – the early on-set of blacking-out. His mind drifted softly to thoughts of his wife and four children – a sense of euphoria was setting-in as Leif was about to pass out. On the verge of consciousness, a soft, gentle resolve washed over him at the thought of never seeing his family again – not so much fear, just acceptance that it was his time. Suddenly, the momentary lapse of mental acuity abated for an instant as Leif took two deep breaths of oxygen and forced himself to concentrate on the here and now. He looked forward and focused on the back of the pilot's helmet… with his last speck of consciousness, Leif assessed the situation – he saw Rabbit's helmet moving from side to side and assured himself,

> If Rabbit had blacked out, his head would be slumped forward or canted to the side. But Rabbit's helmet is moving left and right – he's scanning his surroundings… he's okay and is still in control!

Leif could now hear heavy grunting sounds coming over his headset. Rabbit was instinctively conducting the high-G strain maneuver of pushing air out of his lungs against his glottis while simultaneously contracting muscles in his lower extremities to prevent blood from flowing away from the brain. This trained technique is the only physical performance that a pilot can do to try and maintain consciousness during a high-G maneuver. Leif began to do the same and immediately felt the positive effects of more oxygen to his brain. Then, from what seemed like a great distance, Leif heard a familiar voice – Rabbit's voice – and he was shouting over the intercom, 'HERE WE GO LEIF! ONE… TWO… THREE… YEEHAW!'

Rabbit pulled hard, as hard as he ever had on the attitude control stick, but the aircraft continued its rapid trajectory towards earth and certain death. 'COME ON GIRL – COME ON!' shouted Rabbit into his hot microphone. Another second passed and then, slowly the aircraft began to respond. The aircraft shuddered as if taking on a life of its own – the aircraft was struggling with the competing forces of physics. The jet, with engines still roaring at maximum capacity began to ease out of the vertical and convert all its downward inertia energy into a new plane of direction – the nose of the aircraft began to rise and rise rapidly. As the aircraft pulled-out of its high, negative-G dive, there was a sudden and immediately onslaught of positive-Gs. The pilot and his observer now felt themselves being crushed down into their seats as the blood drained back into their lower extremities. Leif's map, notepad and grease pencil dropped dramatically from the plexiglass canopy above him, and now were plastered to the floor of the cockpit. Rabbit had just pulled their 3-ton Shooting Star out of a 655 miles per hour, negative G dive with eight times the force of gravity being exerted on the aircraft and its occupants. With the sudden onslaught of positive Gs the blood began to rapidly drain from his head to his lower extremities, and Leif's peripheral view narrowed; it seemed as if he were looking through a straw, which was constricting smaller and smaller – consciousness was slipping away. With the speed and G-force well beyond the design capability of the aircraft – with just 500 feet of altitude between them and the ground, the T-Bird pulled-out of its dive.

Below them and their screaming Allison J33-A-35 turbojet engine, cows, sheep and chickens bolted from their pens and enclosures, dogs ran for cover with their ears cocked back and their tails between their legs. Local farmers and pedestrians in the East German border town of Plauen covered their heads and cowered as the sudden, high-intensity noise generated by not one but three fighter aircraft simultaneously assaulted their ears with an overwhelming acoustic energy. Most instinctively flinched and cowered in sheer ignorance at what had just occurred, however, a few East German bystanders caught a fleeting glimpse of the sudden, and almost supersonic, dog fight, but it happened so quickly that the event was over before they realized what had happened. The brief aerial event was virtually indescribable by those in or near the normally quiet rural town. The only physical evidence of the adversarial aerial encounter were the few hundred broken terracotta tiles that had been blown off the roofs of several homes by the wake and jet blast of one of the Soviet MiGs, which had pulled out of their dive even lower than the American Shooting Star and had only narrowly avoided a catastrophic crash. The local police from the village of Plauen later estimated that the MiG had come within 50 feet of the rooftops before it was able to stop its descent and regain altitude and its normal flight dynamics.

After narrowly recovering from the high-speed, high-G evasive maneuver, Rabbit rapidly pulled his T-33 up to an altitude of 1,500 feet and pointed the nose westward with the throttles still fully forward. The T-33 Shooting Star streaked across the East German countryside and entered back into West Germany less than a minute later. The two Russian pilots had taken longer to reorient themselves with their prey after the aggressive, near fatal dive and recovery but quickly reacquired the American intruder and were back in pursuit within a few seconds. The Soviets were now a mile behind the fleeing American aircraft.

At that same moment, observing this aerial chase, one of the 302nd TRS's RF-84 Thunderflash aircraft – known as the 'Thud' in NATO terms, and assigned to fly in a supporting role of Captain Hare's reconn mission, began to vector his aircraft towards the two in-bound enemy MiGs with the intent of challenging them and defending his escaping American colleague. Piloting the second aircraft was Second Lieutenant Orville Buck (call sign Bucky) who had been cruising leisurely at 8,000 feet, slightly below and on a parallel track to Rabbit and The Danish Duke, 2 miles west of them, just inside the West German border. Bucky's assignment on this mission was to challenge or intercept any Russian or East German aircraft who might show up to interfere with the 302nd TRS's mission. Now, Bucky's primary task would make Soviets think otherwise about crossing into West German airspace in pursuit of Rabbit's returning aircraft. Fortunately for everyone concerned, the two Soviet MiGs broke off their pursuit and did not follow the American T-33 across the West German border. On this day, the Russkies would not catch this Rabbit. And once again, Leif had avoided the clutches of his Soviet pursuers.

Why the Soviet pilots had not opened fire with their cannon or launched an air-to-air missile when they had the chance was unknown. Rabbit and Leif later surmised that the nature of the heavily bureaucratic command and control system of the Soviet military required several levels of command approval in order for the MiG pilots to fire their weapons. Their encounter with the American intruder had lasted less than a minute, so there had been insufficient time for the Kremlin to receive and approve a weapons-free aerial engagement request so close to the border. Given the MiG-17's superior speed and firepower, a longer encounter could have been disastrous for Rabbit and his back seater. But on that morning in December 1956, the combination of Rabbit's outstanding flying skills, along with the welcome presence of overcast skies and a bit of luck coalesced just enough to claim victory for the two American aviators over their Soviet counterparts.

The Danish Duke and Rabbit returned to Sembach Air Base where the canisters of film from the T-33 Shooting Star's cameras were developed by the wing's intelligence section, adding to the inventory of Cold War intelligence gathered against their Warsaw Pact adversaries whose forces were amassed just few miles away. Rabbit was debriefed on his encounter with the MiG-17s and asked for his assessment of their capabilities. Though he was able to out fly the Soviets on that occasion, the superior capabilities of these new Soviet aircraft were concerning to Rabbit and the rest of 302nd TRS's pilots, as well as to the Twelfth Air Force as a whole. They realized that their T-33s and RF-84s were no match for the newer, faster and more heavily armed MiG-17s, which the Soviets were now deploying as their frontline fighter interceptor across the European theater. The ten cameras of Rabbit's aircraft had captured the entire intercept, vertical dive and escape maneuvers – all fifty-four seconds of it – providing evidence of the encounter which would be studied by the American intelligence section and squadron pilots. The whole event was a grim reminder that the Americans were facing an aggressive, more technically powerful foe than previously thought.

Captain Bangsbøll had been with 302nd TRS since June 1956 and had flown on more than a dozen tactical reconnaissance missions in the first six months of his tour. However, none was as exhilarating as this mission with Rabbit. This particular mission, Leif's first with Rabbit, would be by far the most harrowing of his entire tour with 302nd TRS. Though their assignment was completed successfully that December morning, Leif now had a better appreciation for just how dangerous, as well as physically and mentally demanding, these types of missions were.

As a grim reminder, just a year later, First Lieutenant Orville Buck, the pilot of the Thunderflash, who had escorted The Danish Duke and Rabbit safely back to base after their encounter with the two MiG-17s, would perish in a mid-air collision with fellow squadron member, First Lieutenant James Bulger during a training mission over Marston, England.

Captain Hare, who had joined 302nd TRS in November 1956, and arrived with far more flying experience than most, in addition to being one of the few combat veteran fighter pilots on the squadron, was designated as the squadron's flight safety officer and crash investigator. Rabbit had the unenviable duty to fly to England to conduct the accident investigation for Lieutenants Buck and Bulger. In a macabre practice, when arranging to send the remains of his squadron's two young lieutenants back to the States for burial, and to compensate for the lack of human remains found at the crash site, sandbags were placed in the two coffins to simulate the weight of the pilots' bodies. Flying combat missions or even training missions were dangerous activities. Though Rabbit was always passionate about flying, he also knew that military flying was a dangerous profession.

As part of his investigation into the crash and when discussing with fellow pilot Captain Paul Hodges the limitations of the American RF-84 Thunderflash compared to the Russians and even other NATO air forces, Rabbit received blunt criticism from Hodges, who stated,

> The thrust to weight ratio of the 'Flash' leaves a lot to be desired… it's an easy airplane to fly, although frustrating when our Canadian allies, in their new Mark V1 Sabres, regularly bounce us from their 45,000-foot perch positions while we're struggling to stay at 35,000 on a cross-country flight. The Canadians, stationed at Grostenquin, Zweibrücken and Marville, bases are located near the air routes we take to go south from Sembach. The 'Canucks' often wait for us in our slower, less versatile 'Flashes' and like sitting ducks they get fifteen minutes of simulated target practice on us while we sit there in our cockpit with clenched teeth… just trying to keep our aircraft airborne at that altitude.

Learning more of the Thunderflash's growing vulnerabilities against enemy aircraft, and recalling the MiG incident that he had experienced, taught Leif, the squadron's ALO, a great deal about the physical and metal stressors associated with intense tactical reconnaissance missions. The split-second decisions that needed to be made and the deadly consequences of mistakes or underestimating one's enemy were almost overwhelming. One of Leif's duties as the ALO was to provide intelligence reports for the pilots and squadron operations officers on where, what type and the combat capabilities of enemy ground forces in the squadron area of operations. As well, the ALO would assess the enemy's likely invasion routes towards West Germany during an attack from the Soviets/East Germans. Though this information was vital for the pilots, Leif wanted to contribute more to the squadron's mission than just analyzing and advising on Soviet ground force capabilities and activities.

Captain Bangsbøll was not one to sugarcoat a situation. After learning of the growing technical disparity between the newer Russian MiG 17s being employed against the 302nd TRS's T-33s and RF-84s lead him to conclude that he needed to better prepare his American pilot colleagues for the eventuality of being shot down. Leif then went to work preparing lesson plans for escape and evasion to provide the pilots with realistic training on how to survive and evade the enemy if the pilots were ever shot down or crash-landed in enemy territory. As a seasoned infantry officer, paratrooper and former OSS agent with ample combat experience and time spent operating behind enemy lines, Leif's expertise was a welcome and vital resource for the squadron. Though 302nd TRS had a handful of combat veterans from the Second World War and the Korean War, such as Rabbit, as well as the CO, Major Ruffin Gray, who had flown P-51 Mustangs over the beaches of Normandy and flew deep into the Rhineland towards the end of the Second World War, 302nd TRS had many young, inexperienced pilots. In fact, the majority of 302nd TRS's pilots like First Lieutenants Orville Buck, Jim Bulger, Monk Everheardt, John Zartman, Edwin 'Ed' Atterberry (call sign Eddy), Don Breedlove and Edward O'Rourke were all first tour pilots. These young pilots were just cutting their teeth on operational reconnaissance missions, having recently been posted in from their initial fighter pilot training in the States. It was up to the veterans like Rabbit to ensure the rookies became not just proficient pilots, but highly skilled fighter reconnaissance pilots as soon as possible. Rabbit would teach them how to operate effectively and survive in the air, and Leif would teach them how to survive on the ground.

There is an intangible and exceptional quality to military life that bonds colleagues and their families together, often for life. But each of the services – army, navy, air force, marines – also has their own characteristics distinctive unto themselves. This uniqueness, based upon specific types of war-fighting capabilities, and long-standing customs and traditions, also creates an underlying rivalry amongst the services. Despite the air force way of doing things, life with Twelfth Air Force, 66th Tactical Reconnaissance Wing, 302nd TRS, nestled in the beautiful pine covered, rolling hills of Germany, would prove to be a remarkably positive experience for Leif, the combat-hardened infantry officer. True to his nature, and as a former pilot, Leif embraced the air force way of life while imparting his army ethos as often as he could, on any pilot who would listen. The best exchanges of views and opinions occurred at the officers' club or during social gatherings within the married quarters. Alcohol was always a factor, as was an abundance of laughter and good-natured rivalry.

The assignment with 302nd TRS brought Leif back to his long-lost love of flying once more. The Danish Duke and Rabbit became close friends in short order. Both men had seen combat in the Second World War – Leif in Europe and Audrey flying combat missions in the final stages of the war in the Pacific.

As well, they both served in the Korean War – The Danish Duke, primarily on the ground as an airborne infantry officer and Rabbit, high above in his fighter aircraft, the F-86 Super Sabre. Both respected each other's leadership and combat experience and their mutual free spirit and love of life. Each of these two officers was an experienced combat veteran who understood the real and present threat of the Soviet armed forces looming only a few miles to the east of their base. They worked hard to ensure they were always prepared for what they believed was the inevitable Soviet invasion of Western Europe. However, when they weren't on duty, they played and played hard. Loud parties at the officers' club or at one or other's married quarters apartments, crowded with squadron members and their families, interspersed with exciting family vacations in exotic locations across Europe and the Mediterranean, kept the families of 302nd TRS occupied and entertained.

Autumn 1956 had been a busy time for 302nd TRS, due to their participation in Exercise Whipsaw, a major NATO exercise in northern Europe designed to practice and evaluate current plans for employment of nuclear weapons, and coordination of Allied forces against the Soviets and their Warsaw Pact forces. Then in November, the 302nd TRS along with the rest of 66th Tactical Reconnaissance Wing and reconnaissance units from 2nd ATAF and 4th ATAF, all of whom staged out of the Canadian base at Lahr, Germany, had come together for the exercise/aerial competition called Royal Flush. It was during these exercises that Captain Bangsbøll began to realize that many of the new, younger pilots did not have sufficient awareness or training in ground survival or escape and evasion, in the event they were shot down or crash landed.

Leif's philosophy regarding the air force was that every pilot on the squadron should be required to complete an annual survival, escape and evasion refresher training program. 'If you jet jockeys are lucky enough to survive being shot down in one of those tin cans you fly', he advised, 'it would be prudent that you have the skills to stay alive once you're back on the ground.' And so, in March 1957, Major Gray, 302nd TRS commander, gave his ALO the authority and the resources to organize survival, escape and evasion training for his pilots. Leif would refer to it as his 'picnic in the Palatinate Forest.' Conversely, the pilot trainees who participated in the training would call the experience something far less benign. For the pilots of 302nd TRS, Exercise Freebier '57 became known as 'The Danish Duke's Revenge'.

The Palatinate Forest was a sprawling expanse of rolling hills, beautiful valleys and gorges covered in thick pine trees located to the south-east of Sembach Air Base. It was an ideal location for Captain Bangsbøll to run a rugged, realistic survival, escape and evasion exercise. Leif had noticed since his arrival in Germany that though the threat of a possible attack or invasion of Western

Europe by the Soviets' red horde was taken seriously, the training exercises or alert responses had often been met with less than enthusiastic participation by United States forces. Though the Americans knew it needed to be practised, it was 'fake war', so many did not take it seriously. Leif, relying on his experience while training with the OSS and SOE, knew the value of making the training as real as possible to maximise its value and ensure that the trainees took from those training experiences valuable, potentially life saving lessons. To that end, with the approval of his Commanding Officer, Captain Bangsbøll organized a small team of officers and non-commissioned personnel to plan and organize a squadron exercise that would set a new standard for realism, training value and, for many involved, the hardest but most engaging military exercise ever. Again, true to his nature, Leif believed that their business was a serious and potentially deadly profession, but that didn't mean you couldn't have fun preparing for it.

* * *

One of the essential components of Leif's success as 302nd TRS's ALO and coordinator of the air crews' survival, escape and evasion exercise was his selection of a clever, industrious young sergeant named Beamer. Sergeant Beamer, also a member of the 302nd TRS, was the consummate scrounger with a can-do attitude. For those two important reasons, Leif had chosen him to be his 'go-to guy' whenever he needed supplies, transportation or any essential service that was not necessarily easily accessible within the normal supply system protocols or within the legitimate boundaries of USAAF regulations.

Oddly enough Leif's first encounter with Beamer was not at work but was rather a chance meeting near the Bangsbølls' on-base apartment just a few days after their arrival in Sembach. While walking up the pavement toward the Bangsbøll family apartment building, Leif saw his three eldest children playing with some of their neighbours' children in the park adjacent to their apartment. The children were all running around, chasing a soldier and crying out with glee as they 'captured' the young man who was feigning distress and begging for mercy with great acting skills. The soldier/airman was Freddy Beamer, a single fellow, and a fun-loving child at heart; all the local kids loved him. As Leif stood watching them play, Beamer told the children that he had to leave, at which the dozen or so kids begged him to stay and play a little bit longer. To the children's dismay, Beamer jumped on his motorcycle, which had earned him notoriety for speeding around the countryside at any chance he got, and rode off, waving to his adoring fans and leaving the children to find a new source of entertainment. Beamer would soon become part of Leif's entourage of eager supporters.

To ensure as much secrecy as possible concerning his intended survival, escape and evasion training exercise, and to ensure the greatest training impact for the squadron's pilots, Leif waited until 302nd TRS's pilots deployed en masse to Cazeaux, France, near Toulouse, for a week of gunnery practice before implementing the training arrangements. During that time, Captain Bangsbøll and Sergeant Beamer and the rest of their exercise planning team made all of the administrative and logistical arrangements for the squadron's first annual survival, escape and evasion exercise. With a sense of humor and for planning purposes, the exercise was named Exercise Freebier '57 and was conducted during the first week of March 1957. The squadron's CO declared four days of no-fly training days during which all thirty of the squadron's pilots were fully dedicated to learning how to survive a simulated ejection from an aircraft over enemy territory and how to escape and evade the enemy. As chief instructor and Exercise Freebier's coordinator, Leif would run the pilots through a day of instruction on survival techniques and military field craft followed by two days and nights of realistic escape and evasion scenarios. With the support of the MP from Sembach Air Base and the local German police from the towns of Hohenberg and Schmidmuhlen, as well as an American infantry platoon lent to him from the United States Army Kaserne at Hoeffel, Leif assembled a series of formidable search parties that would harass and pursue the escapee pilots throughout the Hoeffel training area, which consisted of 150 square miles of dense pine forest, upon rolling hills deep in the beautiful Palatinate.

The first day of training was conducted within the confines of their training area at Sembach Air Base. The pilots were taught how to survive in the wilderness, how to use all the items in the aircraft's survival kit and how to conceal themselves and minimize being seen when traveling. They reviewed combat first aid training and were taught how to build a shelter and ration and supplement their food supplies and how to navigate by day and night. The pilots took it all in but clearly, many of them were only paying lip service to the training being given. The fact that the first day's training was being conducted on base, close to home, where all the pilots were familiar with the training area and the firing ranges that they had used regularly for small arms/pistol annual requalification made them take the training less seriously than they should have. That attitude would change on day two of the training.

On day two of the exercise, the pilots were ordered to report for duty at the squadron's hangar at 0430 hours where breakfast would be provided. However, upon arrival, breakfast was not provided, and the pilots were immediately directed to the flight line where they were loaded onto a bus, which drove them the 90 miles to the Hohenfel training area. Two hours later, the airmen stepped off their bus, stiff and hungry and generally annoyed that the exercise had now become inconvenient. Immediately, each of the escaped pilots was handed the equivalent of everything they would have had with them had they just ejected from an aircraft, less their helmets. They each were given the silk canopy of their parachute and their seat pack, which contained their survival kits (first aid kit, flares and mirror for signaling, waterproof matches, compass and a small amount of emergency food and water). They were told that they would be transferred into trucks and driven into the training area where they would be deposited along the way and expected to survive and evade an enemy force that would soon be looking for them over the next two days. The pilots were divided into various trucks; some chose to leave their parachutes behind, while others took them along. Though the day would be sunny and warm, that evening would become cold and rainy in the Palatinate Forest. Those who had chosen to leave their parachutes behind learned an early lesson: a silk parachute can provide protection from the elements and its many riser cords are ideal for building a shelter. The exercise was only just underway, and the trainees were already hungry and agitated, just as Leif intended.

The next two days and nights were a long, drawn-out nightmare for the pilots. The pilots were hungry and alone in cold, wet weather conditions. Added to that were persistent patrols conducted by the team of MPs with guard dogs, which created enough stress to approach a semi-realistic combat/escape and evasion situation. In addition, there were two enthusiastic infantry squads who were all too eager to harass and make these fly boys suffer a bit. For the first day and night in the Hohenfel training area, Captain Bangsbøll's instructions to the 'enemy force' were to not apprehend any of the escapee pilots, and to divide themselves into shifts to cover twenty-four-hour periods to keep the trainees alert and awake at all times, and to keep them constantly wary of being caught by their pursuers and let fatigue set in. This was accomplished having the patrols fire blanks into the air during their patrols and sending up the occasional flare to distract and disorient the escapees. The patrols had aggressive guard dogs with them, which added to the realism of the exercise. Leif's intent was to create conditions, which would be a semblance of the stress of a combat situation.

That evening, Captain Bangsbøll learned that an effective way to make a guard dog bark aggressively was to dangle a live rabbit in front of them. The ensuing barking and snarling that came from the three MP German Shepherds could be heard for miles. Lieutenant Don Breedlove, one of the escapee pilots later recalled that as he lay in the darkness, under a fallen tree, shivering from the cold, damp air, hungry and alone, that hearing the guard dogs, which sounded like hounds from hell, almost put him over the top. 'Cold, hungry and tired, my imagination got the best of me, and I truly feared for my life.' He continued,

> Despite knowing that this was an exercise, in my mind those guard dogs were tearing something or someone apart and it scared the shit out of me. Leif's exercise was far too real for my liking.

On day three of the exercise, with his pilot escapees hungry and exhausted from their two days of sleep deprivation, Captain Bangsbøll's orders to the MPs and infantry squads were to 'aggressively apprehend and detain as many of the escapee pilots as possible – treat them like enemy prisoners of war.' Leif's enemy force was more than keen to comply. To make things a bit more interesting for his searchers, Leif promised that he would give them a case of beer for every escapee that they apprehended. Soldiers being soldiers, this incentive worked like a charm. By sundown on day three of the exercise, all but four of the thirty escapees had been apprehended.

To make things as real as possible, the captors were not gentle or polite – the prisoners were roughed-up and blindfolded, with their hands tied behind their backs. Local German police were on hand and Leif shouted orders in German, making the situation surreal and uncomfortable to the blindfolded American prisoners who became disoriented and angry. Half of the prisoners were locked in the remnants of a Second World War Nazi ammunition bunker located in the Hohenfel training area. It was cold, damp and foul smelling. The other group of captives were locked up in a heated sauna located in the basement of a local health club/Alpine spa adjacent to the Hohenfel training area. Two different approaches to making prisoners even more uncomfortable.

Captain Ed O'Rourke (call sign Hazy) was part of this latter group of prisoners and made his assessment of the situation clear, and said,

> Despite being initially grateful for the warmth of the detention cell our captors put us in – having just spent forty-eight hours in the cold, damp woods – the heat and humidity quickly became unbearable and in short order we were demanding...pleading to be released by our captors.

He continued,

> Our demands fell on deaf ears I might add. With our hands tied behind our backs and blindfolded, there was not much we could do about our situation except lie on the wet floor, which was marginally cooler, and await our fate. I'm sure Leif wanted to demonstrate as close as possible the misery of being a prisoner. Fortunately, our captors were not allowed to really mistreat us, as would happen as real prisoners of war. Having said

> that, in just a few hours that son of a bitch made us realize just how fast one's stamina can be compromised.

The realism of this training would have a marked impact on the trainees, and for that, Leif was pleased with their efforts. The four pilots who had successfully evaded capture – Rabbit and Atterberry included – had to be convinced that the exercise was really over before they eventually came out of their hiding positions in the forest. These four high achievers were immediately offered hot showers back at the Hohenfels Kaserne and then taken by Leif to a local *Gasthaus* in nearby Schmidmuhlen where they were treated to a hearty meal of *schnitzel* and *spätzle*, fresh bread and a couple of beers each. Following their dinner, the four successful trainees, as well as the remaining twenty-six captured pilots who had been locked up for hours in the dank old bunker or over-heated sauna, were now released and loaded onto the bus for the trip back to Sembach.

As the trainees stepped back aboard their bus, Sergeant Beamer issued each of the pilots a box lunch that consisted of a sandwich on a German *kaiser* roll, a piece of cheese and a piece of fruit, a chocolate bar and a coke. Having had only emergency rations over the past sixty hours, the twenty-six pilots devoured the provisions while the other four pilots, who were still far too full of *schnitzel* and beer, declined to even take the box lunches being offered, which further raised the ire of the rest of the trainees. While the bus made its way through the night back to Sembach Air Base, the exhausted and bedraggled pilots of 302nd TRS rested as best they could. For their efforts, the squad of MPs and the platoon of infantry were given several cases of beer to enjoy, once again thanks to the effective scrounging capabilities of Sergeant Freddy Beamer.

The following Friday, Major Gray, the CO of 302nd TRS, called for an all-squadron officers' assembly at the officers' club during which he, Leif and Beemer handed out free beer to all the exercise participants. From all accounts, Exercise Freebier '57 was a resounding success. Not only did the pilots of 302nd TRS learn some valuable, practical, potentially life-saving skills, but a new sense of camaraderie amongst the squadron members had developed. Though at first many of the pilots that had been captured resented Leif for the hardship they had been put through and for being humiliated by their imprisonment, often referring to him as 'that damn army liaison office', they grudgingly acknowledged the value of the training they had received and the enormous efforts that Leif had gone to in order to plan and organize such a training program on their behalf. The mere fact that the CO of 302nd TRS subsequently ordered that from then on, annual survival, escape and evasion training would be part of the squadron's standing operating procedures was proof enough. In fact, as word of the success of Exercise Freebier '57 got around, it eventually came to the attention of the commander of 66th Tactical Recognisance Wing, Colonel James 'Russ' Tansey, who encouraged the wing's other squadrons to seek out the assistance of Captain Bangsbøll to run similar exercises for their units. The Danish Duke was more than happy to comply.

Weather conditions in autumn 1957 limited effective training and operational reconnaissance flights in central Europe due to too much and too frequent low-lying clouds. In early 1958, the decision was made to use the USAF base located at Nouaceur, Morocco, to its limits to support detachments of USAF (Europe) fighter aircraft as well as several other NATO nations' fighter squadrons. The favorable North African weather provided the ideal environment in which pilots could train. In mid-January 1958, 302nd TRS deployed eight RF-84s and fifteen pilots as well as the squadron's ALO to Nouaceur. The reconnaissance training undertaken by this detachment was even more effective than anticipated. Specific training missions included low-level navigation, all phases of photography, instrument flying, formation flying, aerobatic and evasive tactics as well night flying operations. Every air station and every port in Morocco was photographed by 302nd TRS during this time.

While deployed to Nouaceur, Morocco, Rabbit became enamored with the fact that many of the other nations' fighter squadrons participating in the deployed operating base exercise boasted live mascots with great pride and fanfare. The French squadron had a large black and red rooster as its mascot, the Italian squadron had a magnificent falcon, a British squadron had a ram with huge horns and shaggy, white fleece, which they proudly paraded around the hangar line, as did the West Germans with their adorable black bear cub. Rabbit felt that 302nd TRS had been delinquent in this capacity and intended to rectify the situation.

On his first day off from flying duties on the exercise, Rabbit, accompanied by The Danish Duke and Captain Don Breedlove, went down to the local market in the town of Nouaceur and for a few American dollars purchased 302nd TRS's unofficial mascot: a 3-month-old donkey. With a basic rope bridle, 'Thunder' was led by Rabbit and made his debut on the flight line to great cheers from not only 302nd TRS personnel but also all the other squadrons – the Americans were getting into the spirit of the coalition camaraderie and *esprit-de-corps*.

Two weeks later, as the exercise was winding down, Rabbit, the unofficial squadron chaperone for Thunder, was unsuccessful in his attempts to make arrangements to have Thunder flown back to Sembach aboard one of the USAAF cargo flights, designated to take the squadron's ground support equipment back to base. 'There's no way a donkey is going to be authorised to be transported on this aircraft', the cargo handlers advised. Not to be undone, Leif and Don hastily built a wooden crate, with the requisite air holes drilled into the wood, to ship Thunder home as 'aircraft spare parts'. Regrettably, the loadmaster on the C-119 Boxcar for the designated flight discovered the stowaway and had the crated animal removed from the aircraft. Again, not to be undone, Rabbit led poor, unappreciated Thunder away by his rope bridle and would resort to Plan C – being a good fighter pilot, he always had a back-up plan to the back-up plan.

Two days later, assigned the only two-seater T-33 aircraft on the deployment to Morocco, Rabbit and his back seater, The Danish Duke, prepared to fly home to Sembach. The modest-sized baggage compartment in the nose of the aircraft was enlarged as the four cameras mounted in the nose of the aircraft had been removed, thus allowing ample space for their 'special cargo'. Two hours later, while cruising at an altitude of 7,500 feet over northeastern France (to ensure sufficient oxygen for their live cargo), Rabbit heard a large, dull 'thud' come from just forward of the cockpit of his aircraft. A moment later he and Leif heard another, louder thud. Rabbit realized that it could be only one thing. Clearly the tranquiliser used to sedate Thunder must be wearing off. Knowing that time was of the essence, Rabbit immediately vectored his aircraft towards the nearest NATO fighter base. Marville Air Base, in northern France was only 25 miles to the west of their present position and close to the West German border. Rabbit's radio call to the Marville control tower had to be repeated several times to convince the air traffic controller that he was serious about his intentions. 'Request landing instructions and upon arrival I will need 500 pounds of NATO Jet A fuel, a weather forecast update for Sembach Air Base and please have a veterinarian, equipped with an animal tranquiliser there to meet the aircraft.'

Marville Air Base was assigned to the RCAF, which was home to the 410 Fighter Squadron – the Cougars – which flew the F-86 Sabre fighter aircraft. Rabbit thought, 'Surely the easy-going Canucks would understand his situation and assist him.' Advised by the duty air traffic controller and intrigued by the unusual request for a veterinarian to meet the aircraft, the base duty officer accompanied the local animal physician who had been summoned by the base operations section out to the visiting aircraft. Captain Francois Bessett, the duty officer at Marville that day, thought he'd seen it all, but there in the nose compartment of the USAAF jet aircraft was a young, live, semi-conscious donkey, cramped but nestled in soft blankets. With a brief explanation by Rabbit, and without too much fuss, the local French veterinarian administered a tranquiliser to Thunder. Secured with soft cloth bindings and protected by blankets to keep him warm, Thunder fell back to sleep, comfortably tucked into the nose cone compartment of the T-33. After this unexpected pitstop, the T-33 would be airborne again in minutes and back on course for Sembach Air Base.

With Thunder back in donkey slumber land, Rabbit signed for the fuel and the veterinarian services, thanked all concerned for their efforts, gave a thumbs up to Leif who just shook his head in disbelief. They climbed aboard their jet and took off for home. Less than an hour later he was taxiing his aircraft to the 302nd TRS ramp on the Sembach Air Base, happy to be on home turf again and pleased that he had safely delivered the squadron's first official, live and still-sedated mascot to its new Bavarian home.

* * *

In May 1958, Captain Bangsbøll received orders that he was being promoted to major and would be reassigned back to Fort Bragg. Though disappointed to know that his tour of duty with 302nd TRS was coming to a close, he was pleased with his promotion and was eager for the opportunity to rejoin 82nd Airborne Division – the All Americans. His orders were to report on 1 August 1958, so he only had two months left in this wonderful European assignment with 302nd TRS. One of the things that Leif had wanted to do before he left the squadron was to invite some of his squadron's pilots to Denmark so that he could show them around his beloved homeland and have the opportunity to host them in recognition for the great experience they had given him and his family over the past two years as the squadron's army liaison family.

As luck would have it, Major Ruffin Gray, the squadron CO, appreciated Leif's offer and designated the last week of June 1958 as another ground proficiency training week. This training would be dedicated to 'building relations with fellow NATO members' in Denmark. Major Gray designated Captain Jim Tidwell as the acting CO of the squadron, and with the concurrence of the Wing Commander, the CO of 302nd TRS along with ten of his pilots were led by their trusted ALO on a road trip to Denmark. From Kaiserslautern/ Sembach to Copenhagen was a journey of 600 miles – about an eleven-hour drive. The twelve colleagues in three vehicles set off almost due north towards Denmark as the sun was just coming up over the rolling hills on the eastern horizon of Germany.

After spending two days showing off his beautiful, and beloved Copenhagen, during which they visited the historic seaport, the Royal Palace, where they watched the ceremonial changing of the King's Royal Guard, and then visited the famous Tivoli Gardens, Leif decided it was time to give his American colleagues a history lesson on Denmark's resistance efforts against the Nazis. On the third day, they participated in a private wreath-laying ceremony at the Danish Second World War memorial in Ryvangen Memorial Park in the northern end of Copenhagen. The memorial park had been officially opened by the King of Denmark on 5 May 1950, on the fifth anniversary of the overthrow of the German occupation force and to commemorate the 13,000 Danish Resistance fighters who defied and fought the Nazis and, sadly, the 850 resistance members who died for that cause.

Leif explained to his American colleagues that the location of the Ryvangen Memorial Park had personal significance in two ways. Firstly, it was the location where the Wehrmacht had established a large camp during the occupation of Denmark where hundreds of Danish Resistance freedom fighters had been imprisoned and executed during the five-year occupation. Following the end of the war, many bodies were exhumed from several mass graves at Ryvangen and were then given honorable military burials; the site became the burial site of 197 Danish Resistance members who had been captured, tortured and executed by the Germans. Secondly, Ryvangen was the location where he, Lieutenant Leif Bangsbøll, known as Agent Jorgen Vejlby Bech, had led the assault on and subsequently captured the German garrison on 5 May 1945. Major Gray, the squadron commander, knew that this was also the enemy engagement where Leif had heroically earned the United States Army's DSC for 'extreme gallantry and heroism in the face of the enemy.' His air force comrades secretly made arrangements to have a wreath produced and brought it with them to the memorial site. The wreath-laying ceremony was a poignant moment for Leif. It was a moment that provided a certain emotional closure in that chapter of life for the young Danish soldier.

While standing quietly at the Ryvangen memorial with his 302nd TRS colleagues, Leif recalled another proud moment, three years earlier, during which he had last stood at that very same spot. It had been 9 May 1955, when he, along with a dozen paratroopers from 82nd Airborne Division stationed at Fort Bragg, were selected to come to Denmark to participate in the tenth anniversary ceremonies commemorating the end of the Second World War and the liberation of Denmark. During that visit, Captain Bangsbøll and his small contingent of paratroopers participated in several military parades and memorial wreath lay ceremonies, none so emotionally powerful to Leif as the one at Ryvangen.

* * *

The day following the wreath-laying ceremony at the Ryvangen Memorial Park, the twelve members of 302nd TRS drove across the series of bridges and causeways from Copenhagen to Jutland, passing by the small seaside town of Nyborg where Leif explained that he and three of his resistance fighters had spent a memorable Christmas of 1944 eluding the Gestapo. The small band of Americans drove another forty-five minutes to the town of Horsens where they met Hans Fletcher, the local resistance leader who Leif had worked closely with during his time in occupied Denmark. Leif and his fellow Americans were treated like returning heroes.

On the second evening in Horsens, Leif left his USAF colleagues to enjoy the wares of a local pub along with their host Hans Fletcher and several other local Danes/former resistance members. Leif had some personal business to take care of and drove the 20 miles out to the town of Skive to visit his old friends, Olaf and Ragla Gustavsson, the couple whose farm he had parachuted onto in autumn 1944. They were both now well into their eighties but still living independently on their farm. They no longer worked the land and had leased or sold off most of the arable fields to younger local farmers to cultivate and harvest. The last time Leif had seen Olaf was just after Leif's father's funeral.

The death of Leif's father had been a deeply emotional event for Leif. Frederik died on 6 March 1954 at the age of 64. The cause – lung cancer – five decades of smoking cigarettes had taken their toll. Olaf had heard the news of Leif's father's death – reported in the local newspaper – and though he did not know the man personally, he felt it important enough to attend the funeral and hoped he would get to see Leif there. Olaf did this, not because he knew the late Frederik Bangsbøll, but out of respect for the things Frederik had done in the defense of his nation and, most importantly, he did it for Frederik's son, his good friend, Leif.

Olaf had not been to Copenhagen since before the end of the Second World War, fifteen years earlier. He took the morning train from Horsens to the capital and then a taxi to the Bispebjerg church where the funeral service was to be held. There, he sat quietly in one of the last rows at the back of the church. Olaf was impressed to see so many senior naval officers and former resistance members as well as politicians present at the funeral. Unable to attend in person, King Frederik IX, Leif's childhood friend, sent a letter of condolence that was read aloud by a senior naval representative in attendance. The sentiment from the King was that Denmark had lost a loyal son, a man who had defended his nation at sea as well as through his involvement with the resistance during the war. The letter highlighted the achievement that Frederik's leadership had been critical in the safe evacuation of thousands of Danish Jews to neutral Sweden during the Nazi occupation of Denmark. Olaf was truly impressed by this regal farewell and was equally surprised and gravely disappointed to not see Leif in attendance. The funeral service concluded with Poul Bundgaard, Leif's old friend, a rising Danish entertainer and former resistance member, singing a beautifully stirring rendition of *Ave Maria*. Olaf learned at that moment that Poul had worked with Frederik as part of the Danish Resistance during the Second World War.

At the time of his father's death, Leif was stationed at Fort Bragg. Much to his dismay, Leif had received notification of his father's death by a Western Union telegram from his stepmother almost a week after his father's death. The telegram coldly indicated the basic facts: Leif's father had died and had been buried in Copenhagen. Leif, furious with his stepmother for not contacting him sooner, was immediately granted compassionate leave by his unit and caught the first military flight from the closest air base in Germany to Denmark.

Two days after receiving the news of his father's death, Leif's train pulled into the central Copenhagen train station. He thought that there would be family affairs to attend to. However, he learned, much to his dismay, that according to Danish law, in the absence of a specific will, for which there was none to be found, all of Frederik's worldly possessions were transferred to his living second wife. Distraught at the loss of his father, the greatest man he had ever known, then at being excluded from his funeral service, and now devoid of any access to family heirlooms from his youth – family treasures of unmeasurable value to him – Leif was emotionally devastated. It was a turbulent and emotionally charged time for him. He understood that he needed to clear his mind and console his soul and knew exactly where he needed to go to accomplish those things.

* * *

The day following his arrival in Copenhagen, Leif purchased a ticket and boarded the overnight ferry from Copenhagen to Rønne, on the isle of Bornholm. With his father now gone, not only did Leif feel the deep need to visit the gravesite of his mother and two sisters, he knew he owed a long overdue visit to Jorgen Bech's parents. After an emotional visit to the Bangsbøll family plot at the seaside Lutheran Church at Svaneke, Leif drove the 10 miles back down the coastal road to the seaside town of Nexø. There, in the comfort of the Bechs' small but quaint living room, while drinking tea, Leif explained to Jorgen's parents a remarkable and personal story about himself and their son. Leif explained how he and Jorgen had been reunited at the Danish Maritime Academy and had corresponded many times following Jorgen's departure from Denmark up to his arrival in Hawaii with the United States Navy. Leif then explained that after learning the sad news of their son's death, Leif had adopted Jorgen's name as his wartime identity as an OSS agent. Leif was unsure if Mr and Mrs Bech would understand his rationale for using their son's identity as an Allied secret agent, but he was pleasantly relieved by the obvious pride the Bechs took in knowing that in some small way their son had lived on through Leif's wartime activities and had contributed to the fight against the Nazis after all. For the remainder of the afternoon they spoke of happier days, days when Jorgen and Leif were young, innocent and very much alive. That was the last time Leif ever saw the Bechs and the last time he ever set foot on his beloved isle of Bornholm.

* * *

Although Leif was deeply saddened at the loss of his father and viscerally distraught at his stepmother's cruel actions to exclude him, he was touched and moved to learn that Olaf had attended his father's funeral as his surrogate and was forever grateful for the thoughtful gesture and the profound friendship that had grown between them. Their reunion and evening together at the Gustavsson farm was a wonderful time. They ate, drank and talked of bygone days well into the night. The two men would communicate by letter for almost another decade. But it would be the last time they would ever see each other.

* * *

The next day, Leif rejoined his USAF colleagues in Horsens and they made their way back to the capital. Two days later, on the final night in Copenhagen for the visiting members of 302nd TRS, a formal dinner was held at the Holmen naval officers' mess. It was a fitting location for a farewell dinner and a fine tribute to Leif's father, Frederik Bangsbøll, who had spent so much of his naval career operating from the Holmen base. Regrettably, the commander of the Danish Resistance, the man only referred to as Gold, had died several years earlier. Fortunately, and to Leif's delight, Vagn Bennike, the former COS to the Jutland regional resistance commander who now lived in Copenhagen, was there to host the evening along with the Holman Naval Base commander. Also in attendance that night was Leif's old family friend and fellow resistance fighter, Poul Bundgaard, now a famous actor and singer in Denmark.

* * *

The following morning, the twelve members of 302nd TRS, who had planned to get an early start to their long road trip back to Sembach, were understandably delayed due to varying degrees of hangover. Their Danish hosts at the naval mess the night before had insisted on including the young American aviators in the tradition of imbibing substantial quantities of Danish Akvavit. With each shot of Akvavit, Leif would shout '*Hundebidde*! [dog bite!]', a Danish phrase he had learned as a young sailor. The American aviators soon were joining in with the *Hundebidde*! cheer and had continued into the early morning hours. Aviators, and in particular fighter pilots, are always up for a challenge, especially if it involves alcohol, so they tried to keep up with Leif and their Danish hosts.

Earlier that morning, Leif, who felt no ill effect from the previous night's libations, was glad for the extra time available to him, as he was able to take a long stroll through the city he loved.

Ultimately, he found himself standing in front of the Bispebjerb church. It was mid-morning, 30 June 1958, when Leif sat quietly beside his father's headstone. Leif had wanted to have his father buried at the family burial site in Sveneke on the isle of Bornholm, but his stepmother had chosen otherwise. After long moments of reflection about the man who had made him a man, Leif placed his hand gently on the headstone and bid a silent farewell to his father. Leif left the church yard and continued his leisurely walk through the cobblestone streets of Copenhagen, taking in the sights and sounds of his fellow Danes going about their Sunday morning routines. He enjoyed the delightful smells of bakeries and the open-air markets as he made his way back towards Holmen Naval Base and the officers' quarters. He made a small detour on the way that allowed him to walk past his former school, the Royal Danish Maritime Academy. He stopped briefly and gazed through the heavy wrought iron gate at the main entrance to the academy. Nothing had changed.

'Has it really been 21 years since Jorgen and I walked through the corridors of this old place?' thought Leif. He smiled and shook his head slowly and walked on. Further down the block he crossed the street and looked through the window of the Mayflower Café. This is where Jorgen had introduced him to Sophie Halverson, the innocent young waitress who then became the unfortunate young waitress at the Bygholm Park Inn in Horsens, where she recognized Leif and threatened to expose him and his resistance cell to the Gestapo. That unfortunate encounter had led to her spending the last six months of the war locked up in a sanatorium in Jutland. Leif recalled the moment that Sophie had recognized him in the crowded café, jeopardizing him and his team during an OSS mission. Leif wondered how Sophie's life had turned out. He walked on.

* * *

Half an hour later, Leif returned to the naval base, just as eleven weary members of 302nd TRS were finishing their late breakfast meal and beginning to gather in the lobby of the officers' club. Laughing together as they recalled some of the late-night antics at the bar the night before, they slowly organized their belongings, loaded their luggage into their cars and began their long trek south towards to their base at Sembach. Denmark had been good to the visiting members of 302nd TRS and Denmark, too, had welcomed home its long-lost son who was now at peace with his life. Leif's eleven American traveling companions returned to Sembach exhausted but feeling enriched by the wonderful Danish culture that had embraced them and for the unique opportunity given them to glimpse into the heroic military exploits of their good friend and their ever reliable, squadron ALO – The Danish Duke.

The trip to Denmark in summer 1958 with his American Air Force colleagues had initially been intended to thank his USAF brethren for their camaraderie and for the wonderful opportunity they had given him to be free of the bonds of earth and the laws of gravity, allowing Leif to fly amongst the clouds once more. However, despite Leif's original intention to show his squadron mates Denmark as a way of thanking them for making this army officer feel so at home with the USAF, this trip back to Denmark became more of a healing, cathartic experience for Leif, as he was able to reconnect, in some cases for the last time, with people and places in Denmark that had meant so much to him during a very challenging but rewarding period in his life.

* * *

Many of the fine pilots of 302nd TRS, like Rabbit, who were assigned to Sembach Air Base in the late 1950s would go on to distinguish themselves on combat tours during the Vietnam War. Thankfully, Rabbit came home safe and sound from that combat tour, but regrettably many of his colleagues did not. Ed Atterberry, who had successfully completed Leif's first survival, escape and evasion exercise in Hohenfel, Germany, would be shot down over north Vietnam in 1969 and taken prisoner. In May 1969, Captain Atterberry along with another USAF pilot, Captain John Dramesi, escaped their confinement of the north Vietnamese PoW camp in Hanoi, referred to as *The Zoo*, by American aviators, but were subsequently recaptured. Captain Atterberry would tragically die in captivity from injuries suffered by beatings at the hands of his captors in retribution for his escape attempt. Dramesi also endured horrible beatings by his captors for his involvement in the failed escape attempt but survived and was repatriated to the United States at the end of the Vietnam War.

Thunder's reign as 302nd TRS's official mascot would extend well beyond the postings of all the pilots and crews of 302nd TRS at Sembach during the Bangsbøll tour of 1956 to 1958. Rabbit had become famous for his efforts to secure a mascot for the squadron and had only received two weeks of extra duties as a result of the $20,000 worth of damage done to his aircraft during the transportation of Thunder from Morocco to Germany – damage consisting mostly of dents to the aircraft skin. But a few electrical components, including a navigational gyroscope, had to be replaced as a result of Thunder's temporary confinement.

Rabbit eventually retired from the USAF and he and Ginny relocated back to Oklahoma. After a long and courageous battle with cancer, Rabbit died, at the age of 85, on 7 January 2010, with his devoted wife and loving family at his side. To this date, Ginny, now 91 years young, is still going strong, living close to her children and grandchildren in Oklahoma. She still attends USAF and squadron reunions and visits with members of the Bangsbøll clan from time to time.

Chapter 11

One of America's Best

'Stand your ground men. Don't fire unless fired upon;
but if they mean to have a war, let it begin here.'
Captain Jonas Parker, Lexington, 1775

Above the entrance to the Special Forces Warfare Center's auditorium was the Latin incription 'De Oppresso Liber' – which translates to: "Free the Oppressed". The Chief of Staff (COS) of the Special Forces Warfare Center, also known as the adjutant, entered the auditorium precisely at 0758 hours to prepare the instructors and senior administrators of the school for the address by their Commanding Officer (CO), scheduled for precisely at 0800 hours. 'So, are we all here?' asked the COS, expecting the answer to be a prompt: 'Yes Sir.' There was a delay in response, and the COS looked over at his Senior Instructor – 'Well?'

'All but one, sir' said the the Senior Instructor.

'Who's missing?'

'Major Bangsbøll, sir' said the Senior Instructor.

'For Christ's sake, it's his first day on the job and he's late?' exclaimed the COS. His outburst was clearly rhetorical. Just as those words came out of his mouth, the CO entered from the front door of the auditorium, adjacent and closest to the stage. The room was called to attention by the center's senior sergeant and silence immediately fell over the auditorium.

The CO said, 'At ease.'

The COS added, 'Take your seats.' The audience of fifty or so instructors and directing staff sat down and prepared to listen to their commander's address.

'Are we ready to go?' asked Colonel Ron Speirs, the CO of the Special Forces Warfare Center. 'I've got a meeting to get to, so let's get on with this.'

The COS replied, 'We're missing one instructor, sir, Major Bangsbøll, just posted in from Sembach, Germany.'

Just then, the sound of a heavy exterior wooden door opening at the back of the auditorium could be heard, followed by the rythmical steps of thick-soled jump boots traversing the old wooden floor of the auditorium. The heavy metal door swung open and there, standing in the doorway, was a stocky soldier wearing combat fatigues and bloused jump boots, with his helmet slightly cocked to one side, chin straps dangling on each side of his face, which was sweaty and grimy with dirt. He was unmistakably an airborne soldier.

The CO and adjutant stood and stared, as did all the seated audience who craned their necks to observe the latecomer at the back of the auditorium. They were all wearing their Class A uniforms of khaki-colored slacks and dark green tunic, long-sleeved shirts and ties, as was the custom and dress of the day for the staff of the training center. The back of the auditorium was dimly lit. The adjutant stepped forward and was about to confront the latecomer, but the CO held out his hand and intercepted the adjutant before he could speak. 'Who the hell are you, soldier?' shouted the CO.

"Major Leif Bangsbøll, reporting for duty, Sir," came the reply in a loud, clear and difiant voice.

The CO stepped forward, in front of the adjutant and all eyes turned to him as he inquired sarcastically,

> You're late and out of dress, major. Would you mind enlightening us as to why you are dressed in fatigues? Are you expecting to go jump out of an aircraft this morning, major?

In unison, the audience turned back to observe (newly promoted) Major Leif Bangsbøll and awaited his response to the CO's question. The adjutant smiled, knowing that the commander would deal with this situation effectively and with his notoriously ruthless style. The fifty seated staff members murmured amongst themselves as they awaited the next verbal exchange. 'Sir, I'm dressed like a paratrooper because I am a paratrooper', Leif replied. Leif continued,

> And no, sir, I don't plan to make any *more* jumps today; I've already made two jumps with the 504th this morning and I think it's time for me to figure out what kind of instructing I'll be doing here.

There was more snickering and more than a few uncomfortable stares amongst the spectators to this unexpected intercourse. The adjutant warned the audience to steady up and quiet themselves.

The CO's face scowled, and he shouted the command, 'Front and center, airborne soldier!' Leif immediately straightened his posture and marched smartly down the slight incline of the auditorium aisle towards the foot of the stage where the CO, the adjutant and the top sergeant stood. Leif had inherited his father's naval swagger and confidence, which were evident as he traversed the twenty or so paces to the base of the stage. As he approached his CO, Leif looked directly forward into the eyes of his superior. All the other officers and NCOs in attendance just stared and watched the late arrival approach the 'old man', anticipating the CO was going to chew this new, insubordinate major a new one.

Coming to a sharp halt two paces in front of his CO as military regulations dictate, Major Bangsbøll drew his right arm up in a crisp, military salute, recognizing his superior's rank and authority. Colonel Speirs stared at the dust-covered, sweaty airborne officer for a moment and then returned the salute. Military protocol dictated that the senior of the two officers should initiate any further dialogue, so Major Bangsbøll lowered his salute and stood silently at attention. The two men continued to stare at each other for several more seconds. The tension in the auditorium was palatable. Then, and quite unexpectedly, a broad grin creased the CO's face and his right hand shot out to shake the hand of and greet his old colleague. 'Leif, you son of a bitch! You're as incorrigible as ever!' Leif relaxed and his face lit up with a smile too, and the two old airborne colleagues embraced each other as if they were long lost friends. The two officers had served with 187th ARCT during the Korean War and then Major Speirs had become Leif's company commander in early 1951. During the last six months of Leif's tour in Korea, Speirs had been responsible for sending Leif and his platoon on numerous dangerous special operations missions. One such mission was to recover the Eighth United States Army's lost gold bullion; another was to rescue the American PoWs being held by the North Koreans and the assault mission on the North Korean supply depot. Speirs recalled that it was he who had sent Leif and one of his squads out on the reconnaissance mission where they were ambushed by the enemy and Leif became separated from his men during the firefight. All of which had led to the famous and thankfully premature wake for The Danish Duke.

Speirs knew and respected Leif and was glad to have him as part of his senior cadre at the Special Forces Warfare Center. Speirs was confident that Leif would bring a high level of operational experience to their instruction as well as a unique flare to the methods of teaching that would greatly enhance their results. The Danish Duke will stir the pot alright, but he'll raise the bar as well, thought Speirs.

At this unexpected turn of events, the adjutant seemed to deflate a little, while the rest of the officers in the auditorium began to murmur and smile. Collectively, they were disappointed that they did not get to witness a serious dressing down by the CO. However, most were pleasantly surprised to learn by this public display of affection that apparently, their CO did possess a heart and had at least one friend after all. Following the introductions to the adjutant and the top sergeant, Leif sat down in the front row amongst his fellow instructors and the CO stepped up onto the stage so that he could command a better position to address his cadre of instructors and course administrators. In his welcoming address, the CO reminded both his new and experienced instructors that they represented the best of the best, the elite fighting forces of the United States Army. They were *Sine Pari* – without equal. He reiterated that they would be responsible for training the young men who would be called on to defend their nation in unfriendly places around the world, places whose names many of the audience didn't even know existed. He reminded them that to wear the green beret of the United States Army Special Forces was an honor and a privilege and signified that they had trained and had been tested to the limits of their abilities and proven themselves worthy to take on the toughest military assignments possible – assignments that no other United States Army units would be given. As instructors at the Special Forces Warfare Center, they were expected to weed out those who could not make the grade. They would accept only the best and the brightest, never pass a fault and never settle for 'just good enough'. Colonel Speirs made his next point clear by saying,

> I don't care what your military affiliation is or was. I don't care if you are an 'All American' from the 82nd Airborne Division or a 'Screaming Eagle' of the 101st or even a goddamn Ranger. My point is, once you put on that green beret you represent the special forces and are recognized as an elite warrior – 'America's Best'.

Speirs turned to depart the auditorium, then he stopped and looked back into the crowd of eager young officers. 'If you're smart', he added,

> you'll find the time to get to know Major Bangsbøll, our new, out of dress and almost late for duty instructor. For your information, he was one of a chosen few selected to stand up the Green Berets and set up this training center – we're lucky to have him back. You get to know him and you might learn a thing or two about special operations – things you won't read about in any damn textbook or the army's field manual.

To Leif's surprise and embarrassment, the CO went on to say,

> Remember this, while you were sitting here on your butts in those cushy seats, wearing your Class As, waiting for me, 'The Danish Duke' got two

more training jumps down range. I call that an effective use of his and my time.

At that, the adjutant shouted, 'Ten-hut!' and the room came to attention as the CO departed. The CO gave Leif a wink as he walked past and whispered, 'I'll see you at the officers' club this Friday afternoon. That's an order, airborne soldier!'

* * *

Following the morning briefing, the adjutant looked into the matter. As it turned out, on arrival at Fort Bragg from his previous post in Sembach, with 302nd TRS, Major Bangsbøll had met up with some of his former colleagues from 82nd Airborne Division's 504th Parachute Infantry Regiment (PIR) who were in the midst of their regiment's training cycle and had allowed Major Bangsbøll to join them and get in the necessary number of jumps to requalify and get his jump status reinstated. The adjutant noted that Major Bangsbøll had even used a few days of his own disembarkation leave – personal time off associated with his move from his previous post – to enable him to get the sufficient number of training jumps recorded to regain his "jump status" qualification. The adjutant was impressed and thought, 'Maybe this guy is for real.' Clearly, the CO was a good judge of character, and it appeared that Leif could be a valuable new asset for the Special Forces Warfare Center.

The following day, at the CO's direction, a memorandum from the adjutant's office was circulated to all staff of the center announcing that effective immediately, dress of the day would be combat fatigues. The directive went on to detail that fatigue uniforms would at all times be clean and starched and jump boots would be highly polished. The CO's encounter with his old friend, The Danish Duke, had reminded him that despite being in a training facility, he wanted his troops to look and act like warriors. They would be professional soldiers but always warriors at heart, emphasizing the old military axiom: 'Fight like you train and train like you fight.'

Back once again at the Special Warfare Center, now as as a senior instructor, Major Bangsbøll would teach his eager students, who had all been identified and nominated by their parent units and passed the rigorous screening process to become a soldier of the United States Army Special Forces/Green Berets. They were the toughest, best and brightest the United States Army had to offer. The Special Forces' Warfare Center would make them better and tougher. Its training curriculum, which had originally been based on the experiences of OSS agents from Second World War, had evolved during the seven years of the special forces' existence to incorporate the realities of recent conflicts in

Korea and the initial stages of the anti-communist, counter-insurgency mission in Indochina (Vietnam). Their training still called for intense language and cultural fluency, along with unconventional training in sabotage and espionage. As well, they were taught that a small unit of well-trained special forces could equal or exceed the effectiveness of a vastly larger force, and by employing stealth, agile maneuverability and unpredictability could generate a combat effect far beyond its size and scope. The school also had begun to emphasize counterinsurgency operations and how to not only eliminate an enemy but also win the hearts and minds of an oppressed people to organize and lead them to rise up against their oppressors and the insurgency forces. The Special Forces' Warfare Center's CO and his senior instructors knew that their special forces training curriculum had to evolve with the realities of modern warfare and the new technologies that were emerging.

When not in the classroom or training area instructing his students on the art of counterinsurgency operations and other associated special forces training objectives, Major Bangsbøll could be found on or above one of Fort Bragg's drop zones.

Just that morning, having arranged to join one of 504th PIR's company of 82nd Airborne Division that was in its training cycle and conducting parachute refresher training , Leif had stood at the parachute door beside the jumpmaster and just moments before launching himself out into the slipstream shouted to the jumpmaster,

> NOTHING CLEARS THE MIND OF EXTRANEOUS MATTERS AS JUMPING FROM A PERFECTLY SERVICEABLE AIRCRAFT AT LOW ALTITUDE!

At an altitude of 2,000 feet there is no margin for error. Notwithstanding that fact, Leif recalled that his last combat jump with 187th ARCT during the Korean War was conducted at the incredibly low altitude of 1,200 feet.

Like all new military assignments, this tour duty at Fort Bragg offered new opportunities for friendship within the military community. For the Bangsbøll clan, one new friendship in particular would grow into a lifelong family relationship. Fort Bragg is where the Bangsbøll family met the Meredith family. Captain David 'Dave' Meredith III was from Houston, Texas, and his southern belle of a wife, Anne-Byrd, was a local girl from Raliegh North Carolina. They were two of the kindest, most generous southerners one could ever meet.

Captain Meredith was assigned to the Special Forces' Warfare Center and worked with Leif. Dave and Leif had met briefly just as Leif was preparing to deploy to Korea with 187th ARCT at the outset of the war. Dave was also in the auditorium the morning that Leif made his entrance and had his reunion with the CO. He was one of those in attendance who had expected the CO to chew this new major's head off for showing up as he did. But he was impressed with how Leif had handled the situation and was eager to get to know this uniquely qualified airborne soldier who was able to tame their CO's notorious temper. Dave, with his Texan drawl, and Leif, with his Danish accent, were an odd couple to listen to when they carried on a conversation. But the two immediately became close friends and professional colleagues. Soon after, Dorothy and Anne-Byrd would be spending time together as part of the Officers' Ladies' Club Association, and Dave and Anne-Byrd's two young children, Sutton and Leland, would become playmates with the five Bangsbøll kids. Dave and Anne-Byrd would also become the doting godparents of Leif and Dorothy's youngest son, Brook (the author), who had recently joined the Bangsbøll clan.

Upon Major Bangsbøll's departure from the Special Forces' Warfare Center in July 1960, Colonel Francois D'Eliscu, the new CO, stated in his farewell speech for Lieutenant Bangsbøll,

> Major Bangsbøll is one of the most experienced and highly trained officers in our specialised field of activities. He is the only man in the country, to my knowledge, who has had so many foreign assignments in the field of special or secret operations, which ultimately led him to this important assignment as an instructor in the Special Forces Warfare Center. I would like to thank him for his unwavering dedication, outstanding skills and honorable service to the army, the special forces and to this training center.

In the summer of 1960, Leif and his family – now with five children: Leslie, 11, Chris 10, Wendy 7, Mark 5 and their newest arrival, Brook, who was just over 1 year old, bid farewell to Fort Bragg. Though reluctant to leave his colleagues at 10th SFG and the Special Forces' Warfare Center, and the associated pride and prestige of being a Green Beret, Leif knew this would be his last opportunity to get back overseas (to beautiful Bavaria) and get close to the frontlines to face the 'Russian Bear'. So, the Bangsbøll clan packed up their belongings and moved back to Europe.

Their destination was Ulm, West Germany, a beautiful, ancient walled city on the river Danube, with narrow, winding cobblestone streets and many Lutheran church spires dotting the city. Located in southern Germany in the state of Baden-Württemberg, Ulm was a Bavarian jewel. During his indoctrination to his new unit, Leif learned, among other things, that Ulm's most famous son to date was none other than Albert Einstein.

Major Bangsbøll was assigned as an infantry company commander with 3rd Armored Cavalry Battalion, a highly sought-after leadership position that Leif would cherish and in which he would once again excel. Soon after taking command of his company, the American brigade commander realized that Leif's ability to speak fluent German, combined with his strong leadership qualities and engaging manner, would make him an ideal asset to positively influence the critical working relationship with their host nation's military. As such, Major Bangsbøll was given additional responsibilities as the brigade's liaison officer to the West German Army's II Corps headquarters staff, which was co-located with the American 3rd Armored Division headquarters in Ulm. Major Bangsbøll's proven combat experience and versatile language abilities provided a great deal of credibility with their West German army colleagues. One of Leif's first encounters at II Corps headquarters would define his role and his acceptance amongst the German army officers for the duration of his assignment.

Keeping with Major Bangsbøll's stead-fast belief to never pass a fault, his initial contact with his German hosts was anything but routine. On his first day as the liaison officer with the German II Corps, as he waited to meet Colonel Sonnek, COS of II Corps, for their introductory meeting, Major Bangsbøll sat in the German colonel's outer office. While waiting for his appointment, he overhead a heated dressing down, in German, emanating from the COS's office. The COS was shouting slurs and insults at one of his officers. A few minutes later the unfortunate and much berated German major departed the COS's office red-faced and in a rush to put as much distance between himself and his angry colonel as possible.

Moments later, the COS, his demeanor now calm and friendly, welcomed his new United States Army liaison officer into his office with a broad smile and extended hand. Leif, who had seen enough of this kind of German totalitarian attitude and leadership style during the Second World War, decided to do something brave. Leif extended his hand but did not release their handshake. While gripping the Colonel's had tightly, Leif confronted the German colonel using perfect German dialogue. He said,

> My colonel, sir, I could not help but overhear your admonishment of that officer who was just in your office. Sir, you must realize that those days are over (his hand gripping tighter). Addressing subordinates – or anyone for that matter – with such a Nazi-like fervor is unacceptable and will not be tolerated by me or my American commander. Can we agree on that Sir?

Leif released his iron grip on the German Colonel's hand. Taken aback, not only by Leif's bold rebuke, which was well beyond insubordination, but also with

Leif's impeccable application of the German language, the colonel was caught completely off guard. Disarmed by this brazen United States Army officer, the German colonel had been placed in an embarrassing, almost humiliating position with his new liaison officer. But the colonel knew this bold American, combat veteran was right and had been brave enough to confront him directly, in his own office, at their first meeting. The COS respected such boldness and integrity, and he immediately knew that this was an officer who had a steel backbone and deserved, no – needed to be treated with respect. This American Officer might just be perfectly suited to help II Corps get out from the shadow of its past and help it flourish amongst its NATO allies.

From the outset of his assignment with II Corps, Major Bangsbøll had proven himself worthy and from that moment onward, Colonel Sonnek ensured that he and the rest of the II Corps headquarters staff treated Major Bangsbøll as one of their own. They would seek his advice on technical military matters, and on more ways to improve their command and control and enhance their interactions with the American forces in the region. Leif's unwillingness to overlook an overt leadership transgression, even though it was technically concerning his superior's conduct, had immediately established him as a credible and reliable officer with the highest moral standards, who would provide candid, professional advice.

Combat readiness training for American and NATO troops in Europe was always a critical part of being prepared to face an expected Soviet invasion, and none more so than for the German II Corps, whose area of responsibility lay directly in one of the expected invasion routes of the Soviets. One of Leif's most dramatic and ingenious accomplishments during his tenure as liaison officer to the German army's II Corps was the role he played in a large American-Germany exercise in the autumn of 1960. The exercise was designed to help facilitate and practise mutual command and control and intelligence sharing capabilities between the two NATO allies. It was one thing for an American Army headquarters to be able to convey strategic level intelligence to a partner German army headquarters, but to be truly effective in close-quarters combat operations – even during an exercise – communications and intelligence sharing needed to be effective at the operational level to provide the tactical commanders with vital and timely information and vice versa. It is essential that commanders have situational awareness in the battle space, within their area of operations and with other nearby Allied supporting units (other friendly forces in their area of operations). With these critical elements in mind, Major Bangsbøll began to build his plan to demonstrate to both his American Army and West German army superiors that effective communications and liaison, combined with a bit of ingenuity, could produce superior results.

For the purposes of this exercise, Major Bangsbøll was assigned to the American-West German Blue Force (AKA the good guys) who would be defending a large swath of German countryside against an aggressive adversary composed of American Army Red Force troops (AKA the bad guys). Leif had been assigned Captain Gerhart Stoddard, a German army intelligence officer from the II Corps headquarters, to be his exercise counterpart/liaison officer. Several days before the commencement of the exercise, Stoddard had reported to Major Bangsbøll at his 3rd Armored Calvary Battalion headquarters office. Stoddard was the consummate professional German army officer, demonstrating a high level of military bearing, protocol and technical competency. Leif's only concern was that the German staff officer would not appreciate some of the non-NATO standard procedures that Leif intended to employ during the exercise. Leif planned to engage in some unorthodox activities that would, most assuredly run contrary to the German officer's strict military sensibilities. Leif guessed he would have to cross that bridge when he came to it. The week prior to the exercise, the two officers explored how best to support the exercise to ensure both the American and West German forces of the Blue Force involved in the exercise would glean the most benefit and experience from the training.

* * *

The day the exercise was to begin, the late September morning was cool, the air crisp, and the sky a cloudless, vibrant blue. A young boy, aged 9, wearing his American Boy Scout uniform sat in the back of a jeep with a green, wool, army blanket wrapped around him to keep him warm. He watched the smoke-like wisps of breath emanating from his father's mouth as Leif gave directions to his driver as they navigated the narrow and winding cobblestone streets of the Bavarian town of Ulm to pick up their German liaison officer.

After only a ten-minute drive from the joint American-West German Kaserne, Leif, his son, Chris, and their American sergeant driver arrived at Captain Stoddard's home on the outskirts of Ulm to pick up the German army intelligence officer for the start of the NATO military exercise. Stoddard was visibly surprised to see that, in addition to Leif and his driver, there was a young, blond boy sitting in the back seat of the jeep.

> Good morning, Captain Stoddard. This is my son, Christian. You can call him Chris. Chris, this is Captain Gerhart Stoddard, you call him Captain or Sir. You two are going to be traveling buddies back there, so get comfortable and get to know each other.

With a michevious gleam in his eyes and a nod of his head to the driver, Leif exclaimed, 'Now we're off to play war!' With the introductions completed, the jeep sped away northwards towards the designated Blue Force exercise assembly point an hour away, within a military training area in the 'Swartzwald [the Black Forest]'.

The first day of the scheduled five-day exercise, Leif and Stoddard spent much of their time in the large Blue Force operations tent, listening to exercise intelligence and operations briefings about their own troop dispositions and reports of enemy Red Force movements in the designated training area. Meanwhile, Sergeant Daniels, Leif's driver, and his young Boy Scout companion were sent out to locate a couple of good observation posts to observe the likely Red Force approach routes and a suitable nearby campsite for the night.

By sunset, Major Bangsbøll and Captain Stoddard had joined Chris and Sergeant Daniels at a remarkable campsite amongst the ruins of an ancient Germanic castle overlooking a bridge across the river Brigach, a few miles north of where it joined the magnificent river Danube. To young Chris, this was just like Boy Scout camp, except for all the guns and tanks. They slept in army-issued, down-filled sleeping bags under the stars and ate army-issued field rations and cooked over an open fire. As the resident Boy Scout, Chris was naturally put in charge of the campfire and maintaining fire security until bedtime.

Several of Leif's colleagues at the headquarters who were involved in the exercise wondered amongst themselves why Major Bangsbøll had taken his son out of school to observe and participate in a military exercise. Like his father, Leif had learned through experience that exposure to real life events and the challenges that come along with those experiences make up the true and most important lessons in life. Spending a year as a cabin boy on a Royal Danish Navy light cruiser at the age of 11 and voyaging to Greenland on a three-mast sailing ship to rescue National Geographic explorers when he was but 15 years of age had opened Leif's eyes to the expanses of the world's beauty and dangers and the intrigue of its remote regions. Those experiences that his father had facilitated for him taught young Leif many important life lessons. Leif believed that it was time to give his eldest son the same opportunity to explore some aspects of his father's grown-up world too, while under the close supervision of both him and his sergeant. Arranging to have his son miss a day or two of school seemed a small price compared to the value of the investment of spending a few days camping in the beautiful Bavarian countryside with his father and being able to witness and participate in an international military exercise.

Over the following two days and nights, this small, oddly assembled American-German intelligence liaison team traversed the military training area north of Ulm, wearing the appropriate blue arm bands to designate their official Blue

Force affiliation. However, from time to time, as the situation dictated, Leif felt that there were justifiable requirements to switch to the unauthorised red arm bands of the enemy Red Force – an act that was strictly forbidden according to the exercise regulations. In the first circumstance where Leif felt this 'adaptation' was required, Stoddard vehemently protested, reciting the page and paragraph number of the exercise operations order and procedural instructions, which indicated that such conduct was '*verboten* [forbidden]'.

With a serious and stern look from Major Bangsbøll, Captain Stoddard was told to be quiet and follow his lead, and blue arm bands were switched for red. When they pulled up in their jeep at the Red Force roadblock/checkpoint in the early evening hours, the presence of the young boy in an American Boy Scout uniform quickly became the focus of the checkpoint guards' attention. Leif had explained to his son what he was about to do and then explained to the Red Force guards that they were Red Force exercise staff officers who had found this lost American boy in the forest several miles back and were attempting to get the boy to a safe, designated exercise assembly point to facilitate returning him to his distraught parents. The facts seemed reasonable: the occupants sported the appropriate red arm bands and there was a young Boy Scout in obvious distress, and so without hesitation the guards allowed the foursome to pass with wishes of 'Good luck!' and 'Don't worry kid, you'll be fine... you'll be home with your parents soon.'

As the jeep proceeded through the checkpoint into Red Force territory, Leif's German colleague, despite being surprised and, to a degree, impressed by the boldness of the bluff he had just witnessed, was heard to say partially under his breath, 'You Americans really are cowboys.'

Despite hearing Blue Force radio communications indicating various small movements of Red Force units in the area, the foursome of Blue Force intelligence agents had not observed more than a couple of Red Force reconnaissance vehicles maneuvering across the German countryside. However, later on the second evening, now well behind Red Force enemy lines, the foursome observed a convoy of army trucks loaded with dozens of assault boats that were being positioned and assembled in a large clearing close to the river Brigach. Both Major Bangsbøll and Captain Stoddard immediately knew what the Red Force was planning. Not wanting to broadcast their findings across the airwaves back to the Blue Force command, Major Bangsbøll handed out a new set of arm bands and ordered his driver and German colleague to switch their arm bands from enemy Red Force to the white exercise official armbands. Years later, in 1967, having just watched Robert Aldrick's movie, *The Dirty Dozen*, with its star-studded cast, including Lee Marvin, who pulled-off the same exercise scam, my father would say: 'That's just the way I did business – unconventional and sometimes a bit screwball, but it always worked!'

Shortly thereafter, and just before they drove through two additional Red Force checkpoints, as well as one Blue Force checkpoint, Major Bangsbøll told Sergeant Daniels to pull over. Leif got out of the jeep and walked a few feet into the woods beside the road. Using his combat boot, he cleared a patch of earth of pine needles and twigs, bent over and grabbed a handful of moist Bavarian soil. Chris, still sitting in the back of the jeep looked quizzically at his father as he approached him. His father smiled. 'Dad's going to put some make-up on you, Christian.' Leif took his son's face between his dirty hands, smudging Chris's face with the fragrant, moist earth and then giving his son's strawberry-blond hair the same treatment. Chris was instructed to lie down in the back seat of the jeep with a blanket covering his torso and legs, and "act sick".

Five minutes later the daring foursome approached the first Red Force checkpoint, again using the lost and injured Boy Scout rescue routine to facilitate their urgent passage. For this version of the ruse, Chris, now looking a bit like a street urchin, was laying down on the back seat of the jeep and acting like he was sick or injured. Declaring a 'no duff' emergency with an injured young American Boy Scout allowed Major Bangsbøll and his marauders to quickly pass through all of the exercise checkpoints with impunity. Within the hour, the foursome was back within Blue Force territory and Stoddard had reported the suspected enemy Red Force's river crossing location, with precise grid-references and marked the location on the Blue Force operations map along with the location of the pontoon boat assembly area to his German II Corps intelligence officer. The information was in turn communicated to the American Blue Force commander.

At approximately 2300 hours that night, Major Bangsbøll, Captain Stoddard, Sergeant Daniels and Scout Bangsbøll watched from a perfect vantage point on a nearby hillside as approximately 1,000 Red Force troops in portable assault boats paddled into an ambush set by waiting Blue Force troops. Using dozens of star-burst illumination flares to simulate an artillery and mortar barrage and expending thousands of blank rounds of ammunition simulating live-fire rifle rounds, the Blue Force enfiladed the Red Force in the midst of its clandestine river crossing assault into Blue Force territory. 'That's the coolest thing I've ever seen!' gushed young Chris. Even Stoddard, the stone-faced German officer broke into a broad grin at the spectacle unfolding in the valley below them. "I never imagined that we,…ah, the Blue Force could have accomplished this" said Captain Stoddard. Major Bangsbøll smiled and look over at his young German accomplice and said: "There are more things in heavan and earth, Horatio, than are dreamt of in your philosopy." Captain Stoddard stared back at his Danish-American mentor with a quizzical look on his face as he tried to register this odd, yet vaguely familiar phrase. Leif smiled knowingly and continued…"Hamlet?"… With that, a large grin spead across the German officer's face…"Ja [yes] – Shakespeare!"

According to the real exercise officials (judges), Red Forces involved in the early morning river assault would have been annihilated by the Blue Force. How the intelligence about the river crossing was obtained by the Blue Force was an issue of great contention, but the facts were the facts. The foursome making up one of the Blue Force intelligence parties had breached the Red Force security network, identified the river assault threat, and were able to convey this critical information to the Blue Force commander in a timely manner to ensure a successful defense of the Blue Force territory – a win is a win, be the war real or pretend. Leif looked at his German colleague and said, 'Sometimes the ends do justify the means.'

Stoddard received much praise for his initiative and effective liaison and intelligence gathering efforts during the exercise. Major Bangsbøll ensured that Captain Stoddard received full credit fo their success…Leif had no need for personal recognition; he was there to pass along his knowledge and seeing its success was reward enough. The following day, a Sunday, Major Bangsbøll arranged to have his driver take Chris back home to Ulm where he would have time to get cleaned up and complete his homework for the following school day. Chris did so, but only after he called on all his close buddies to tell them how he had just spent the weekend. To this day, Chis cherishes being included as part of his father's joint American-German military intelligence team and still wonders what Boy Scout merit badges he could have earned for participating in a NATO army combat exercise at the age of 9!

Leif went on to fulfill his liaison duties with the German army with the highest degree of professionalism possible and thoroughly enjoyed the experience. As the II Corps liaison duties were secondary to his 3rd Armored Cavalry company commander duties, much of his engagement with the German staff and line officers was after hours, at social and ceremonial functions, during which Leif could really pour on the charm. With his lovely and entertaining Canadian wife often at his side, Major and Mrs Bangsbøll established important friendships among II Corps of the West German Army, and within the local civilian community. So effective was his tour as the liaison officer that upon completion of his duties in Ulm, Leif would be recognized by the West German army with the prestigious II Corps Commander's Commendation. At the time, he was the first and only United States Army soldier to have received such an honor.

* * *

Contrary to the growing harmony within the American and West German militaries, in particular in the Bavarian region, political tension between the United States and East Germany/NATO and the WARSAW Pact had progressively deteriorated since the end of the Second World War. The early half of the 1960s brought forth a series of destabilizing events. The rise in critical tensions began on 1 May 1960, when former USAAF pilot, then reconnaissance/spy plane pilot for the CIA, Gary Powers and his ultra-secret U-2 aircraft were shot down over Soviet airspace. As a result, the political and military threat levels in Europe ratcheted up. Then, in summer 1961, the Berlin Crisis would bring the Warsaw Pact and NATO forces to the brink of armed conflict. Known as the Berlin Crisis of 1961, this development saw the Kremlin dictate an ultimatum to the West, demanding the immediate withdrawal of all Western armed forces from Berlin. The ensuing crisis culminated in the city's *de facto* partition and the erecting of the Berlin Wall by East German forces.

With the Cold War intensifying, provoked by American-Soviet tension, Europe became the most likely epicenter of the next world war. At more than one point during these days of impending crisis, the Bangsbøll family car sat for days fully loaded with suitcases and essentials in anticipation for an impending evacuation order. With their children asleep in their beds, Leif repeatedly reviewed the European roadmaps with Dorothy to verify that she knew the fastest primary and secondary routes west towards the French and Spanish coasts. If the balloon went up, Leif and his company would deployed eastward to fight the oncoming Soviet forces while his family, like many others, would race westward towards the presumed, relative safety of Western Europe.

Amidst these growing international crises, Leif found himself once again at the forward edge of battle space. All American troops in Europe were placed on high alert. At the outset of the Berlin Crisis, understanding the severity or at least the potential severity of the situation, the Bangsbøll family packed-up the Buick station wagon with their get-away kit and waited for the word to bug out. Dorothy and her five children remained at home in their on base apartment at the Kasern in Ulm while Leif and his infantry company deployed forward to take up their assigned defensive positions at the border of East Germany as part of the NATO first line of defense as outlined in its General Defence Plan (GDP). There, for nearly four months, NATO and Warsaw Pact forces stood face to face waiting for the other side to blink.

Major Bangsbøll's company's forward fighting position was no more than 200 yards from the Soviets' frontline troops. His troops could routinely hear the movement of Soviet logistics vehicles moving troops, equipment and supplies forward and could see the ominous silhouettes of many Soviet T-55 main battle tanks moving into their various fighting positions adjacent to the border with West Germany. At night, when the day's military activities were winding down, the Americans soldiers could hear their Soviet counterparts speaking amongst themselves. It was unnerving to say the least. The assignment of 3rd Armored Calvary in this situation was simple: be the first echelon of defense for NATO. These frontline American troops were to resist and delay the expected Soviet armored onslaught to allow the NATO counteroffensive to be implemented. In short, delay the enemy until tactical nuclear strikes options could be considered. The reality was that the life expectancy or perceived operational effectiveness of those frontline NATO forces, including 3rd Armored Cavalry was estimated at twelve to twenty-four hours at the most. The initial efforts of the American frontline units, such as the 3rd Armored Cavalry would provide the NATO commander with enough time to assess the magnitude of the assault and objectives of the Soviet attack and initiate the appropriate NATO counterstrikes.

For Major Bangsbøll and the other combat veterans in the American Army stationed in Europe in the early 1960s, the seriousness of the situation and the danger it posed was not unfamiliar. However, for the vast majority of the post-Korean War American Army soldiers, this frontline stand-off was a frightening and surreal experience for which they had no other reference point to help them understand the true gravity of the situation. It took a great effort and continuous vigilance on the part of Major Bangsbøll and the rest of 3rd Armored Cavalry officers to keep their troops calm, focused on their duties and at a high state of readiness for such a prolonged period of time. Drawing on his previous combat and operational experiences, Leif ensured that he spent the maximum amount of time with his troops, visiting each one of their defensive positions on a daily basis. Knowing that guard duty at night was particularly tough on the morale and nerves of the young troops, he and his first sergeant would make a point of regularly visiting these troops, usually bringing a canteen or two of fresh, hot coffee and a box of Hershey chocolate bars, the troops' favorite. As Leif and his First Sergeant shared a cup of coffee at one of their advance fighting positions, he addressed his troops. 'It's alright, gentlemen', he assured them gesturing over towards the Russian frontline,

> I know you're scared. But just remember, those Russkies over there are just as scared as you – more so, because they have senior NCOs and officers who don't give a damn about their wellbeing and treat them like dirt – like mindless, meaningless second-rate instruments of war. You, on the other hand, are the best equipped, best trained soldiers on earth. You are intelligent men, defending freedom, and have been taught to fight and to think. Taught to out-think your enemy and outfight those mindless hordes over there.

To lighten up the mood, Leif added,

> You know, if you were to throw one of those chocolate bars anywhere near those Russian soldiers, they'll drop their weapons or jump out of their tanks to get one. Those poor bastards don't know how bad they've got it.

With smiles and nods all around, Major Bangsbøll and his First Sergeant bid goodnight and moved on to the next defensive position to carry on their inspection and chat with their troops. He and his first sergeant drank a lot of coffee on those nights.

Good leadership can take many forms. Major Bangsbøll had ensured that through rigorous and realistic training, his infantry company was as or more technically proficient and physically fit than any other Allied troops in the theater. Being able to keep the troops focused on their assigned duties and confident in their abilities was essential. As their CO, he needed to convey calm, cool confidence. Leif wanted to assure his troops that if they were going to defeat their enemy and survive their assault, they would have to instinctively rely on their training. He emphasized that they should take comfort in the knowledge that they could fully depend upon their fellow soldiers on either side of them and they, in turn, were relying on them. Leadership in situations like this can take many dimensions and styles. Some leadership tactics can be taught, while others are inherent in one's being. For Leif, leadership had been bred into him and put into practice and tested at an early stage of his life. Along the way, through the various life events he had experienced, he had drawn many lessons on how to train and motivate troops. There on the East-West German border, standing toe to toe with the great Soviet Army in autumn 1961 had provided yet another valuable, practical leadership experience for the members of his infantry company.

While American and Soviet politicians made threats and ultimatums in a dangerous game of international brinksmanship, heavily armed American and Soviet troops stood fast, just yards apart, along the East-West German border. It was during this stand off that Major Bangsbøll heard one of his sergeants use a phrase for the first time that he liked. Speaking to his squad, the sergeant said, 'We won't fire until we see the whites of their eyes.' Amused by the poignancy of the phrase, Leif inquired as to its origins. The sergeant, a military history buff proudly explained to his company commander that the phrase was attributed to Colonel William Prescott, American Continental Army. They were instructions given to his American militia who faced the British Army in Boston at the Battle of Bunker Hill, in June 1775. Giving the scholarly sergeant a friendly slap on the shoulder, Major Bangsbøll said, 'I like the way Colonel Prescott and you think, sergeant.' Major Bangsbøll then moved on to inspect the next defensive positon of his company.

Though the Berlin Crisis would be considered over in November 1961 without any significant military incidents occurring, the landscape of central Europe, and particularly Germany, would undergo an enormous transformation. With the building of the Berlin Wall, rapidly yet methodically erected by the communists, the Iron Curtain fell into place with devastating effect. The wall would physically divide the Warsaw Pact Eastern European nations from the NATO alliance of the West. The Berlin Wall would psychologically and ideologically drive a deep wedge between Eastern European communism and Western European free-state capitalism that would have ripple effects around the world. Fellow citizens, friends and families would be forcibly separated by the threatening and ugly presence of barbed wire fences and concrete walls. The landscape was scarred with hundreds of armed guard towers along with thousands of tank obstacles and millions of land mines. It was an ambiguous and surreal situation – it was unclear if the communists were trying to keep the West out or keep their population in.

* * *

During his military career and, arguably, during his entire life, Leif had never backed down from a confrontation. However, given the close proximity of his young family, and knowing that retirement from the military was just a few years away, he was relieved that a conflict with the Soviets had been avoided. In December 1961, a few weeks following the stand down from alert status of the 3rd Armored Cavalry, Leif was promoted to Lieutenant Colonel and reassigned to 10th SFG at the NATO Special Forces' School in Oberammergau, Germany, as the Director of Special Operations.

Nestled in the Bavarian Alps, Oberammergau is located 180 miles southeast of Sembach, Leif's former assignment with the USAF and 302nd TRS, and 60 miles due south of Munich and barely 40 miles from his most recent assignment with 3rd Armored Cavalry in Ulm.

The village of Oberammergau, affectionately referred to as O'Gau by many American service personnel and by the Bangsbøll family, would be the Bangsbølls' new and final military family home. O'Gau was the quintessential, picturesque alpine village, boasting traditional Tyrolean chalets complete with moss-covered roofs, window boxes full of colorful flowers, immaculately tended properties and gloriously painted murals adorning the exterior walls of homes and businesses. All this lay nestled amongst high mountain pastures – it was paradise.

While there, assigned to the NATO Special Forces' School on his final military posting, Lieutenant Colonel Bangsbøll would once again use all his career expertise in special operations and from his time at the Special Forces'

Warfare Center to help develop NATO's special forces doctrine and training program. He would accomplish this while offering his family the unique and wonderfully enriching experiences of a Bavarian lifestyle and ample mountain-living adventures – skiing and hiking. The American military's rest and relaxation center, called The Edelweiss, was located just thirty minutes away at the beautiful town of Garmisch-Partenkirchen, located under the massively spectacular mountain called the Zugspitze – a place the Bangsbøll clan would frequent often. Oberammergau was not only the Bangsbøll family's final military assignment but one of their fondest.

* * *

Then, in October 1962, the events of the Cuban Missile Crisis would greatly increase international tensions and bring the world to the brink of nuclear war. These events had an immediate and significant impact on the balance of power and the readiness levels of the military forces facing each other in Europe and around the globe. With the ever-looming threat of a possible attack or invasion by Soviet and Warsaw Pact forces, contingency plans – both official and unofficial – had to be made to take care of the non-combatant (family members) of the United States' military forces in Europe. Despite the tranquil appearance of the Bavarian village in which they now lived, Leiutenant Colonel Bangsbøll, the consummate military planner, continued to take the Soviet threat and the safety of his family seriously. As a result, he would routinely insist that his family practice a 'family bug out' drill to ensure that Dorothy and their five children could pack up the car and 'get outta Dodge' without delay if and when the time came. For the kids, it was an adventure. Somehow, they managed to make the bug out drills seem like an exciting family adventure rather than a desperate plan to dash for survival.

Neither the Gary Power's U-2 spy plane controversy and his subsequent trial, the Berlin Crisis nor the Cuban Missile Crisis ever precipitated a war. The Soviets remained poised behind the Iron Curtain and never crossed the West German border as expected. By early 1963, a new stalemate had formed between Eastern and Western Europe but seemed to be stabilizing. As a result, Leif gave the okay for the Bangsbøll family to unpack their station wagon and life in Oberammergau returned to a new normal – a Bavarian paradise in the shadow of the Soviet Bear.

* * *

In spring 1963, with the welcome de-escalation of tension between NATO and Warsaw Pact forces in Europe and his retirement from the United States Army looming, it was time for Leif and Dorothy to begin thinking about their future, a future outside of the military.

Leif's good friend and colleague, Dave Meredith, had been posted from Fort Bragg to the NATO Special Forces' School in Oberammergau in summer 1962. As a result, Leif and Dorothy's last year in the military would be spent with their closest friends, the Merediths. Dave, now a newly pomoted Major, would eventually rise to the rank of colonel in the United States Army and would distinguish himself in combat during the Vietnam War. Colonel Meredith, the author's Godfather, would be seriously wounded during the Tet Offensive in January 1968, defending his base, which was nearly overrun during the Viet Cong's surprise attack. Dave's presence, years later, at Leif's funeral brought great comfort to the Bangsbøll family. Sortly after Leif's passing, Colonel David Meredith III died and is buried alongside his wife, Anne-Byrd, at Arlington National Cemetery – just down the ridge from Leif and Dorothy's final resting place.

Chapter 12

Moments Before Midnight

'He who uses up his life without achieving fame leaves no more vestige of himself on Earth than smoke in the air or foam upon the water.'

Leonardo Da Vinci Quotes
by
Walter Isaacson

It was early in the morning on 30 April 1963 in Oberammergau, Germany when Leif rose from bed to the sound of reveille being played by a lone bugler on the American military Kaserne. Leif knew that the bugler would be standing in front of the headquarters building while the duty NCO of the day ran the crisp red, white and blue of the Stars and Stripes up the Kaserne's main flagpole. It was the start of a new day, and it was familiar and comforting. However, Leif knew that everything would be very different tomorrow.

Later that morning, after several cups of coffee and now wearing his freshly pressed Class A uniform and highly polished black military issued shoes, Leif stood in front of the full-length mirror in the hall of their apartment. Although, throughout his career he had bent and even broken the military dress code on numerous occasions to disguise himself from the enemy or trick Red Force troops during an exercise, on his last day in uniform Leif wanted to look as sharp as possible and be dressed by the book – the U.S. Army Dress manual.

Knowing that her husband was growing increasingly anxious about that morning's retirement parade, Dorothy walked up behind him and reached her arms around his broad shoulders. At first Leif thought she was going to hug him, then he realized that Dorothy, standing on her tiptoes, was just reaching around his shoulders to adjust his necktie. The two looked into each other's eyes in the reflection of the mirror and a knowing smile passed between them. There was a silent message of love and contentment that once again joined them as one. To Leif, Dorothy's fleeting glance said to him,

Despite the numerous and prolonged absences because of military duty that have put your life in harm's way, your amazing military career has provided

> me and our five wonderful children an exciting and fulfilling lifestyle with an array of wonderful friends and scrapbooks full of cherished memories from around the world.

Leif smiled and gave his wife a wink. He tried to convince himself that despite the fact that everything was about to change, it did not matter. He and 'Dottie' would tackle this retirement thing together just like they had taken on every other obstacle life had thrown at them during their fifteen years of marriage. Dorothy kissed the back of his uniformed shoulder and lay her cheek against him and hugged him tightly – just like he had initially expected. It felt good.

After a moment, Dorothy relaxed her arms and said: 'You look great, Leif'. And then she continued,

> And you will do fine out there. But now, I must get these children of yours out of bed and dressed for the parade. After all, it's not every day they get to see the army bid farewell to one of its real-life heroes.

Dorothy smiled, then whispered, 'Don't forget we have Brookie-san's [Brook's] birthday celebration this afternoon too, Leif.' Leif felt her arms release him and he watched his beautiful wife walk back down the hall in the reflection of the mirror. A few minutes later, Leif could hear their children's voices coming from their bedrooms as they began to stir. Leif looked back to his own image in the mirror. 'Did she mean I'll do fine out there on the parade square this morning? Or I'll do fine out there in the civilian world for the rest of my life?'

Leif did not relish the idea of retiring from the military. Quite the contrary, he viewed it like the scene in *Hamlet,* his favorite Shakespearean tale, in which the Danish prince anxiously waits atop the castle battlements for the reappearance, in the gloom of night, of a ghostly apparition. Leif's impending retirement from military service had become something like that dreaded spectre, which approaches at the darkest hour, the stroke of midnight. At his very core, and in his own way, Leif did not want to let go of his military career; he lamented the things he would be leaving unfinished and feared becoming simply a faded memory. His military career had defined the man he had become. It had been rife with danger, challenges and accomplishments, laughter, love and tears… so many tears. Now it felt as if his military career was the fleeting existence of foam upon the water or the dissolving wisps of smoke in the wind. Was life really so fleeting, is our existence mere wisps of smoke in the wind?

Two hours later, as Leif stood on the edge of the parade ground while the troops assembled, memories of the defining moments of his military career flashed through his mind like a kaleidoscope…

> Leif's mind drifted back in time, to a place when he was a cabin boy on a submarine tender and a member of a submarine crew at the age of 13. Then adrift on a disabled schooner and rescued along with his father from the North Sea aged 16; sailing on a three-mast ship with the Shackleton expedition from Greenland; being one of lucky but an unlikely participant in the Dunkirk rescue mission; earning his pilot's wings with the Norwegian Air Force; the fateful meeting with Colonel Donovan and entering the mirky world of secret agents; the excitement of combat and the adventures of harassing the German occupiers in Jutland, culminating with his battle at Ryvangen and the Allied victory over Nazi Germany. Peace did not last long…the KGB incident in Berlin still haunts. And then there was Korea…fuckin' God-forsaken Korea and its devil's harvest. Then the happy times and the thrill of being a parachutist and member of 82nd Airborne, being a member of the elite Green Berets – the awesome sense of pride at being referred to as 'one of America's best'… so much… so much… and gone by so fast…

Suddenly the military band began to play. The music brought Leif's attention back to the present – the parade…his retirement parade. He took a deep breath, and the cool, morning air of the Bavarian Alps filled his lungs. It was intoxicating, and he closed his eyes briefly and drank it in: the clean mountain air, the smell of pine, meadow grass and edelweiss, the unmistakable scent of farm manure mixed in – an exquisite blend of olfactory delights that pulled him across time and space. He would miss this.

Leif, standing at attention, gazed across the valley to the mountains beyond. There before him, dominating his view was the Kofel; the distinctly shaped mountain loomed over the villages of both Unterammergau and Oberammergau and the river Ammer below, which ran between them. The Kofel, the mountain that he and his family had hiked to the top of countless times, commanded the vista of everyone on parade and those in the viewing stands. The Laber, the sister mountain to the Kofel, was at his back. That too, he and his family had climbed and skied upon many times. He stood overlooking the parade square, located slightly down the slope from the NATO Special Forces' School, and his final military assignment. The day had come: his final day in uniform – and the setting was magnificent.

The United States Army troops assigned to the retirement parade had assembled and were in formation, row upon row. Flags fluttered, the band played, and the spectators waited and watched. There in the audience were Leif's fellow NATO officers and instructors from the NATO Special Forces' School, including his old friend and fellow Rakkasan, Major David Meredith

III, and his wife Anne-Byrd, as well as his close colleague Major Hal Demoya. They were all there out of respect for the distinguished warrior, and to bid farewell to this sometimes bombastic, but always dependable, officer and a true airborne soldier known fondly by his long-standing moniker, The Danish Duke. Of course, Leif's wife and five children, along with their nanny, Rosie, looking after the youngest – Brook – were there too, in their front row seats.

Leif knew he would be called forward by his commander in a few moments. Complimentary things would be said about him and about his career. They would speak earnestly, and with respect for his proven courage, dedication and selfless service in the defense of the United States and his native Denmark, and in the liberation of Europe during the Second World War. His valor on the battlefield in the defense of South Korea would be highlighted. His leadership role with the creation of the United States Army's Special Forces, Green Berets, and with his NATO Allies would be extolled. He would march past the Honor Guard and their brightly colored flags and would be asked to inspect the troops one last time.

As Leif gazed across the front rank of the soldiers on parade, he noted how young they all seemed. 'Was I ever that young?' Leif asked himself. 'I'm only 45 years old but feel like an old man compared to these kids.' Leif knew it was his time to bid farewell to the profession he loved. He knew it would all be over soon. The parade would take just a few minutes of time and then his services would no longer be required. He would be demoted to the civilian rank of 'mister' or, at best, 'lieutenant colonel (retired)'. It was a stark reality he was facing. He was familiar with and understood the dynamics of facing an armed adversary but was totally unfamiliar with the realities of life outside of the military. Mr. or Lieutenant Colonel (Retired) Bangsbøll would have to face the prospects of being a former military member for the rest of his life, which to him seemed more daunting than anything he had encountered during his years of service. The things that he knew best and was most comfortable would be gone. What lay ahead was the great unknown.

Leif's final words as a commissioned officer were not overly sentimental nor deeply profound. However, they were spoken directly from his heart and accurately conveyed his true character and his beliefs:

> I thank you all for being here this morning. To my friends, family and colleagues, I appreciate your presence as a meaningful show of support. For the fine troops on parade who were ordered to be here today, thank you. It has been an honor to serve with you all and I promise that my comments will be brief so that you can get home to your families and enjoy the weekend in this beautiful Bavarian paradise.

As you have heard, I was raised in the military community, but you need to know that it has been my life's honor to serve in the defense of my countries, both my native and beloved Denmark and my wonderful, adopted country, the United States of America. I hope that in some small way my efforts as a loyal soldier have contributed to the peace and security of a free and just world.

I will reserve my comments about my lovely wife Dorothy and our wonderful young family to a time and place that is more private. However, I do wish to acknowledge now, in front of you all, how much I owe to my family, and in particular my parents, for their love and guidance, for setting me off on a meaningful path to adulthood, and for the many life lessons they taught me. My deep spiritual connection to my ancestral bloodline back to the age of Vikings remains strong within my soul and always steeled my confidence when times where tough.

As well, I owe so much to my military family – the brave soldiers and the fellow officers who I have served with in peacetime and in war and who have valiantly supported me and taught me so much throughout my military career. From the wise words of my father, the Danish commodore, to my commander on the Danish light cruiser *Hekla* when I was but a boy, to the captain of the formidable sailing ship *Dannebrog* of His Danish Majesty's fleet, which took me to the frozen expanses of the Arctic circle, Greenland and beyond as a young man. I must acknowledge my Norwegian wing commander who had the patience to train me, in the skies above Canada, to be a pilot in the Norwegian Air Force. My everlasting gratitude goes out especially to General William Donovan of the OSS who saw something in my character that I did not know existed and whose offer to join the United States Army and the Office of Strategic Services profoundly changed the trajectory of my military career and my life. If it were not for him, I surely would not have had the chance to fight alongside the Danish Resistance to help defeat the Nazis and liberate Denmark.

I must acknowledge my enduring gratitude and respect for Colonel Aaron Bank, a fellow Rakkassan of the 187th Airborne Regiment Combat Team, who led me in battle during the Korean War and who subsequently gave me the opportunity to be part of the initial [United States Army] Special Forces Unit and the notorious Green Berets who are now and will always be the vanguard and tip of the spear of America's elite warriors.

Lastly, I solemnly and respectfully remember my childhood friend Jorgen Bech, a loyal Dane who died an honorable Viking death far from home, and in the defense of his adopted homeland – the United States of America on December 7th, 1941. It was his spirit and his identity that carried me through some very dangerous times in the execution of my clandestine OSS missions. To these indomitable men and women, I stand in their shadow in awe and have nothing but admiration and a deep sense of gratitude and undying respect for them all.

And now, at this moment, as I reflect back over my career, I am content. I am proud of my accomplishments, and I regret absolutely nothing, save for the loss of so many close friends and colleagues who met their fate bravely facing the enemy, honorably defending democracy and freedom. My conscience is at peace as I have done my duty to the best of my abilities, and I can do no more. I will always cherish my time in uniform and will remember this bittersweet moment forever.

As I stand here amongst and admiring the majesty of the snow-capped mountains of Bavaria, I am reminded just how beautiful our world can be. But make no mistake, there are dark forces and dangers lurking out there, dangers that threaten our peace, security, freedoms and our very existence. Remember, a very wise person once proclaimed, "for evil to prevail in this world, all that must happen is for good men to stand idly by and let it happen." Lieutenant Colonel Bangsbøll took a step back from the podium, facing the troops and brought his right arm up in a sharp military salute. He held the salute longer than standard military protocol, not wanting the moment to end. But end it must. Lieutenant Colonel Leif Bangsbøll, The Danish Duke, the soldier's soldier, slowly and reluctantly lowered his arm and completed his final salute. He then turned with crisp military precision from the dais and marched back to his position in the parade formation. The deed was done; the final salute had been given; the hour had struck midnight.

Epilogue

'Thank God I have done my duty.'

Lord Horatio Nelson,
Battle of Trafalgar,
21 October 1805

On that April morning in 1963 – when my father took his final salute and removed his uniform for the last time – it was the day Lieutenant Colonel Leif Bangsbøll, sailor, aviator, soldier and secret agent ceased to exist. But his life story does not end there. My father would go on to experience many wonderful years of civilian life following his retirement from the United States Army, until his death and final journey to Valhalla on the 20 November 2001 at the age of 83. However, his estrangement from military service was like having an essential part of himself ripped away, creating a wound that would never completely heal. My father had spent virtually his entire life associated with the military. He had lived well, accomplished much and enjoyed an extensive, impressive and challenging military career, surviving without significant injuries and with a plethora of incredible stories to tell. And while his post-military years were rich in domestic routines and family events, for my father it would always pale in comparison to that of his richly fulfilling military life. Retirement lacked the indescribable thrill of combat operations in the face of the enemy or of clandestine missions behind enemy lines, as well as the sublime camaraderie that grows amongst soldiers, sailors and aviators in the midst of imminent danger. Retirement and 'real life' was, to put it simply: boring. Thankfully, there were many joyous occasions at various military affiliation reunions that my father and mother attended in the years that followed his retirement, where my father could reconnect with former military colleagues and relive those bygone days. However, there was always an underlying, bitter-sweet sadness, an emptiness of sorts, that these reunions were always about the past. The days of living on the razor's edge between life and death, of being given almost insurmountable challenges and being expected to overcome them, had brought such meaning to his life. Now, they were only memories.

In spring 1963, as much as my father was sad to leave his military life behind, there were aspects of his impending retirement from the United States Army that somehow felt right. The politics of war were changing, and just as he was preparing to leave, members of the United States Army Special Forces – soldiers he had led and trained, close friends and colleagues – were being sent to Vietnam. Initially, they were sent as military advisors to the South Vietnamese military. But eventually, as the conflict intensified and expanded, United States Army Special Forces would play a major part of a massive and prolonged United States' military presence in Southeast Asia in an effort to expel and prevent the spread of communism in the region. This situation conflicted my father greatly. As part of his assignments at both the Special Forces' Warfare Center and his final assignment at the NATO Special Forces' School, Leif, who understood Karl von Clausewitz' axiom of 'know your enemy', had studied the impressive military careers and insurgent tactics of such communist leaders as China's Mao Zeodong and North Vietnam's Ho Chi Minh and General Nguyén Giáp in depth. Though he did not agree with their ideologies, he admired their military skills, respected their leadership and unwavering dedication to their cause, and recognized that these men were brilliant strategists and logisticians, who had honed their skills of communist revolution and insurgency operations in the harshest conditions imaginable. He understood that their guerrilla warfare strategy embraced a level of patience and commitment that would far outreach and outlast what the American government and the American people were prepared to endure. My father felt that entering such a war would be like walking into quicksand. The more you struggled, the deeper you would be drawn in. Sadly, he was right.

My father had considered extending his career by volunteering for service in Vietnam with the United States Army Special Forces, but his deep-seated reservations about the questionable American aims, objectives and methods of involvement in this conflict would not let him do it. There is no question that he was prepared to return to combat, but he had an unsettling feeling as to its futility. The United States was waging a limited war halfway around the world against a determined and resourceful enemy who appeared to be absolutely committed and prepared to invest unlimited resources towards their cause – to wage total war. To my father, it seemed like an endeavor that was bound to fail and cost too many lives on both sides. He felt it might not be America's war to fight, or his to volunteer for. So, he didn't.

Following Dad's retirement, the Bangsbøll family moved to Toronto, Canada to be closer to Mom's family. For as long as I can remember, my Uncle John Henry's cottage on Eels Lake was one of the most wonderful places to be. Located near Bancroft Ontario – about a 2½ hour drive north-east of our family home in Toronto – it was a family gathering place for many summers, nestled in the pristine pine forest of the Canadian shield, with massive Precambrian granite outcroppings along the shoreline of a beautiful, crystal-clear lake. With the gracious hospitality the Henry family (John – my mother's younger brother), the Bangsbøll and Grey clans would join the Henrys during the summer months and build memories – wonderful memories. Along with our friends and lakeside neighbours – the Kifts, the Wilsons, the Bradshaws and the Sikorskys, long summer days and those wonderful, star-filled nights spent at John and Fay's cottage were always full of life's celebrations – swimming, water skiing, canoeing and fishing, catching cray-fish and frogs, laughter, laughter and more laughter. Campfires, and hikes deep into the forests, building secret tree forts, trying our first beers and fumbling through our first kisses. And magical, historic moments – being captivated by Neil Armstrong making one giant leap for mankind on 20 July, 1969 – witnessed by forty neighbors and family members, all viewed from the Sikorskys' grainy black and white TV, via the only TV on the lake. It was wonderous.

I recall with great fondness and a sense of intimate belonging one evening during the summer of 1970 which stands out as a memory of great importance to me and to this story of my father's life. I was eleven years old, just on the cusp of puberty – still thinking girls were a nuisance but intrigued and a little annoyed by their growing presence in my life. At the time, there was nothing more fun than fishing with my buddies and spending time building forts and having adventures on the lake. That summer, my God parents, Dave and Anne Byrd Meredith, along with their teenage daughter Leland and son Sutton, drove up from Virginia to visit. It had been two and a half years since Uncle Dave had been wounded in Vietnam, something I was vaguely aware of at the time, but not mature enough to understand what he had gone through and how my father had dwelt on his friend's near-miss with death. That summer, the Merediths came up to celebrate life with their Canadian friends. I recall that they brought a wonderful southern comfort and the largest and most delicious Virgina Ham as a gift to the hosts. On the Saturday night, after a long week of cottage activities, and wonderful family feasts, a lakeside bonfire was made by our host to the delight of all. The bonfire was a magical event that created its own excitement and awe – a gathering of the clans. The children got to stay up late, adults indulged their children's excitement, and the spirits of the lake and surrounding forest came forth.

We were mesmerized by the glittering carpet of stars above, and the sparks from the bonfire dancing up into the night sky. The children's faces glowed with the flickering light from the fire, some, the younger ones, inched closer to their neighbor sitting beside them on the wooden logs encircling the fire, seeking some reassurance as they listened to a variety of ghost stores from various, creative story-tellers amongst the gathering. The adults created a ring of safety and assurance around the enthralled gathering of children. Camp songs were sung, stories told, and marshmallows were roasted on long pointy sticks to the delight of everyone. But as the evening approached its conclusion, all became unusually quiet when Uncle Leif, the gruff old uncle, stepped forward to tell his story of the Clabowder Man…the true ghost story that was always a highlight of the evening. One child whispered to their cousin beside them, "Do you think it's true?" The other child responded in a hushed tone, "I don't know, but look at Uncle Leif's face – he looks so serious – it must be true… he doesn't joke around." The two cousins glanced at each other and back to their infamous storyteller who continued towards the tale's eerie conclusion…

"Finally, our ship, the Dannebrog, battered and broken limped into the harbor in Oban, Scotland. We were alive and had survived the terrifying North Atlantic storm that the Clabowder Man had warned us of. And that my children," Leif concluded, "is the only ghost story I ever tell…because it's a true one!"

With the story of the Clabowder Man told, the gathering of a dozen cousins, aged eight to eighteen, did not say a word. Only the sounds of the crackling fire could be heard. Then the silence was broken when Paul Henry, the youngest of the clan shouted, "Tell another one Uncle Leif, tell another one!" This was immediately echoed by similar, pleading demands from the gathering of children. Some truly wanted to hear another ghost story, but most just wanted the night to continue, to stave off bedtime.

It was at this moment – late in the evening when no one wanted it to end, that Dave Meredith, standing beside Leif leaned over towards his long-time comrade and said: "You know Leif, I've heard y'all tell that story a time or two bout that apparition or ghost that y'all saw on that ship of yours. To be honest with ya' Leif, I ain't never really believed in that sort of thing. But something happened to me there in Vietnam that has changed my mind". Leif looked at his old friend with an expression of…so, what happened?

Dave gave a motion to Leif that said: wait for it. Dave moved forward from the perimeter of the circle of friends surrounding the crackling bonfire and with his raspy southern drawl got everyone's attention. "Pardon me y'all, I know I ain't kin, but you've sure made me and my darlin' Anne Byrd and our kids feel like we are. I thank you for that – it feels like real southern hospitality, right here in Canada. I hope you don't mind if I contribute to tonight's story-tellin'"….there was a pause as he gathered his thoughts on how to approach his next sentence. "I hope you don't mind if I tell you a story, a story that only my wife has heard…it ain't no ghostly story, but it's the strangest dang thing that has every happened to me. When I tell ya, you may think I'm crazy as a rabid coyote, but this story is true.

"I was fortunate enough to meet and spend time with your uncle Leif while he was still on active duty with the Airborne. His nick-name back then was the Danish Duke. He was a seasoned combat veteran with a great reputation in the Army and amongst the Airborne and within the US Special Forces communities. Over the years I got to know Leif and other colleagues that knew him real well. I consider myself privileged to have heard some of his stories first hand, about his life and career that were truly incredible. Stories about challenges that life can throw in your path. Stories about hardship and intrigue. Stories about soldiering and about spies and such. He had a myriad of war stories to tell and they always included an underlying theme about life's simple pleasures and goodness. They were stories about honor and commitment, stories about successes and about failures and some tragic losses. But what I remember most of that old soldier was his enduring spirit of camaraderie and esprit de corps in the face of danger, and his absolute undying will to never give up until the mission was completed. He taught me all about soldiering".

Dave's thoughts drifted back to his own combat experience in Vietnam. "Strangely enough, it was this fighting spirit that Leif taught me that I believe saved my life back there in the jungles of Vietnam." After a moment's pause, he went on to say, "The only moment in my military career or in my whole life, when I truly thought I was about to die came during my tour of duty in Vietnam – just three years ago. You may not believe this, but this story is true, as God is my witness.

"My legs were busted up pretty dang bad from an explosion from a suicide attack by a North Vietnamese soldier who had run into my command post bunker and detonated an explosive in his ruck sac". Fortunately, the sentry had shot him at the entrance to the bunker before the enemy soldier was fully into the operations center – otherwise I wouldn't be here today. At the time, I was the Battalion Commander with the 27th Infantry. We were known as The Wolfhounds and were located at Firebase Mahon, in the southern part of South Vietnam, in the district called Cu Chi. It was late January 1968 and my base had come under a massive surprise attack from both the Viet Cong and North Vietnamese regular army units. It was the early stages of their Tet Offensive – the Lunar New Year holiday. I was in my Command Post as you might expect. One moment I was leaning over my map table with my operations officer standing beside me. I was giving orders to be relayed by the battalion radio operator. The next moment there was a commotion at the bunker's entrance and a tremendous explosion of light, heat and sound – dang, it was loud! Sometime later – I don't know how long – I regained some degree of consciousness and as I lay there, smoke and debris still floated in the air in what used to be my command post. I was temporarily deaf – my ears were ringing, my mind spinning, my leg expelling blood out of a dozen gaping shrapnel wounds. I was going into shock and all I could hear was this voice in my head – that man's voice". Dave pointed at Leif and continued. "I heard his voice in my head as sure as I'm standin' here before ya'll. He was saying over and over, 'Meredith, what the hell are you going to do now? Meredith! I'm talking to you! GET UP YOU SON OF A BITCH, IT'S TIME TO FIGHT!'"

"Call me crazy, but that's what happened. Leif, with that dang Danish accent was shouting inside my head, ordering me to get back into action. His shouts brought me back to my senses and up on my feet – well, partially on my feet. With my injuries, which would soon take me out of the war, I fought. I fought for about three hours until my fire base was able to recover and eventually kill, capture or expel the enemy that had attacked and partially overran our base. My Wolfhounds fought with such tenacity that night. As the Fire Base Commander, protected by hundreds of American soldiers with massive air power and artillery support, I never expected that I would find myself fighting at close quarters with the enemy within the perimeter of my own camp. But that's what the enemy did right across South Vietnam during the '68 Tet Offensive. They caught us with our pants down and put us back on our heels that day and it served as a shocking wake-up call for the United States – we were fighting an enemy that wanted to win – no matter what the costs. And I'm here today because the Danish Duke told me to get up and fight". Silence hung over the crowd and only the crackling of the fire could be heard.

The night ended as always, with our bonfire tradition – with Uncle John Henry and Paul Kift, John's childhood friend and long-time cottage neighbour, singing their incredibly chilling version of Ghost Riders in the Sky. With the flickering light of the bonfire reflecting off their faces, Uncle John and Paul sang their hauting song to the delight of all.

As my father got use to being a retired soldier and a full-time father, Leif took great pride in his five children as the grew into adulthood. Leif was especially proud that three of his children and several of his grandchildren chose to serve their countries in a military capacity. His son, Chris, served in the Royal Canadian Navy, Mark in the United States Army and yours truly, in the Royal Canadian Air Force. In addition, his grandchildren served: Bryce in the Canadian Army, Brandon in the United States Army, 'Big' Garrett in the Canadian Army, Russell in the United States Air Force and Michelle in the United States Army (Reserves).

From time to time, my father would quote Ralph Waldo Emerson, 'The apple doesn't fall far from the tree.' Surprising to many, save for the example that follows, my father did not steer or pressure any of us onto these career paths; military service just seemed to be a natural progression for each of us.

The one exception to my father's 'none-involvement' in our career choices came in the 1970s when one member of our extended family was at crossroads with dangerous, anti-social leanings in his future. At that place and time my father decided he needed to 'encourage and guide' one of his nephews towards a military career. Leif's sister-in-law, Peggy Grey, had two young children, Elliott and Gail, and was pregnant with her third, Dadja, when she lost her husband. Captain Elliott Grey, USAF, who died on 5 August 1959 when his F-86D Sabre fighter jet had a mid-air collision with a target drone during a training mission over the Caribbean Sea off the coast of the United States Virgin Islands. Unquestionably, Elliott's loss had a significant impact on the entire family, but none more so than 6-year-old Elliot Jr, fondly known as 'Chip'.

Following her husband's tragic death, Peggy tried to make a go of it on her own in St Thomas, Virgin Islands, but in 1968 she moved the Grey family to Oshawa, Ontario, to be closer to family and the support it lent. Fatherless, Chip grew into his teens on a rebellious and ever darkening path and lifestyle. By the mid-1970s, Chip was in the midst of being indoctrinated into the local chapter of the Hell's Angels motorcycle gang known as the Shea Satans. It was at this point that my father, Chip's Uncle Leif, decided he needed to take action – to intervene for the sake of his nephew.

My father had always believed that it was the parents' responsibility to give their children the love, confidence and decision-making tools to make their own way in life. Chip was given that, however, during his formative years, he lacked that important father figure and the paternal guidance that only a father can bestow. In the summer of 1976, with the Shea Satan's motorcycle gang vying for Chip's allegiances, my father picked up his nephew, an American citizen, from his home in Oshawa, Canada and drove him across the border into New York State, delivering him to the United States Army Recruiting Center in Buffalo. Whether he liked it or not, Chip was going to grow up and my father knew that becoming a soldier would make an honorable man out of him. My father's parting words to Chip at the recruiting center were, 'Chip, you want to be a gang member? Well, the United States Army is the biggest, baddest gang on earth – show them what you've got.' And my father walked out the door and drove back to Toronto.

Twenty years later, Chip would retire from military service as a master sergeant in the United States Army's Military Police Corps, having served honorably and with distinction. To this day, at virtually every family occasion since Chip joined the army in 1976, under a degree of duress from his uncle, he has made a point of acknowledging to all those in attendance that "My Uncle Leif saved my life and I will be forever grateful for his bold and unsolicited intervention and lesson in tough love he taught me."

My father was not only a good husband, a good father, good uncle, he was a good friend. Although his years as a United States Army Special Forces/OSS agent made him inherently suspicious of everyone at first, once a person earned his trust, they had no better friend or ally. A shining example of this was the close friendship that grew between my father and our next-door neighbour in Toronto – a former German soldier from the Second World War.

Following my father's retirement from the army in April 1963, the Bangsbøll clan settled into our new Canadian home, a modest suburban five-bedroom house at the north end of Toronto, adjacent to farmers' sprawling fields and apple orchards, and just a few minutes drive down Highway 401 from Oshawa where my grandmother (Dorothy's mother, Margaret) still lived and where, in 1943, Leif had met the Henry family. It was there, in Toronto that Leif met our new neighbor, Heintz 'Henry' Pfizer.

As it turned out, Heintz was equally wary of strangers, and at first did not feel comfortable around his new Canadian-American neighbor and former United States Army officer. Heintz, who had emigrated from West Germany in the 1950s, eventually confided in my father that he had been a boy conscript in the German Wehrmacht during the final stages of the Second World War. At the age of only 15, Heintz had been a corporal and squad leader of a ragtag bunch of conscripts who were ordered to confront the onslaught of Allied forces overwhelming Germany in spring 1945. His ill-equipped Volkssturm battalion consisted of frightened young boys and injured old men had been badly mauled by the battle-hardened American troops when they crossed the Rhine River and broke through the Siegfried Line near the city of Wesel. Heintz's last recollection of his brief period of command was the act of surrender. With his weapon on the ground and his hands held high over his head, he was smashed in the face with the butt of a rifle by an angry American soldier. Dazed and in pain, he recalled seeing through blurry tears a gruesome mass of blood, teeth and bile on the ground below him as members of his squad picked him up and carried him away. That was Henry Pfitzer's first face to face encounter with an American soldier.

Now, safe in Canada years later, his next-door neighbour was an American infantry officer and decorated hero who had methodically and without prejudice contributed to the lethal vengeance levied upon the German Wehrmacht during the Second World War. Remarkably, and as a testament to true warriors who had fought to defend their nations, yet now held no malice towards their former enemy, Leif Bangsbøll and Heintz Pfizer became close friends. Whenever the opportunity arose, my father would converse with Heintz in German, recognizing that our neighbor missed his homeland and enjoyed the opportunity to speak his mother tongue. And though they would only seldom speak of their wartime experiences, Leif and Heintz had an unspoken bond that only two former enemies now at peace could share. And so they did, over a cold beer or a glass of wine or simply friendly chats over the fence that separated our properties – they would reminisce, in German, about their trials, their loves, their losses and their mutual love for Bavaria.

As I look back, I can only imagine the actual thoughts that were going through my father's mind on that last day of April 1963, as he stood on parade for the last time. But I do know that it was his time to bid farewell to the uniform that he loved so much and place behind him the military career that had made him the man he was – a defender of his nation, a dedicated and loyal soldier in the United States Army and a faithful son of Denmark.

I also know that my father deeply desired to leave behind a legacy before his death. I can only hope that he realized that even then, he had already achieved this goal; not only in the lives of those who knew and served alongside him during his military career and the friends he made along the way, but also within his family, where his enduring presence is ingrained in the lives, characters and the very DNA of his five children, twelve grandchildren and his future descendants.

In April 2019, my father's legacy took a significant step forward when he was posthumously awarded the United States Army Special Forces' Commando Medal and was inducted in the Commando Hall of Honor at the United States Special Forces' command headquarters in Tampa, Florida. In a stirring tribute to his remarkable military career and his unique and significant contribution to the creation of the United States Army Special Forces, Green Berets, Lieutenant Colonel Leif Bangsbøll joined the hallowed halls of the Commando Hall of Honor. On that day, The Danish Duke joined his former commander and mentor, Colonel Aaron Bank, widely known as the father of the United States Army Special Forces and my father's recruiter into the clandestine world of shadow warriors, Colonel William 'Wild Bill' Donovan, the director of the OSS.

* * *

According to ancient Viking lore, a Viking warrior has two deaths. The first death, which all Vikings hope will come in battle, sees the slain warrior chosen by the Valkyries – the mythical female beings – as worthy of a place in Valhalla and taken to sit and feast with their god Odin in the great hall of their Viking ancestors. The second and final death of a Viking warrior is deemed to come when his name is spoken on earth for the very last time; hence the importance of the oral tradition and Viking clan stories passed from generation to generation, which create, in essence, Viking immortality.

Leif Bangsbøll made his only, unfinished attempt at an autobiography in spring 1963. His intent was clear. My father's retirement was only weeks away. He knew he would soon part ways with the United States Army: an army that had defended the nation that had adopted him while his native country was under siege; an army and a nation that he loved so dearly. Now, as he approached the end of a rewarding and profoundly meaningful military career, he had something to say.

Like his Viking ancestors, my father wanted to leave some meaningful record of his journey upon this earth... he did not want, in the words of Leonardo da Vinci, 'to use up his life without achieving fame – leaving behind a memory which is no more than foam upon the water or smoke upon the wind.' (*Leonardo da Vinci Quotes* by Walter Isaccson.) Accustomed to conveying his life experiences orally, however, the written word did not come naturally to my father. As such, his initial draft consisted of only ten pages detailing his plans for the written history of his life: 'a gift to his family and its descendants.' The document was found just days following his death on 20 November 2001 and provided the inspiration for me to write his story: *An O.S.S. Secret Agent Behind Enemy Lines* and *US Special Forces Commando.*

Though my father's first Viking death was not in battle as all true Viking warrior's aspire, I truly hope his valiant life's achievements have earned him his rightful place amongst his Viking ancestors in Odin's great hall in Valhalla. I also hope that his second Viking death will never occur. Like our great Danish ancestors, King Harald 'Bluetooth' Gormsson, the great communicator and first king of Denmark and Norway, and his son, Svein Haraldsson 'Forkbeard', the First Viking King of England, whose names are etched in history and adorn Scandinavian and English lore, and whose names continue to be spoken more than 1,000 years after their first Viking deaths, I pray the name Leif Bangsbøll will continue to be spoken and his story told over and over again – for generations to come, staving off his second Viking death, and thus granting him Viking immortality.

Viking Immortality

If Leif Bangsbøll's story, presented to you on the pages of *An O.S.S. Secret Agent Behind Enemy Lines* and *U.S. Special Forces Commando*, has resonated with you, which I truly hope it has, I convey to you the opportunity to contribute to his quest for Viking immortality… whisper aloud the name Leif Bangsbøll as you close this book.

Like his ancient Viking forebears, Leif Bangsbøll,
the descendant was the master of his fate
and the captain of his soul.
Now, the end is nigh, so gently lay the brave warrior
onto the wooden ship with the dragon-headed bow.
Place his sword and shield by his side.
Gather his people and alight the funeral pyre.
Set loose the vessel upon the fjord
and witness the old Dane sail onward to Valhalla.

Brook Bangsbøll, 2025

Bibliography

Books

Bangsbøll, Brook G., *An O.S.S. Secret Agent Behind Enemy Lines*, Frontline Books/Pen & Sword Books Limited, Barnsley, 2024

Brown, Anthony Cave., *The Last Hero: Wild Bill Donovan*

Dunlop, Richard., *America's Spy Master*

Shakespeare, William, *Hamlet*

Shakespeare, William, *Macbeth*

Shakespeare, William, *Twelfth Night*

Films

The Dirty Dozen

Magazines

Stars and Stripes

Mottos

187th Airborne Regiment

Green Berets, United States Army Special Forces

Special Operations Group

Special Forces' Warfare Center

Newspapers

Nationaltidende

Photographs

United States Army, United States

The Bangsbøll family photo collection

World Wide Web – Stock Photos

Poems

Henley, William Ernest, Invictus, 1888

Rudyard Kipling, If, 1943

Quotes

Child, Julia

Da Vinci, Leonardo, 1480

Donovan, Colonel William, 1943

Emerson, Ralph Waldo

Griffith, General S.B., United States Marine Corps, 1961

Herbert, George, 1640
Hooke, William, 1640
Nelson, Lord Horatio, Battle of Trafalgar, 21 October 1805
Parker Captain Jonas, Lexington, 1775
Shakespeare, William
Washington, General George, 1776

Research
British Army, United Kingdom
Canadian Army, Canada
Danish Royal Family, Denmark
National Geographic Society, United States
Norwegian Air Force, Norway
Royal Canadian Air Force, Canada
Royal Danish Navy, Denmark
Royal Canadian Navy, Canada
Sølvgades School, Copenhagen, Denmark
United States Air Force, United States
United States Army, United States
United States Army Air Corps, United States
United States Army Military Police, United States
United States Army Special Forces, United States
United States Army Special Forces' Warfare Center, United States
United States Government, United States
United States Marine Corps, United States
United States Navy, United States

Songs
Ave Maria
Ballet of the Green Berets